Wisdom
Hunter

Wisdom Hunter

RANDALL ARTHUR

DEDICATED...

*foremost to my outstanding and patient wife
and my two lovely daughters, who sacrificed me
to this lengthy writing project;*

*to my wonderful mother and father
who years ago sacrificed me to the foreign mission field;*

*and to the people of the FIBC (from '78 to '85)
whom God used to teach me HOW to think.*

ACKNOWLEDGMENTS

*I want to thank the twenty-eight test readers of the original manuscript
who gave me invaluable editing suggestions, and who gave me
the needed encouragement to pursue publication.*

*I especially want to thank the Questar staff for their
vision for WISDOM HUNTER, and for the energy and hard work
they have displayed while trying to turn their vision into reality.*

WISDOM HUNTER

published by Multnomah Books
a part of the Questar publishing family

© 1991 by Randall Arthur
International Standard Book Number: 0-88070-580-9

Printed in the United States of America

For information:
QUESTAR PUBLISHERS, INC.
POST OFFICE BOX 1720
SISTERS, OREGON 97759

93 94 95 96 97 98 99 00 01 — 15 14 13 12 11 10 9 8 7 6

PART
ONE

1971-1972

1

Jason cleared his throat. His wife knew what was coming next, and the pain within her rose again. At every evening meal for the last five hundred and fifteen days he had prayed aloud for their daughter, always working his way slowly through the prayer, emphasizing each word as if to prove his sincerity.

"O God," he said tonight, "wherever Hannah might be right now, we ask that she'll know your protection. Thank you for watching over her. And thank you even more that one day you'll honor our faith and bring her home."

He paused, as if to arrest the Almighty's attention, then continued with a faltering voice. "Just—just make it soon. We miss her..."

≈ ≈ ≈

LYING ON THE living room couch, Hannah Freedman proudly realized once again that she was the reason Cody had emerged from his loneliness. He was absolutely consumed by her—and the thought was enthralling. Admiring her diamond-studded wedding band, she gratified herself with the reminder that Cody always treated her like a princess, as if by royal decree she had somehow granted him a new life.

At this very moment, alone in their suburban Miami home, she could feel his infatuation. It lingered in every room, echoing in the easy recall of Cody's loving words and embraces.

Hannah turned heavily upon her side, the baby in her womb preventing her from rolling all the way over onto her stomach. She smiled. It was like a fairy tale. She and Cody had met only ten months ago—she a runaway, not yet eighteen; and he a well-bred, 25-year-old professional. Now they were together forever. How could it be real? How could they have it so good?

She reached over her head, retrieving from behind her a framed photograph of Cody that sat alone on the end table. The picture had been taken only weeks before she met him. It was the same handsome face, the same green-eyed, ash-blond man who was now her husband—but he had been so different then. There was a smile on the face, but it was hiding a sense of loss that had governed his life ever since the death of his parents in a plane crash two years earlier. From that seemingly unshakable disorientation, she had rescued him. Likewise, Cody had taken her from a miserable existence and placed her on a lofty pedestal of fulfillment beyond her wildest dreams.

Her spirit soared with gratefulness as she pressed the photograph to her chest. Lost in blissful thoughts, she relived for the thousandth time the nonstop passion of the last ten months. First, the explosive romance—the instant chemistry, like gunpowder contacting fire. Then came the unplanned but welcomed pregnancy, followed by the exchange of wedding vows seven and a half months ago. Every day had been glorious. If she could live all of it over, she would not change a single detail.

A wall clock across the room began to chime the hour, and Hannah closed her eyes and stilled her thoughts to listen: Four o'clock. It was four o'clock, Friday afternoon, December 15th. The "Christmas spirit" with its commercialism was in full swing—and she, Hannah Freedman, had everything in life a woman ever dreamed of: a large and beautiful home, a flaming love life, and emotional security. In only forty minutes her lover would be home from a day's work at his veterinary clinic, ready for their usual early and intimate dinner together. And in only fourteen days, according to the doctor's calculations, she and Cody would cuddle their first child.

She lifted the photograph and contentedly stared through tears at Cody's picture. For the first time in her eighteen years, she knew what it was to live and to love.

She slowly reached over her head and carefully returned the photograph to its place. She contemplated getting up from the couch. But due to an early morning burst of energy she had already put in a full day of cleaning house and baking Christmas cookies, and the work had left her exhausted. Her small frame, now carrying an extra twenty-six pounds, simply refused to rise.

≈ ≈ ≈

AT 4:40, CODY came in the back door. He slipped quickly through the kitchen, moving his six-foot-three, 170-pound athletic body with the fluidity of a cat, and began singing: "Jingle bells, jingle bells, jingle all the way. Oh what fun it is to live with a blue-eyed Georgia girl, *hey!*"

On the living room couch Hannah awoke from her light sleep, and broke into a smile as Cody continued singing heartily off-key: "Jingle bells, jingle bells, jingle all the way. Oh what fun it is to love my blue-eyed Georgia girl!"

When Cody poked his head around the corner, Hannah was applauding. "Coe," she said, extending tired but inviting arms, "you can love this blue-eyed Georgia girl anytime you want to."

Like a moth to a flame, Cody was drawn into her arms. Kneeling on the plush gray carpet beside her, he kissed her full, moist lips as if he had been starving for her for weeks. When he finally withdrew, he looked into her eyes and said with intensity, "Hannah, you're so beautiful—even when you're tired"

So often before he had told her she was beautiful—and had never stopped, even after her pregnancy began showing. Spreading her arms playfully like wings, Hannah nodded toward her body. "You like it, huh?"

Cody smiled his reply, then ran his fingers slowly through her long, thick auburn hair. "Hannah," he moaned in earnest, "I'm missing you, bad."

"How much?" she asked with delight.

"You really want to know?"

"Yeah."

Cody grinned. "Well, I'll tell you. I accidentally gave overdoses of antibiotics to four different dogs today and killed them all," he joked, "simply because I couldn't get my mind off you. All I've done today is dream about being with you."

Feeling aroused, Hannah slowly pulled him into another fiery kiss.

It took every ounce of self-control Cody could muster to keep from going further. When Hannah finally released him, he fell re-

13

luctantly to the floor and stretched out on his back. "Just you wait," he said with gusto, "till we're able to be together again. I'm going to make it unforgettable."

Hannah laughed seductively. "Are you sure you can hold out until then?"

With surprise, she watched Cody's mood turn sober. He rose to kneel beside her again, and took her hands in his. "Hannah, if I had to, I'd be willing to wait the rest of my life for you."

There was no doubt in Hannah's mind that he meant every word. She felt his sincerity as certainly as if it were rain pouring down on her. Instinctively she pulled him into another tight embrace.

"Cody," she confided in his ear, "this will be the best Christmas I've ever had. And the reason is *you...*"

≈≈≈

AFTER DINNER Cody raved as Hannah placed the tray of Christmas cookies on the dining room table beside him. "Better looking than Mother's used to be," he said. Taking a bite, he nodded, "And every bit as good!"

An LP of instrumental Christmas music was playing softly in the backbround. Hannah sat down to hear Cody finish telling her about his day: setting a German shepherd's broken leg, diagnosing an old tomcat that was refusing to eat, bobtailing a four-day-old boxer, and giving an array of shots.

"And Mrs. Gravitt brought in her Dalmatian again," he said, then paused.

"And?" Hannah asked.

"And it should be the last time!" he smiled with satisfaction. "He's fully recovered, and Mrs. Gravitt is as happy as any client I've ever had."

"She should be," Hannah reassured him. "That dog was nearly dead two months ago when she first brought him to you. It was a miracle anyone could save him. But what can I say? You're the best!"

"Well, maybe not *the* best.. But..."Cody tucked his thumbs beneath imaginary suspenders, in a mocking pose of greatness. They both erupted into laughter.

"Say," he said after finishing another cookie, "I called Reed's

Travel Agency this morning. They promised they could reserve the cabin—"

Before he could complete the sentence, he saw Hannah suddenly gasp for breath, tense in her chair, then let out a low groan. Cody was immediately face to face with her, gripping her shoulders. "Are you all right?" he demanded.

She finally began breathing, then looked him in the eye and gave the most surprisingly beautiful smile he had ever seen. "I think so...I...uh...yeah, I'm okay," she answered. "My water just broke." She could feel the warm fluid puddling around her buttocks and running down her leg. For a moment she was embarrassed, but the feeling was quickly overcome by an acute surge of pain.

Still trying to figure out what to do, Cody saw Hannah tense again. He gripped her hand in silence, stunned by the piercing hurt locked on her face.

Several seconds later, Hannah relaxed and took a deep breath. "I'm not positive," she said, "but if that was my first contraction, we may be mommy and daddy two weeks earlier than we thought."

Elated, Cody held her in a big hug and said, "Can you believe it?" He started dancing around the table. "We're going to be a family!" he shouted, as Hannah laughed.

≈ ≈ ≈

THEIR CELEBRATION was soon tempered by the quickly recurring pains, and the rush to leave for the hospital. Within twenty-five minutes from the time Hannah's water had broken, she was seated beside Cody in their Ford station wagon. He was timing her contractions, which now came at less than three-minute intervals. The quickly paced labor pains, coming so soon, made Cody nervous. He tried to relax, but it was all so new. And this was *his* wife, *his* baby.

This is happening too fast, he thought, calculating that the trip to the hospital would normally take twenty-five to thirty minutes. This time, he decided, it would have to be less than twenty. No stranger to speeding, he was confident he could meet the challenge.

He glanced at his wristwatch—5:51—just as they were leaving

their residential area and approaching the nearest main road. One look ahead quickly confirmed a rising worry: *It was rush hour.* Traffic on the main road was packed, moving at only a fraction of the normal speed.

For the first time, Cody felt panic. To hide it, he forced a grin and said to Hannah, "I love adventure, but this is a little too much of the good stuff."

She smiled briefly, before yielding to the start of yet another contraction.

Soon the eruptions of pain were less than two minutes apart. Hannah bravely fought back. *Everything's under control,* she kept telling herself. *Be strong, be strong.* Impossible as it seemed, each contraction hurt worse than the last, worse than anything she had ever felt in her life.

"Just hang in there, babe," Cody said. "I'll get you there."

The line of cars crept forward to an intersection which he realized was approximately their halfway point to the hospital. The flow of traffic halted again as he saw the same set of stoplights change to red for the second time. With mounting fear he looked at his watch: 6:16.

Suddenly, Hannah leaned forward, grabbed the dashboard with both hands, and screamed. Cody reached out and touched her shoulder. He was now almost beside himself with panic. "Are you going to make it?"

When her pain had passed its peak, she found her breath and shot back, "I don't know…Just hurry!"

He knew then what he had to do. And on impulse, as if the adrenaline surging through him had switched on a machine, he did it.

Trying to take charge of this desperate situation, he lurched the station wagon out of their traffic lane. Sounding his horn and flashing his headlights, he charged through the intersection and down the avenue, straddling the middle line.

Hannah did little more than flinch. The thought of how crazy it all seemed flashed in and out of her mind.

"I'll get you there," she heard Cody say again.

2

JASON FAIRCLOTH looked sternly at the young man sitting on the other side of his desk, and thought, *How dare he defy me?* A lecture began forming in his mind, ready for his lips: *Apparently you don't understand that you're dealing with a spiritual leader, an individual appointed by God to...* But Jason quickly realized the man before him probably didn't care.

The thought only increased his anger. Jason decided to teach him a lesson he should have learned long before.

"Your tenure on the faculty at our school has just ended, Mr. Myers. You're fired."

"Fired?" the teacher retorted in unbelief. "Just because my hair is touching my ears and my collar?"

"It's your *attitude,*" Jason corrected him. "The length of your hair is only indicative of your defiant heart."

"But—"

"No buts!" Jason interrupted. "I don't have to remind you that you've been reprimanded twice already."

The teacher was in shock. "Shouldn't this go before the board, before the principal, or something?"

"That only goes to show your problem, Mr. Myers. You've never understood the chain of authority around here. I'm the one who built this school, I built the church that runs it, and I'm the one who hires and fires. Every person on the payroll answers to me."

The teacher was furious enough to scream, but his throat was tied in knots. He shot toward his pastor a look of bitter frustration, then silently turned to walk out. *God help the man,* he thought.

As Jason watched him silently leave, a shadow of regret crossed his mind: Mr. Myers, a man for whom Jason and the school and the church had done so much, now seemed filled with resentment toward him. Jason's mind ran immediately to others as well who had shown the same dislike, for reasons of their own.

17

But that wasn't the whole story, he reminded himself. Most of his congregation and school staff loved him. Hardly a day went by without Jason hearing the words "We thank God for you" from one or more of them. And they meant it. They appreciated a minister who was willing to stand for something.

Jason took a deep breath, shut his eyes, clamped his brawny hands behind his head, and leaned back in his chair. His light brown hair was clipped in a crewcut. His five-foot-eleven form was hard and hefty, presenting a steel-man image even in this rare moment of attempted relaxation.

When he reopened his eyes, he let them rest on an oak-framed brass plaque on his office wall, engraved with these words:

With loving appreciation for
THE GENERAL

The General. By now almost all the people around him called him that, instead of "Reverend" or "Pastor." Six years earlier, the *Atlanta Journal* used the word in a feature article about him, referring to his tireless energy and his no-nonsense approach to church management. The characterization generated so much positive laughter and conversation that it stuck. "He may be the toughest pastor in Atlanta," the article had said. Those who knew him well agreed—and most of them with genuine admiration.

Jason turned his attention back to his desk, and spent the next hour reviewing his notes for the Sunday sermon. When he next glanced at his watch, it was 4:40. It was Friday afternoon, and feeling quite satisfied with his work for the day, he decided to go home.

As he packed his briefcase, he looked up to see his secretary appear at his open door, holding a sheet of paper. "It's the new visitors' letter. Want to proof it before you leave?"

"Thanks, Helen," Jason nodded as he met her at the door. He took the paper from her, and Helen went back to her desk. It was a revised letter to be sent to first-time visitors to the church, and Jason wanted it ready for mailing to the many guests expected to visit in the next few Sundays, before and after Christmas. "Dear Visitor," the letter began,

The congregation of North Metro Church of the Bible wishes to thank you for the honor of your recent visit. As one of the largest churches in Atlanta, we have a well-rounded program designed to provide for your spiritual needs at every level. In addition to our three inspiring worship services each week, we offer instructive Sunday School programs for every age group, a church-operated elementary school providing the best in academic discipline for grades K through 8, a Sunday morning and Sunday evening bus ministry with eleven convenient routes, a bimonthly Christian newsletter that is both informative and thought-provoking, and the popular radio broadcast "Fire of God" at 8:30 each weekday morning on WAEC (AM 970).

Our pastor, Jason L. Faircloth, offers you strong leadership and dynamic charisma. A seminary graduate with a master's degree in theology, he has effectively guided our church's growth from 48 members to 2,232 in just under eleven years. He is a leader who will make you proud.

Thus we extend to you this personal invitation to join us and our pastor, and make North Metro Church of the Bible *your* home for spiritual growth.

"It's good," Jason called as he walked out past Helen's desk. "I see only one mistake: Our present membership is 2,236, not 2,232. I accepted two more couples for membership last night." Without further comment he placed the letter on her desk, and left.

≈ ≈ ≈

JASON CAME DOWNSTAIRS and into the dining room at 6:15, twenty minutes after Lorene had called him to dinner.

"It's not my fault I'm late," he called out curtly to his wife in the kitchen, as he seated himself at the table. "I've been on the phone with that hopeless fool of a congressman we've got. I made it absolutely clear why he can't vote for the Equal Rights Amendment, but Branley cares more about catering to the masses than he does about principle. He's weak."

Lorene showed no emotion as she brought in a platter of fried fish and potatoes, and set it down on the table. She knew he was not talking directly to her, but only expressing his thoughts aloud in a vague acknowledgment of her presence. She answered him gingerly: "Well don't let it make your supper any colder. If you're going to be up to par for the big wedding tonight, you'll need a good meal."

Jason continued fuming about the congressman. Lorene sat down across from her husband, making no further attempt to lighten the mood. Looking into his face, she saw his tightly creased brow, his hardened jaw as he spoke, and his dull, narrowed eyes. More and more she had become afraid of him. His tension, she realized, had become a permanent part of their life.

She lowered her head and stared into her empty plate. Jason was becoming less of a human and more of a machine. And he was destroying her.

For the hundredth time, it seemed, she was acutely reminded of what their marriage had become. She was only a house servant now. The occasional night out he gave her, or a new dress—they came surely from his sense of duty, not from love or desire. Yet she had kept on being the model pastor's wife that everyone expected of her. Always submitting unequivocally to her husband's authority. Always selfless. Always lay-down-and-die. *That's exactly what I'm doing: dying.*

She felt numb. Deprived of his intimacy and sensitivity, she knew she was near the breaking point. *Would he drive away his own wife,* she wondered, *just as he has our daughter?*

The fearful voice within her was quickly silenced by pain at the thought of Hannah. Lorene bit her lip, determined again not to give in to the hurt. She knew she could not believe in the future unless she also believed Hannah would be there to share it with her. Her motherhood had been on hold for almost a year and a half, yet it was the only part of her life that still held meaning. She had to keep hoping for Hannah.

"Didn't you hear me?" Jason asked in a raised voice.

"I'm sorry," Lorene said quickly. "What did you say?"

"I asked if you picked up my suit from the cleaners this afternoon. I'll need to wear it tonight."

She tried to sound cheerful. "It's hanging in your closet."

"All right," he said coldly. "Let's pray." Lorene bowed her head, as Jason lifted his and closed his eyes.

"Dear God," he began, "I first want to pray for our inept Congressman Branley. I beg you to judge him for his lack of courage. Force him to repent. Make him see what's right."

Lorene sat stiffly and listened as Jason prayed in the same vein for the fired schoolteacher, Mr. Myers, then in cold routine requested God's blessing on the church.

He paused, and cleared his throat. The wave of inevitable pain rushed again over Lorene. When Jason continued, his voice was suddenly tender and earnest—a father longing to see his daughter.

For the five hundred and sixteenth consecutive evening, in slow and heartfelt words, he prayed aloud for Hannah's return.

3

"STAND TO THE SIDE PLEASE!" the lead paramedic demanded as he and two team members stepped briskly from the ambulance and pushed their way through the crowd. According to the initial dispatch, formulated from a call made from a nearby service station, the team had been sent to deliver the baby of a woman stranded in a ditched car.

In the bluish glow of a streetlight overhead, the thirty or so people who were gathered by the road and down the embankment quickly stepped back to give the men room.

Equipment in hand, the emergency crew hurried to a Ford station wagon buried to its axles in sand about thirty-five feet from the shoulder. Near the car they spotted a man kneeling beside a woman, frantically pressing on her abdomen. She was lying on old blankets stretched out on the weed-infested sand. They appeared soaked in blood.

The lead medic's experienced eye told him they faced a problem far more serious than a natal delivery.

Cody, fighting to stay calm, looked up only once to see the men approach. With blood dripping from his hands and forearms he explained with machine-gun release the events of the last several minutes.

"The baby's already born and looks healthy," he nearly shouted. "But Hannah's hemorrhaging. I've tried to cut off the circulation around the vaginal area, but I can't."

As the medics went quickly to work, Cody bent down to Hannah's face to reassure her. But she was unconscious. Cody found himself starting to shake.

"Where's the baby?" the chief paramedic asked aloud to everyone nearby, without breaking his attention on Hannah.

An elderly woman quickly stepped forward from the crowd, holding the baby. It was snugly wrapped in a collection of sweaters and jackets, and as she loosened the makeshift coverings it let out a wail.

One of the assistant medics quickly rose to examine the child. Moments later, content that the baby girl was healthy, he unfolded a small pad on the ground and gently laid her on it. He removed the string used to temporarily tie off the umbilical cord, properly clamped it, then rubbed a salve on the stub. He rewrapped the baby securely and gave her back again into the elderly woman's safekeeping. Then he rejoined his teammates. Working furiously with Hannah, they had packed her vagina with sterile gauze to impede the bleeding and were starting an IV solution.

"Give me the pulse," the chief paramedic commanded, racing to set up the compact defibrillator.

"It's forty-three and dropping," his assistant said tightly, his eyes moving to the portable vital-signs monitor.

"Forty and dropping," he spoke again, louder.

"Come on, Hannah," Cody begged, as he held her head between his hands. Hysteria was entering his voice. Sweat coated his face, mingling with tears on his cheeks.

He heard the medic's tight voice again: "Thirty-eight and dropping—*we're losing her!*"

Cody flinched involuntarily, as if he'd been shot through his midsection.

A few feet away, the woman holding the baby began to cry, and hugged the child closer.

"Get ready for CPR," the lead medic ordered, tearing open a packet of adrenaline-filled syringes.

He reached up to help the others strap an oxygen mask to Hannah's face.

"Thirty-two and dropping!" came his assistant's voice again.

"Hannah!" Cody yelled through tears. "Come on, Hannah!"

The watching crowd stood transfixed. A few eyes were shut tight in quick, spontaneous prayers.

"Thirty and dropping!"

≈ ≈ ≈

A FEW MINUTES AFTER Hannah took her last breath, the paramedics tugged Cody's arms, trying to pry him loose from her body.

Staring up into their faces, he took in what he had been refusing to hear from them. "I'm sorry," he heard one of them say again. "We did everything we could possibly do."

Resisting them as they helped him to his feet, he felt the crushing reality of her death wrenching away from him his one happiness, his only possibility for happiness. *This can't be happening*, he tried to force himself to believe.

Finally standing, Cody aimlessly took a few steps. Then he stopped, realizing he and Hannah hadn't even had the chance to exchange last words.

With no notice of the watching circle of tearful faces or of the blood that soaked his clothing, he looked down at his wife and shouted with all his might: "I love you, Hannah! *I love you!*"

He continued to stand there, the sound of his farewell fading slowly over the the crowd of crying, motionless onlookers.

As the paramedics prepared to carry her dead body up to the ambulance, Cody trembled in a daze of horror. At that moment he felt with absolute certainty that he, too, wanted to die, that without Hannah he could never really live. *"No!"* he started shouting over and over. *"This isn't happening!"*

Beside him a white-haired woman slowly approached, cradling a bundle in her arms. "I'm so sorry," she said in a choking voice. "The girl didn't even get to hold her baby…"

Lost in grief and guilt, Cody didn't seem to hear her. All he could manage to do was bury his face in his hands and vent his hopelessness with a primal scream.

4

SCATTERED BY an early afternoon wind, a moderate snow was dressing Atlanta with its accumulation of white flakes. It was the first Christmas Eve snowfall in the city in seventy-five years, and its promise of a white Christmas the next morning put most of the city in a jovial mood.

Lorene was standing at her kitchen sink, her hands in Sunday dinner's dishwater. Staring out at the falling snow, she wondered if she was the only Atlantan who felt void of any childlike excitement. If anything, the family holiday season seemed only to heighten her growing loneliness. She looked back down at the dishes and began washing again, trying hard to shake her depression.

Jason, whistling a Christmas carol, had just come in from collecting an armload of pine logs. During a cold snap years ago one of his church members had given them an enormous pile of firewood as a Christmas gift. But due to the short Atlanta winters, consisting of weather that northerners wouldn't call winter at all, most of the wood had remained stacked against the back side of the house and was beginning to rot. Jason was grateful for the opportunity to use some of it now. The snowy afternoon was begging for a cozy blaze.

He entered the den, laid down the logs, and began to build a fire. In the fireplace, upon a small mound of paper and pine cones, he laid small pieces of wood with larger ones on top. He arranged them strategically, as if he were a boy trying to impress his scoutmaster. He lit a match to the paper at several points, blew some puffs of air to encourage the tiny flames, then sat back to watch them grow.

As he watched, his mind critiqued his annual Christmas sermon that he had delivered to a packed auditorium two hours earlier. The sermon had required little preparation, but he was convinced it was a classic. He had zealously called his people to a sacrificial level of Christian commitment. Tomorrow was Christ's birthday, he had reminded them, and they should give their Savior a birthday gift—a gift that would truly cost them something. Like a valiant leader rallying his troops, he then instructed them on the very thing they should give: their *obedience*. To make it easy for them, he had even explained *how* they should obey. He had entrusted to them a list of do's and don'ts.

Jason took a fireplace broom and began sweeping into a pile the wood debris that had fallen around the hearth. In an age of moral weakness, when the name of the game was self-indulgence at any cost, he had shamelessly given his people God's no-compromise code of ethics. The list included things he had preached about unnumbered times before, things that demanded constant repetition.

These were the things, he proudly recalled, that had become the staple subjects of his ministry: Christians should not attend public movies; should not engage in mixed swimming; should never be found dancing or playing cards; should without excep-

25

tion shun alcohol and tobacco; and should avoid rock music like the plague. The men should never allow their hair to grow over their ears, the women should not wear slacks, and mothers should never work outside the home.

Of equal importance were the things he expounded on from the list of do's: Christians should faithfully attend every church service—in North Metro's case, Sunday school and the worship service on Sunday morning, the Sunday night Bible study, Wednesday evening prayer meeting, and any other special meetings that might be announced. They should have a personal time every day for prayer and Bible reading; should give no less than ten percent of their net income to support the church; should be militant soul-winners; should be unquestionably patriotic; and should use only the King James Version of the Bible.

He had been thorough, Jason now concluded, in covering all the points. And he had done so with passion and dedication. There was no doubt he had been in good form.

And he had not forgotten how to build a good fire, either. The pine logs on top were crackling, and a burst of warmth radiated into the room.

"Are you about finished, Lorene?" he beckoned. He wanted her to come see the fire and enjoy it with him.

"Almost," she answered. "I'll be there soon."

Left to himself for a few more minutes, he stretched out on the sofa. The fire, the snowflakes on the tree branches outside, and a red-ribboned wreath above the mantle gave him a heart-warming reminder that Christmas was his favorite time of year. Just one sad thought blemished his perfect moment: *If only Hannah were here to share it.*

His eyes turned automatically to the high school photograph of Hannah that set on the mantle. This was their most recent picture of her, taken during her junior year, just before she ran away. He stared. He never ceased to be struck by her beauty. Her long, thick auburn hair hung to her shoulders with an innocent but luring sensuality. Her blue eyes were set in a delicately sculptured face that most professional models would envy.

It was impossible, he reckoned, for anyone not to stare at her, or at least not to want to. He remembered more than once when her attractiveness had caused him embarrassment, when they were together in public and strange men would stop and gawk at her and lose awareness of their surroundings. In an effort to make her appearance less captivating, he had restricted her use of makeup and enforced a rule against wearing snug-fitting or overly fashionable clothes. It was only right that she save her beauty for her marriage partner. "God will be honored," he repeatedly preached to her, "if you direct attention away from your body." Loose-fitting, dull-colored clothing was the way to do it.

He gazed longer into the wood-framed picture. Through the years he had found it necessary to be stern with her. From childhood on she had shown audacious tendencies to question everything, and to be obnoxiously vocal about her opinions. She had a vigorous and independent spirit that seemed to scorn authority. He remembered the many heated confrontations they had as a result. He was convinced those incidents had only been reflections of her immaturity. Refusing to let her go wild, he had consistently doled out discipline in an effort to make her a God-fearing young lady.

He had been left no choice, he felt—mainly because it was what God expected of him, but also because he could not depend on Lorene to do it. She was too soft, as proven during her occasional brave moments when she suggested he was being too harsh. He did not doubt Lorene's trust in his wisdom; it was just that she was a mother.

And he was certain his way had been right. Just before Hannah ran away, after years of his consistent discipline, he felt he had finally succeeded in breaking her will. She had mellowed, and shown a well-rounded spirit of cooperation.

That made her unexpected disappearance all the more jolting. Running away from home amounted to an act of extreme rebellion, and was therefore a cold slap to his pride. But he had long since been willing to forgive her. *She's not a foolish girl*, he often thought. *One day she'll come home. She'll have learned her lesson, and things will be different.*

The FBI had included her on a nationwide missing persons list, but there was no clue to her whereabouts. Jason, though, never lost hope.

He rose now from the couch, stepped over to the fireplace, and added one more log atop the nicely burning fire. *She'll come back*, he thought again, looking more closely at her portrait.

Then he pulled his billfold from the back pocket of his trousers, and retrieved a nearly worn-out sheet of folded stationery. It was the runaway letter Hannah had written on the eve of her disappearance. Lorene found it taped to Hannah's vanity mirror. Jason had carried it with him ever since, removing it only when he or Lorene wanted to read it.

Kneeling beside the fire, he read it again for the hundredth time.

> Dear Mom and Dad,
>
> Let me start by saying that I've tried to be a good daughter. I really have tried. I've tried more than anything else in the world. But I can't try anymore. It's hopeless. You want me to be something I'm not.
>
> Please try to understand me. Dad, I've tried to talk to you about my feelings, but you just don't listen. You always say I'm just trying to make trouble. And you, Mother—you act as if Dad is the only one who has any authority. You just play deaf and dumb. So I gave up a long time ago trying to make either of you understand. For the last six months I've just been pretending. I've tried to go along with all your rules and I've tried to act happy. But I can't do it anymore.
>
> So I'm leaving. My decision to run away is not meant to hurt you. It's just that I want to live and be normal, that's all.
>
> This might sound stupid, but just try to pretend I've only moved away to college somewhere.
>
> In spite of what it might seem, I do love you. I really do.
>
> > Your daughter,
> > Hannah
>
> P.S. Don't worry about me. I'll get a job. I'll be okay.

Returning the letter to his billfold, he whispered another prayer for her, reminding himself that only his rock-solid faith had enabled him to handle the whole ordeal so far. Even Lorene had been sustained by his faith. Jason was assured that God would honor his loving sternness as a father by bringing Hannah home safely. Not for one moment did he doubt it. After all, he reasoned, God is bound by a Christian's faith, and had no choice but to respond affirmatively to persistent praying.

His thoughts were distracted when he heard the phone ring in the kitchen. He waited for Lorene to answer it, though he expected her to call him to the phone right away. The caller was likely some church member wanting his counsel or instruction on a matter, or wanting to unload a troubled conscience after being convicted by this morning's sermon. Jason readied himself to respond. He had always told his people that he was their pastor twenty-four hours a day, and they should never hesitate to call him whenever they needed him.

Faintly, he heard Lorene say, "Yes it is....Sure, just a moment and I'll get him." He was already moving toward the kitchen when she lifted her voice and said, "It's for you, Jase."

He walked casually in and took the receiver from her hand. "Hello," Jason said in a professional tone, as Lorene turned away.

"Hello," came the serious reply. "Is this Pastor Jason L. Faircloth—the father of Hannah Renée Faircloth?"

Without taking time to think, his answer came spontaneously: "You found her!" His feelings zenithed.

Lorene pivoted, and locked her gaze on her husband's face.

"Mr. Faircloth," the voice continued soberly, and then paused. "This is the Florida branch of the FBI Missing Persons Bureau. I'm sorry to have to give you this news, but Hannah is dead. Her death was recorded ten days ago at a hospital in Miami."

The words exploded in Jason's mind. He instantly craved more information, but his mouth struggled to form words. "What? ...De—..." Absorbing the shock, he willed himself to regain composure as alien feelings swept through him. Everything—beliefs, plans, assurances—seemed instantly out of focus.

Confusion and anger finally overpowered him. Dropping the phone, he shouted, "No! She can't be! *She can't be!*"

Lorene froze with horror. She watched Jason drop to his knees, bury his face in his hands, and curl into a fetal position. He let out an agonizing cry, and it shook her from her daze. She lurched for the phone.

"Who is this? What's happened?" she asked frantically. After a half-minute of quiet listening, she began a steady stream of questions.

Jason heard Lorene talking. But through the darkness that had seized him, she sounded unintelligible, remote.

Her voice eventually drifted out of range. Lost in the obscurity of his soul, he found himself firing a torrent of accusations at God. He knew it was wrong, irrational, out of place, maybe even blasphemy. But he could not stifle it.

For the first time in his life, he felt controlled by unnatural forces.

≈ ≈ ≈

A SHARP PAIN in his shoulder summoned Jason back to reality. He turned, broke Lorene's grip, and looked into a pair of eyes displaying a hypnotic stare of nothingness.

She spoke slowly, mechanically. "The FBI is sending an attorney to our house. He'll be here Tuesday around ten. He'll give us the details, and answer any legal questions we have. And he'll help arrange for Hannah's body to be sent back to Atlanta."

She reached down stiffly and helped Jason stand erect.

"Jason..." Her voice still sounded ultra-controlled. Jason realized she was in shock. He wrapped his arms around her rigid shoulders, and locked her in an embrace.

≈ ≈ ≈

A PHONE CALL from Jason launched a flurry of others that carried the tragic news to the entire church within a matter of hours. Several heartbroken members hurried to the Faircloth home to offer support and consolation.

Lorene was sitting in a corner chair in the living room, emotionally and verbally closed in to herself, like a cocoon. She felt dead.

She heard several ladies trying to talk to her. In a way she wanted them there, yet even more she wanted to be left alone. So she made no effort to listen or respond. She had long ago mastered the art of masking her loneliness and depression, but now she didn't care what anyone thought.

"Let's pray for her," one of the women suggested. They stood in a group that encircled her, and prayed for her, their friend and pastor's wife. Then, sensing her mixed feelings about their presence, they broke into various pockets of whispered conversation across the room, expressing to one another their concern for her. "She might come out of it any time," one of them said, "and maybe she'll want someone to talk to or cry with." They agreed together to stay, at least until the arrival of Lorene's sister, Betsy, who had been summoned from Macon.

In the den, Jason was a great deal more self-conscious than Lorene. A half-dozen of the church's deacons and most faithful laymen were standing around him, groping for something therapeutic to say. In a sense they felt odd even trying; they were sure the General was in full control.

As their leader and their tower of spiritual strength, Jason felt no liberty to discuss the dark vacuum still gripping his heart. He felt pressured to act saintly. But with neither the mood nor the motivation, he found the performance terribly draining. His anger and bitterness cried out for release.

For years he had preached about the right Christian response in times of trauma: Simply relax and trust God. His convictions about the rightness of that formula had deepened since Hannah ran away. During the last year and a half he had always been able to keep his emotions under control and to retain a calming faith, even in the face of grief and anxiety.

But back then there was always the hope of seeing Hannah again. Now there was none. Faith seemed worthless.

Jason succeeded, however, in keeping his dark feelings well out of sight of these men. As they each left him with a firm handshake later in the evening, not one would have believed him if he said he was already on the edge of disillusionment.

5

IN THE MASTER BEDROOM, Betsy sat at Lorene's bedside. It was past midnight, but Lorene was wide awake, staring silently at the ceiling, apparently hearing nothing her sister said to her. Betsy felt helpless.

She had started the ninety-minute drive from Macon as soon as she heard the news. Five years older than Lorene, she had not been particularly close to her while growing up. But in recent years, mainly due to Betsy's initiative, their relationship had deepened.

Never religious, Betsy had always been considered the family's black sheep. Recently, however, Lorene had seemed to find a sort of awkward refreshment in her older sister's honesty, humor, and independence. "You're like a long-lost treasure chest that I've finally discovered after all these years," Lorene told her privately when they were together at Thanksgiving.

Betsy had jokingly nicknamed her younger sister "The Quaker," amused by what she considered the centuries-old mentality of Jason and Lorene. With harmless intentions she sometimes kidded them about it. Actually, although she didn't agree with them, she respected anyone who had convictions and lived by them. And besides, she thought Lorene possessed a rare and simple innocence that she herself had lost years ago. Betsy felt almost protective of her—especially now, as she beheld her sister stretched out in sleepless grief.

She doesn't deserve to hurt like this, Betsy thought.

≈ ≈ ≈

IN THE GUEST BEDROOM, Jason was awake, tossing and turning on bed sheets damp with sweat.

Sleep seemed absurd now anyway. He got up, dressed, then stepped out and took a coat from the hall closet.

He saw the light in the master bedroom, but decided not to

drop in. He was thankful Betsy was there. At the moment he didn't have the capacity to do what she was doing.

The air outside was brisk. Jason looked up into the clear sky. Stars sparkled by the thousands. Normally the sight would have been enchanting, but tonight it held no appeal.

He walked aimlessly in the white, silent street. The devastating flood of loneliness and uncertainty refused to recede. It was Christmas Eve, supposedly the happiest night of the year, but he could not even think about joy or peace, much less experience them.

He had given God his entire adult life. Now God had taken the life of his only child. Why? He asked the question again and again and again. But there was no answer. The skies were quiet. The streets, the trees, and the houses were all silent and white. For the first time in all those years, Jason felt he did not know God at all.

His slow, dragging steps made long tracks in the snow. Eventually they made a full circle around the block that included his house. In front of it again, he turned mindlessly up the driveway, then shuffled across the lawn and behind the house.

Almost instinctively he was drawn toward a wooden structure that stood deep on the far side of their lot, nestled under pine trees. He had built it the same year he and Lorene and Hannah moved here—as a birthday present for Hannah. It was her childhood playhouse.

He stood under the snow-laden pine limbs and stared at it, transfixed by his memories. He remembered playing house with his little girl.

"Hannah dear, what are you making for supper tonight?"

"Well...how 'bout ice cream and cookies?" came the precious reply.

"Don't you think we need to have some meat and vegetables?"

"Nope. We eat that stuff all the time in Mommy's house. In my house we'll eat ice cream and cookies."

"Too many sweets will make holes in your teeth, you know."

"Ah, Daddy, we're just pretending!"

For the first time in ten hours he smiled. It lasted only a second or two before he burst into tears.

≈　≈　≈

BETSY WAS THERE the moment he opened the kitchen door leading in from the carport.

"Jason," she said with concern, "I think we need to get Lorene to a doctor. She's burning up with a fever, and she's acting delirious."

"Delirious? What do you mean?"

"She's lying there in bed just staring at the ceiling and talking nonsense. And she still won't acknowledge that I'm in the room with her. Something isn't right."

Without bothering to take off his coat, Jason headed for the master bedroom. Betsy was right behind him.

When he walked through the bedroom doorway he was almost certain he could smell the sickness. Eerily, he even thought he could sense from across the room the feverish heat radiating from Lorene's body.

"Lorene, are you all right?" he asked automatically as he sat next to her on the bed.

She was swaying her crossed arms back and forth as if rocking a baby. She was singing a quiet lullaby, almost in a whisper, and kept right on as if she hadn't heard Jason's question.

For several minutes, as Betsy applied an icepack to Lorene's head, Jason tried in vain to establish communication with his wife. Worried, he finally turned to Betsy. "You're right. She needs a doctor. I'll get Ray over here right away."

Betsy nodded. "I'll stay put and try to keep her calm."

Jason made the phone call, and within half an hour Dr. Ray Meade, the Faircloth family physician, was at their front door. He was one of Jason's dedicated church members, and a loyal friend for more than ten years. It was three o'clock in the morning, but Jason knew Ray didn't mind coming over.

Jason and Ray entered the bedroom, and after a brief introduction of Betsy, Ray stepped over to the bedside and went immediately to work. Jason felt a slight bit of relief. *If anyone can know what's wrong with her,* Jason thought, *I'm sure Ray will.*

After only a moment, Ray lifted his head and said in a soft but authoritative monotone, "If you don't mind, let me be alone with her."

≈ ≈ ≈

JASON WAS PACING the kitchen floor, drinking a cup of instant coffee Betsy had made for him. She stood silently staring out the window above the kitchen sink, lost in her thoughts.

Jason wanted urgently to pray for Lorene. But when he thought about the hundreds of times he had prayed fervently for Hannah, always with a secure belief that God would keep her safe and bring her home, he was now tempted to believe the whole concept of faith was only an ill-conceived hoax. He tried praying for Lorene anyway—but he could not believe.

Another new pain—the pain of insecurity—was growing within him, the result of his eroding faith in a prayer-answering God. Already it was beginning to plant fear in his heart. He gave a shiver, and gulped down the last of his coffee.

He and Betsy heard the sound of a door opening. They both turned and went out immediately, meeting Ray in the hallway.

His expression revealed deep concern. "Jason," he said pointedly, "I hate to unload more bad news on you. But to be honest, Lorene's situation appears to be serious. The fever is due to nothing more than a common virus. It's been complicated by an ear infection. I'll leave you some antibiotics that should take care of that.

"But the real problem is that she's in a state of mental shock, and it appears to be rather severe. There's no medicine I can give her for that. I'm going to recommend that you put her under the care of a psychiatrist. I believe she's had an extreme reaction to Hannah's death, and it scares me. I may be wrong, you understand—but my experience tells me a person suffering to her extent has been damaged to the point of needing professional therapy."

Jason's mind was reeling. Betsy started to weep.

"Listen," Ray said, trying to ease their distress. "Let her rest here today. Stay with her, keep her fever under control, and give her the antibiotics every five hours. Then tomorrow you can get her to the hospital."

Jason nodded.

Ray gave them further instructions about the antibiotics, packed his doctor's bag, and left. Betsy took up her position at Lorene's bedside. Jason retreated to his study.

He left the lights off. He sat on his desk and examined the pale stripes of light showing through the window blinds. It all seemed so senseless. "Don't you love me, God?" he begged aloud. He paused, then repeated the question in anguish.

The silence he received in answer was maddening. He didn't know exactly what he expected God to do or say, but Jason knew he couldn't handle the silence. Why couldn't God speak audibly just this once, and offer an explanation or a word of comfort? Why? Why? Was God so heartless?

As he faced the dawn of Christmas Day, he had only one consolation: In less than thirty hours, the mystery of Hannah's death would begin to unravel.

6

PEN AND PAPER IN HAND, Jason sat at a desk in the den. He had been waiting nervously all morning for the attorney's scheduled ten-o'clock arrival. It was now 9:45, and still finding it impossible to relax, he decided to write out a list of questions for his visitor.

Yesterday, Christmas, had been the longest and bleakest day of his life. He had endured unwanted conversations with a parade of grieving friends and relatives who either dropped by or phoned to express their condolences. He had to repeat endlessly an explanation of Lorene's condition, while she spent most of the day shut up in the bedroom sleeping. Betsy nursed her constantly, trying to keep the fever in check. By nightfall both Jason and Betsy were exhausted, and they decided together not to take Lorene to the hospital until after the attorney's visit.

Jason had now been wide awake since 6:30. He'd eaten grapefruit and toast for breakfast—the first meal he remembered having since Sunday's after-church dinner. He decided he couldn't face the office for a few days at least, so shortly after eight he telephoned the church and talked with his secretary and the three assistant pastors. He assigned each of them various jobs he wanted done during his absence.

Soon afterward, Betsy had succeeded in getting Lorene to take some warm cereal and milk in bed. Lorene still was noncommunicative, however, and was now sound asleep.

Jason had started his second page of questions when the doorbell rang at 10:03. Fighting hard to look composed, he answered the door. The stranger he ushered in was dressed in a well-cut three-piece suit. Jason judged him at once to be a high-caliber individual, one who could be trusted to deliver an honest and thorough account of the facts.

The man extended his hand. "Reverend Faircloth," he said in a clear and intelligent manner, "my name is Slade Wakefield. I'm an attorney in Miami, and a personal friend of Rex Lehman. As you recall, Mr. Lehman is the man you've corresponded with a few times at the national headquarters of the FBI Missing Persons Bureau. At his request, I've come to give you information you've probably been waiting a long time to hear."

Jason nodded wordlessly, and directed Slade into the living room.

When the two men were seated—Slade on the sofa, Jason in an armchair beside it—Betsy served coffee. The conversational formalities were courteous, but brief and to the point.

Betsy had just taken a seat when, without a sound, Lorene walked in unexpectedly from the hallway. She looked frail and thinner than ever in her nightgown. Jason and Betsy were speechless. Before they could react, Lorene sat down in an antique rocking chair across the room from the sofa. Sensing the awkwardness, Slade remained quiet.

Lorene broke the silence. Staring at Slade, she pleaded, "Tell us everything, *please.*" Her voice was strained and broken.

Encouraged at hearing her first coherent phrase in a day and a half, Jason recovered his speech. "Honey," he said with a ray of optimism, "are you feeling okay?" He got up and moved toward her.

Before he could take three steps, Lorene jerked her head in his direction and stopped him cold with a venomous glare and an order given like a growl: "Stay away from me, you *murderer!*"

Jason's optimism about her condition dissolved on the spot. He stood there in shock. What she meant by her last word escaped him for the moment; it was her hostile tone and blazing stare that astounded him. Had he been alone with her, he might have tried to force from her an explanation of this behavior. But in the presence of Betsy and Slade he did not want to take the risk of creating a scene. He felt himself turning red with embarrassment.

Betsy quickly took the initiative to ease the tension by scooting her chair next to Lorene's. Comfortingly, she placed her hand lightly on Lorene's arm. She could feel Lorene begin to relax.

Slade, accustomed to seeing heated emotions in courtrooms and law offices, appeared unaffected by the outburst, and said nothing.

Jason, still unnerved, retreated to his chair. Then Lorene pleaded once more with Slade. This time her voice was soft and teary, like that of a frightened child wanting a parent's reassurance: "Please...just start from the beginning. I want to know everything."

Slade looked to Jason for a nod of approval, which Jason quickly gave.

"Certainly, Mrs. Faircloth," Slade began. "First of all, let me say that most of the information I'm about to share with you has been supplied by Hannah's husband—"

"Her husband!" Jason interrupted. He had considered before the possibility of Hannah's having married during her long absence, but hearing it as fact was jarring.

Lorene sighed. She started rocking slowly in the chair, her forearms resting loosely on the rocker's aged wooden arms. Betsy cupped the back of Lorene's hand in hers.

"Let me try putting your mind at ease," Slade continued, "by saying also that there was no foul play involved in her death. She died of natural causes. Her husband's statements, along with those of witnesses, have already been verified." He hesitated, looking for a sign of questioning. When there was none, he continued.

"When Hannah left Atlanta in July of last year, she hitchhiked to Miami, where she found a job as a hotel maid. Her income was minimal, but it did allow her to rent an inexpensive apartment not far from the hotel." Slade purposely avoided mentioning that the apartment was in one of the poorest and roughest areas of the city. "She was still working there seven months later when she met her husband at one of the beaches. Apparently there was a very strong attraction between them, because two weeks later Hannah moved in with him."

"Unmarried?" Jason asked, again bewildered. Already he'd been torn up inside by the thought of his beautiful daughter hitchhiking hundreds of miles, then working the dreg job of a hotel maid.

"That's correct. They didn't marry until two months later, after they found out she was pregnant."

Until that moment, Jason had never considered whether he might have been a failure as a father. He had always attributed Hannah's problems to her refusal to submit to authority. But hearing of her immorality triggered in him the numbing notion that all the standards and values and convictions he'd spent years drilling into her had never registered with her in the slightest. It was suddenly clear: At some vital point he had failed. His pride wanted to deny this truth, but his broken heart forced him to admit it.

He stole a glance at Lorene. Rocking slowly, she was staring distantly out the picture window behind the sofa. "So...she had a child?" she said slowly, returning her eyes to Slade.

"Yes ma'am, there is a child, but I'll explain more about that later." He carried on: "The young man comes from a well-to-do background, and had finished graduate school last December. He had just begun his own business—and was doing well with it. Shortly after Hannah's pregnancy was confirmed, he proposed to her and she accepted. They were married on her birthday, in a civil ceremony. And their marriage, by all accounts, went along very smoothly..."

As Jason followed the scenario in his mind, he tried to imagine Hannah's daily life and feelings. It brought yet a different kind of pain, a new and angry hurt: The last eighteen months were a chapter in her life that he would never be able to share with her. They were gone, forever.

In tense anguish he shifted in his seat, and turned to Lorene. She was again staring quietly out the window. She looked drained.

"Apparently," Slade continued, "Hannah's pregnancy also went well, right up until a week and a half ago. They were at home on the evening of Friday the fifteenth, when Hannah's water broke. Her due date, I understand, was supposed to be this Friday—the twenty-ninth—so the baby came early. Anyway, she immediately began having strong contractions at quite close intervals, and she and the young man set out for the hospital. Unfortunately they encountered rush hour traffic which held them up. As her labor intensified, the young man panicked. He started taking chances to gain time. As he attempted to drive through a red light, he had to swerve to miss another vehicle; he lost control and ran off the road. No one suffered injuries, but the car got stuck in some sand. The young man waved some people down and solicited their help to get the car back on the road, but they couldn't move it. He then asked someone to call an ambulance. By the time it arrived, Hannah had already delivered the baby—a little girl—with the help of her husband and some bystanders. The baby was fine, but due to complications with her uterus, Hannah started bleeding severely from the moment she delivered. By the time the emergency team arrived she had already lost too much blood. She died there, beside the road."

Slade paused. Lorene collapsed onto Betsy's arm. Both sisters were weeping. Jason's stiffened lips were trembling as he struggled to hold his tears inside. A thousand questions were rising in his soul, but before he could speak, Lorene lifted her glistening eyes and asked one of her own: "Where is my granddaughter?"

"Still in Miami," Slade answered, offering nothing more.

Lorene fired her next question like a bullet: "When can I see her?"

Slade reflected no emotion. "I had hoped, Mrs. Faircloth, that we could wait and discuss that later."

"Why?" Jason broke in. "Is there a problem of some kind?"

Slade could tell from Jason's tone that he wanted nothing less than an immediate, straightforward answer. "Yes...there is a problem."

"Well?" Jason prodded, impatiently.

"It seems," Slade answered, "that your son-in-law has waived your rights to see the child."

"What do you mean?" Jason retorted with unbelief.

"For personal reasons," Slade related, "the young man has requested that both his and the baby's identity and location be withheld from you."

Jason now realized why Slade had been referring to his son-in-law as "the young man" instead of giving him a name. Unable to stay seated any longer, he stood and began pacing a tight circle in the center of the room. Then he turned to Slade. "But why...I mean, she's our granddaughter. How can he do that? *Why* would he do that?" His exasperation filled the room.

"I do want to say," Slade calmly replied, "that he contacted the police himself, and he personally volunteered your name and address and asked that you be notified. He also decided on his own to let you have your daughter's body. But for his own reasons he's chosen to raise his daughter himself. There's simply nothing the law can do to force him to share the child with you."

Aghast, Jason nearly shouted: "So you're telling us we'll *never* get to see our own granddaughter?"

Slade answered with empathy. "I'm afraid that's the situation, unless the young man reconsiders and takes the initiative to contact you on his own."

"Well—you've been with him. What do you think? I mean, isn't his decision just a temporary hang-up of some kind?"

Slade shook his head and sighed, his own feelings obvious in the silence.

Jason sat back down in his chair, engulfed in agony and

mounting rage. He had never imagined the nightmare could grow any worse. He buried his face in his hands, and did not see or hear Lorene as she slowly pulled herself forward, leaning on the rocker's arms for support, then stood up.

When Jason lifted his head, her eyes were focused at his feet, as if she were laying something there. With the look of death, she turned and staggered out of the room, with Betsy at her side.

≈ ≈ ≈

BY EARLY AFTERNOON, Slade had answered every question Jason in his despair could think to ask. He also obtained Jason's signature on paperwork authorizing Hannah's body to be flown back to Atlanta, and stood at his side while Jason made a lengthy call to a local funeral home to make the arrangements.

Jason said goodbye to Slade, thanking him for his help and concern. When Slade was out the door, Jason immediately headed down the hall to lie down. He decided he needed a moment to rest and regroup before getting Lorene to a hospital. He also determined to give a phone call later to Steve Mitchell, his primary assistant, and ask him to give the upcoming sermons for Wednesday night, Sunday morning, and Sunday evening. For the first time in his ministry, he had no heart for preaching.

He closed the guest bedroom door behind him, and threw himself face down on the bed.

The adversities that had assailed his life since Sunday afternoon had consumed his every thought and feeling. They had become his world. He could not deflect them, and they would not release their pressure. He had been a puppet to their power. The whole of his life outside the realm of these thoughts and feelings had been put on hold.

Everything had gone numb. Only pain remained, a pain that seemed just moments away from the total conquest of his sanity.

He wanted to scream, but resisted. The effort produced a throbbing lump in his throat, followed by an explosion of tears.

Just when his cries had quieted, the door swung open, banging against the doorstop on the wall. The unexpected noise frightened him. As he jerked and rolled over, he found himself staring into Lorene's eyes, only inches from his own. They were the eyes of an enemy intent upon revenge. Her fists were already aiming their blows.

As he lifted his arms to block the swings, her shrieks filled his ears. "You killed my daughter! You *idiot!* You killed her!" He recalled in an instant her accusation from this morning, the meaning of which registered with him only now.

Fighting like a wild animal, she was almost impossible to handle. After Jason managed to get off the bed and stand firmly on both feet, it took all the strength that he in his weariness possessed to finally pin her to the floor. Straddling her writhing torso and trying to hold down her arms, he felt his lungs stretching for every breath.

He thought of yelling for Betsy to come and help, but changed his mind, not wanting her to see them like this.

Suddenly one of Lorene's arms fought free. Before Jason could pin her again, she slashed at him and clawed open his left eyelid with her sharp nails. The cut went all the way through the eyelid and up into the eyebrow. An excruciating pain shot through Jason's head. The blood at once started rolling down the contour of his face and dropping off at the chin. Her hand still free, Lorene kept delivering blows.

With his ripped eyelid squeezed shut and gushing blood, Jason erupted with anger. He slammed Lorene's arms to the floor as if they were broomsticks.

She groaned in pain and exhaustion. For a few seconds she lay there breathing heavily, with Jason's blood now splattered on her neck, face, and chest.

Jason thought the fight was over. But when she gained her breath she lashed out again, this time with words.

"You...you killed her!...You know that...don't you, Jason?"

"What are you talking about?" he demanded angrily.

"Exactly...what I said, Jason!" she screamed between labored breaths. "You killed her!"

He shouted back: "You're not making sense, Lorene!"

"All right, I'll make sense!" she snapped. "Hannah would still be alive in this house if it hadn't been for your stupid rules. No pants! No being alone with her boyfriends! No rock music! No makeup! No dancing! No cheerleading! No mixed swimming! No movies! Everything was No! Jason, can't you see it? You were a heartless, legalistic, know-it-all dictator! You forced her to leave—you and your damnable know-it-all attitude!"

Jason leaned back his head in frazzled astonishment, his hands still locked on her arms. "You're falling apart, Lorene!"

"*NO!* No, Jason—I've just never had the courage to confront you before. Like a fool I've played the submissive little housewife who keeps her mouth shut. But I really don't care anymore, because it's over!"

"For heaven's sake, Lorene! Try to—"

"You *still* don't understand, do you? You really *are* blind! I don't believe the thought's ever crossed your mind that you could be wrong about anything, has it? You think you know it all. And anybody and everybody who disagrees with you or challenges you is wrong! Isn't that right, Jason?"

"Lorene...I think you're...I mean..." He was loosening his grip on her.

Emboldened by the experience of seeing Jason incapable of a comeback, she continued her tirade: "Talking to you is like talking to a rock, Jason. You don't listen to people. You never have. You disregard people's feelings as if they were trash! And what about *me?* You've walked all over me for years. You didn't listen when I said I didn't want that tubal ligation surgery. You forced it on me! It's always been that way! About everything! First with me, then with Hannah. *That's why she left*, Jason! She couldn't stomach you anymore. You should know—you've carried her letter around for more than a year. But have you ever really understood it? *No!* Your stinking, almighty pride won't let you! You're just too..."

She was stopped abruptly in mid-sentence by a heaving sensation. Her chest rose twice. Frightfully, Jason began lifting his weight from her. Reflexively, she sat up, erect. And then it came. The vomit spewed forcefully. Jason felt it splatter over his chest and arms.

Lorene went limp, closed her eyes, and fell back again to the floor. Jason promptly felt a sick churning in his own stomach. He was nearly overcome with the stench and the repugnant sight of

Lorene covered with blood and vomit. But this was no time to be weak-hearted. Shaking nervously, more from confusion than anxiety, he instinctively pressed his fingers lightly to the side of her neck. Her pulse was dangerously accelerated. He felt her forehead. She was burning.

Quickly he searched for Betsy, leaving a trail of blood and regurgitation on the carpet.

He finally found her outside, in the laundry room off the carport. Both the washer and dryer were running noisily. He scared her as he walked in. *Good,* he thought, *she didn't hear us inside.* "I'll explain about the eye later," he said. "But Lorene is sick—collapsed—and I need you to help me get her to the car. We've got to get her to the hospital."

Betsy needed no second urging. Almost in panic, she followed on Jason's heels as he turned and ran back into the house.

They said little as they madly rushed about, wiping up the foul mess, putting on clean clothes, and filling a small suitcase with essentials for Lorene. They carried her to the car, laid her on the back seat, and were off. Betsy drove, while Jason sat in the front seat beside her and kept a towel pressed to his bleeding eye.

Jason's sustained grimace told Betsy the wound was causing lots of pain. After a few minutes of silence she expressed her concern. "That cut looks like it needs a doctor, too. What happened, anyway?"

"Oh, it's not much," Jason shrugged. "Lorene...accidentally pushed the door open in my face as she came into the guest bedroom."

Betsy asked innocently, "Why was she going in there? I left her sound asleep in bed."

"She must have been trying to let someone know she needed help," he suggested. "She got sick on the spot. That's when she collapsed. I never got a word out of her."

It was the first time in his adulthood that he remembered telling an intentional lie. But it had come quickly, without hesitation; he was determined not to disclose the bedroom brawl. Besides, he rationalized, letting Betsy know the truth would be an injustice:

The incident in no way reflected his and Lorene's normal behavior.

Satisfied, Betsy took a quick glance over her shoulder at Lorene, and let out a sympathetic moan for her suffering sister as she continued toward the hospital. She asked nothing more.

In the silence, Jason wondered about Lorene's accusations. Was she coherent when she made them? Did she know what she was saying? Did she really mean all of it? If so, was there any truth to it? Was he really blind, unlistening, heartless? Was he a know-it-all dictator?

Am I really to blame for Hannah's death? he asked himself.

If so, he concluded angrily, then it was God's fault. He was the one who had misled him.

7

UNSHAVEN AND IN his old brown housecoat, Jason held his face a few inches from the bathroom mirror, forcing sight through one eye. He watched the reflection of his finger as it lifted to the other eye, then slowly moved over each of the twelve stitches rejoining the torn edges of the gash across his eyelid and eyebrow. Three extra stitch points kept the eye temporarily shut, so the main stitches would not be batted loose.

"You're a lucky man," he heard the echo of the doctor's voice ringing in his head. "You came within a sixteenth of an inch or so of losing your eye. You'll wear a scar for the rest of your life, but at least you'll be able to see."

He dropped his finger, pulled his face back slightly from the mirror, and noticed how beaten and miserable he looked. *You have ceased to be the strong man*, he told himself. He stepped away, walked back into the master bedroom, and slumped back down on the bed.

It was early Saturday morning. He was alone in the house, and feeling alone in a world that was no longer easy. It was chaotic, depressive. Answers he once had lived by had now vaporized and vanished. Nothing made sense anymore.

The sudden ring of the telephone shook him from his introspection. It rang again. He reached over to the bedside phone, hoping it was the call he had been waiting for. "Yes?"

"Good morning, Reverend Faircloth, this is Dr. Waterman." *Good*, Jason thought. It was the expected call from the hospital. Now he would get his answer.

"I know you wanted your wife to be able to attend your daughter's funeral with you this afternoon, but it just isn't going to be possible. Dr. Weber, the psychiatric specialist I told you about, has agreed to examine her today. It was the only time he could work it into his schedule. As I explained to you earlier, his evaluation is absolutely vital to our diagnosis. So we've gone ahead and planned the tests for later this morning and throughout the early part of the afternoon.

"However, even if Dr. Weber couldn't see Lorene today, she's in no condition to leave the hospital. Two nurses are in her room right now trying to cool down one of her flash fevers. And she—"

"So there's been no sign of improvement?" Jason interrupted tiredly.

"She's still not coherent. And as I just indicated, she's still suffering from the frequent fevers that for some mysterious reason we haven't been able to eliminate. So to answer your question: No, there has been no sign of improvement."

"But she...Doctor, it just isn't right for her not to be there," he said with a quivering voice, trying not to sound disagreeable. He stood up from the bed. "It's...It's not fair. This is her *daughter!*"

"I understand, Reverend Faircloth. I know how you must feel. Anyone would agree it's an unjust set of circumstances. And I assure you, if it was in my ability to change those circumstances I would certainly do so. Let's just cross our fingers and hope Dr.

47

Weber's tests will prove to be the breakthrough we need to understand your wife's sickness."

"Yeah...okay then," responded Jason, trying to sound hopeful. "We'll do that."

"Let me also say, Reverend Faircloth, that from Lorene's point of view she'll not be aware of missing the funeral." His tone was compassionate. "Perhaps that will help you endure for the moment, until we have some good news."

The conversation ended after Dr. Waterman told Jason he could extend his daily five-minute visits with Lorene to fifteen minutes, beginning tomorrow.

Jason thanked him, hung up the phone, and sank to the bedroom floor. He drew up his knees and dropped his head between them. Dr. Waterman, it seemed, cared more about his plight than God did.

≈ ≈ ≈

DRESSED IN HIS recently cleaned best suit, Jason looked at his watch. He still had well over an hour until the funeral. He sat down again on the bed, and decided to try praying for Lorene. Moments later he gave up, feeling once more that his prayers were impotent.

He walked vacantly from the bedroom and began pacing the house, wanting to squeeze memories of Hannah out of every room. But the terrible, sickening realization came to him that there were not many detailed memories to draw upon. He had always been too busy to give her enough time, enough *good* times. It was always "Later, Hannah." Later never came—and now, later never would.

He drifted into the living room. Lorene's accusations were taking root. He was forced to admit that intimate father-and-daughter times with Hannah had been unforgivably few and infrequent. Behind his priestly cloak he had been a decrepit father.

He walked by the coffee table and stopped. Picking up the family Bible lying there, he slung it across the room.

He stalked out, found his topcoat in the hall closet, and made his way to the carport. Yanking open the Buick's door, Jason paused. Before leaving he felt compelled to go once more to the far corner of the back yard and visit Hannah's playhouse.

48

The walk across the lawn and under the pines came close to driving him crazy. It was an intentional assault against himself, a tortuous reminder of what his relationship with Hannah could have been.

He reached the structure, paused before it, and ran his hand along its blue-painted wood siding and white trim. Inside the door he could see a stack of three or four miniature red plastic plates that had been there since Hannah's childhood.

The floodgates of memories were beginning to open. Soon he was overcome with images from the past—Hannah running, Hannah laughing, Hannah falling, Hannah crying, Hannah sleeping, Hannah talking. Hannah breathing...Hannah lving...

The pain built again in his throat. *"My God! Somehow help me redeem myself!"*

≈≈≈

THE WORKERS FROM North Brothers Funeral Home, dressed in matching dark-brown polyester suits, were unloading the casket at the church when Jason drove up in his Buick. He parked in his designated spot, the one closest to the main building's side entrance that led to the church offices. He was glad to be early, hoping that when the casket was set up inside the sanctuary he could spend a few minutes there alone.

He watched the workers quickly roll the casket inside on its collapsible four-wheel transporter, then close the church doors behind them. Inside that box, Hannah was lying stiff.

Into his throat came the pain again. *It's over!* he raged silently to himself. *It's really over. She's really dead. God—I can't face it!*

He prayed aloud in a wrenching whisper: "Why have you done this, God? I begged you day and night for eighteen months to keep her safe. And I believed in you. O God, why? What did Hannah do to deserve this? And what did *I* do? Don't you know what this is doing to my faith?"

Jason dropped his head on the steering wheel. "All I've done is give up my entire life for you!" he shouted as he squeezed the wheel. "Is this what I get in return?"

For long moments of sweat and tears, Jason waited till the brown-suited workers exited the building and drove away. Then he got out of his car and walked around to the building's front entrance, through the huge white double doors, and across the quiet, spacious foyer. He was struck immediately by the strong fragrance of flowers.

He stood looking down the auditorium's carpeted center aisle. At the other end was the maroon-colored coffin, surrounded by a massive and varied array of blooms that filled the area below the pulpit. The top half of the coffin was open, with the lower half covered by the customary flowered sheath.

Dizzily, slowly, he started up the aisle. He felt his legs growing weak as he moved closer.

Finally, after a year and a half of separation, he stood looking down on Hannah's face. With his heart and throat feeling ready to burst, he stood there, motionless, fighting to breathe.

She was more beautiful than he had remembered. Dressed in her favorite color, lavender, she looked more like a mature and elegant lady than a rebellious runaway teenager.

Almost hypnotized, he watched her for what seemed like hours. When he finally moved, he kissed the fingers on his right hand, then slowly, reverently, placed his fingertips to Hannah's forehead.

"If only..." He whispered aloud to her. "If only I had another chance, Hannah..." His voice was tight. The grief was indescribably intense, nearly paralyzing. Yet he still forced out his words: "You tried to tell me, didn't you? But I wouldn't listen. I was just a blind fool, honey. Just a blind old fool."

Through tears he kept staring at her, trying desperately to will her back to life. The more he stared, the more his anger swelled against God. A voice inside him was roaring his animosity: "You're heartless, God. You're outright heartless!"

His grief, his contempt for God, and his hatred toward himself seethed until they were more than he could manage. He sat down on the carpet and cried uncontrollably.

It was over. He would never be a father again.

≈ ≈ ≈

MOST OF THE FIVE HUNDRED PEOPLE attending the funeral proceeded afterward to the burial site where, in sunny, fifty-degree weather, they paid their final respects.

Following the last prayer, Jason was immediately swarmed by

scores of church members feeling the need to express encouragement. "You can trust God, General," he heard from several. "He knows what he's doing." "God is on the throne, General; he doesn't make mistakes." "There's a reason why it all happened, General; we'll be praying for you." "Remember, General: All things work together for good to them that love God."

He wanted to believe they really cared, but found it impossible. Did even one person there comprehend the pain that was shredding his life into pieces? Was any one of them sincere? He grew more resentful by the minute, until it dawned on him that most of these expressions were simply echoes of what his people had heard him offer up as consolations so many times before.

Shaking the hand of his would-be consolers one by one, he kept watching out of the corner of his eye as the grave-diggers threw shovels of dirt on the coffin vault below. He wanted to run.

So he did. When the crowd dispersed, he got in his car, found the closest freeway entry ramp, and drove aimlessly for hours. He cried till he could cry no more.

His subconscious kept the car on the highway while his mind traveled a million miles down other roads: Had he been a self-deceived fraud in his ministry? He did not feel like a general anymore; instead he felt like a private in generals clothing. How was it that others considered him a spring of knowledge, when he now saw nothing in himself but a dry, empty well?

He wanted someone to talk to. But was there anyone? He needed someone with a listening ear, someone he could spill his heart to, someone with whom he could share his real feelings, someone who could understand and accept his newly discovered weaknesses and not be disillusioned by them. But there was no one. For years he had distanced himself from everyone, allowing himself to be idolized. He'd let himself be put on his pedestal alone. Now he would have to suffer alone.

With an aching head, he eventually decided to go home. When he finally drove into the darkened carport, it was almost 7:30.

He unlocked the door of the house, pushed it open, and heard the annoying sound of the phone ringing. He steped inside, de-

51

ciding not to answer it. But it kept ringing. Finally he picked up the receiver, for no other reason than to kill the bothersome noise.

"Hello. Pastor Jason Faircloth," he answered moodily, sounding boorish and detached.

"Just a moment, please," a female voice responded. There was a long, irritating silence. Jason waited impatiently before another female voice came on. "Reverend Faircloth, this is Georgia Baptist Hospital. Listen to me carefully, please. Dr. Waterman says you need to come to the hospital right away. Your wife has taken a severe turn for the worse, and it's possible she may not make it through the night. Do you underst— Reverend Faircloth? Reverend Faircloth?"

Jason had hung up before she finished. He was running out the door and heading for the car.

≈ ≈ ≈

THE BUICK'S SPEEDOMETER indicated eighty miles per hour, but Jason wasn't watching it. "God, don't do this to me!" he started shouting. He found himself beating the dashboard and cursing God at the same time.

Suddenly he saw blue rotating strobe lights reflecting their pulsing beams in his rearview mirror. He had no intention of stopping, however, until he reached the hospital. He pressed down harder on the accelerator.

Almost instantly he heard the blast of a siren. His heartbeats quickened. Glancing up into the mirror, he saw the patrol car closing the gap between them.

He looked ahead. He was bearing down on a traffic light that had just flashed red. He held his breath, his foot pushing the accelerator all the way to the floor. In that same split-second, when there was no more chance of stopping, he spotted headlights merging from the street to his right. His heartbeats halted. He tensed himself for the impact.

Above the blaring siren he heard the tires of the other car grab the asphalt and start skidding. He knew it was over.

Suddenly it was as if everything went into slow motion: the lighted intersection, the headlights of the merging car shining in his eyes, the brilliant, flashing blue from the police car behind him

—and his clear and precise thoughts that life was ending, and in such a ravaged state.

But the collision never happened. Just as quickly as it had come to threaten his life, it was gone.

His car engine continued whining. The scene of the would-be disaster faded in his rearview mirror. Jason was safe. But he did not unfreeze until in his mirror he saw the pursuing patrol car make it safely through the intersection as well. Then, realizing how close it had all been, a hot, uncomfortable tingling ran the length of his spine.

Still he made no attempt to slow down. Despite the distractions he could think of nothing except Lorene crying out for him from a bed of pain. He was forced onward by his husbandly bond of more than twenty years.

Under hot pursuit he kept his lead all the way to the hospital. As he slowed down to make the turn into the parking lot, he noticed another set of sweeping blue lights coming from in front of him.

Jason sped to the parking row nearest the hospital's main entrance. His car screeched to a sliding halt, straddling a parking space dividing line. In the second or two it took to switch off the ignition and unbuckle his seatbelt, two patrol cars had stopped behind him, with blinding lights and deafening sirens.

He threw open the car door and stepped out to run. A voice shouted, "Freeze!"

Tempted to ignore the order, he quickly changed his mind when he saw four policemen move quickly from behind their blazing car lights. He stopped. Three were bearing pistols, and the fourth was shouldering a shotgun. All four guns were aimed at him.

He heard a second order: "Turn around slowly, mister, and put your hands in the air!" The officer sounded serious enough to shoot.

Jason obeyed. As he turned around he was forcefully pushed up against the Buick. Quick hands searched him for a weapon.

"Officer," he almost growled, "You don't understand. My

wife..." His hands came down to gesture his words when the officer's shout cut him short.

"I said put your hands up!"

Jason shot them back into the air.

He tried again: "Just listen to me, please! I was just notified that my wife is dying—she's a patient in this hospital. I've got to get to her! Don't you understand?"

Jason was aware that these were experienced men who constantly heard lies and excuses. They knew better than to just let Jason walk. And his damaged, hoodlum-looking eye probably only heightened their leeriness. But he had to get to Lorene.

"You what?" he heard the angry demand.

"I've got to get to my wife. She's a patient here. She's dying!" Jason shouted impatiently. "I've got to get to her!"

There were a few seconds of silence behind him. Then a burly officer edged closer to him and growled through clenched teeth. "Listen to me, man. If you're lying, you're gonna wish this day never existed!"

Jason cringed, then raised his voice emphatically. "I'm not a criminal. I'm a pastor. And if my wife dies while we're standing here, *you're* gonna be the one who wished this day never existed!"

"Let me see your driver's license," the officer ordered, his gun still aimed. Jason pulled out his wallet, found his license, then impatiently handed it over.

The officer turned to the others. "Harris! You and Bob search the car." He looked at the license for a moment, then said, "Fitz, you come with me." He grabbed the back of Jason's jacket collar and gave a shove in the direction of the sidewalk leading to the hospital entrance.

Nobody spoke during the short jaunt. All three men were breathing heavily.

The receptionist in the hospital lobby gaped with alarm at the sight: an obviously angry policeman holding his pistol to the back of a defiant but nervous-looking man with a terribly ugly eye injury, and another policeman at their side toting a sawed-off twelve-gauge shotgun.

"What's your wife's name?" the officer barked at Jason, as they neared the desk.

"Lorene. Lorene Faircloth," Jason snapped back.

Once at the desk, the officer turned to the receptionist. "Do you have a patient here by the name of Lorene Faircloth?" he asked without explanation.

"Uh...let me, uh...check my patient directory," she stammered. Her own heavy breathing matched that of the men for several seconds while she searched through the file cards.

"Yes," she finally said, her puzzlement combined with fear. "Yes, we do. Room 333."

"Have you ever seen this man before?" the officer asked her, as he jabbed the gun barrel into Jason's back.

"No, I haven't," she answered without hesitation.

Jason interrupted, asking her calmly, "Can you just ask Dr. Waterman to send someone down, please?"

"I'm not sure he's on duty right now," she said, turning from Jason to the officer. "But I can find out." When the officer nodded his approval, she looked down at her telephone extension directory.

"If you reach him," said the officer, "ask if *he* can come down."

She picked up the phone and punched out three numbers. There was a slight pause as she waited for an answer.

"Hello," she said coolly. "This is Reception. Can you tell me if Dr. Waterman is on duty?" Five seconds later she spoke again. "If he's not occupied with an emergency situation can you please ask him to come to the lobby? There are two police officers standing here who have asked to speak to him."

She hung up the phone and eyed the officer. "Either Dr. Waterman or one of his assistants will be down in just a moment."

The officer started to say something to her, when everyone's attention was stolen by the other two policemen rushing into the lobby.

"The car's clean," the oldest-looking officer said as he approached. "And we got a make on it. It's registered in the name of a Jason L. Faircloth."

Jason sighed. He hoped desperately the chaotic circumstances would now begin to make sense to the man still training a gun toward his back.

Soon the sound of a doctor's shoes filled the silence in the lobby with their high-pitched squeak. Dr. Waterman spoke first, in bewilderment: "What's going on here?"

"Are you Dr. Waterman?" the chief officer responded.

"Yes, I am."

"Can you verify that this man's wife is a patient here?"

"Yes, she is. She was just moved into ICU about two hours ago. She's in critical condition, and Reverend Faircloth was contacted and asked to come immediately."

"Thanks, Doctor. That's all we needed to know." For the first time since Jason heard him speak, the officer's voice came across with a gentleman-like quality. Turning to his comrades, the officer said, "Let's go, fellows."

While the others moved away, he turned to Jason.

"Reverend, I hope you realize you nearly got us all killed back there. The next time you have an emergency situation, please call for a police escort." He turned to join the others.

Jason looked at Dr. Waterman and explained, "I got a little carried away trying to get here." Not caring to talk further about it, he quickly asked, "How's Lorene?"

8

"I'M NOT SURE I UNDERSTAND," Jason mumbled as he stepped from the elevator onto the third floor.

He had been listening with undivided attention while Dr. Waterman explained Lorene's condition. Dr. Weber, the psychiatric specialist, had spent four hours with her today. His diagnosis: Lorene was suffering from hyper-extended shock, a rare condition Dr. Weber had seen only a handful of times. The symptoms included a mental detachment from reality, a termination of the survival instinct, and a psychic overrule of the immune system.

Her temperature for the last two hours had read 106 degrees, Dr. Waterman related, despite maximum medication. Her vital signs were showing a slight improvement compared to earlier in the evening, but they were still at dangerous levels.

Outside the elevator, Jason leaned against the wall of the corridor and repeated aloud Dr. Waterman's phrases: *"Termination of the survival instinct. Psychic overrule.* What does that mean, doctor?"* His voice reflected his desperation to understand.

Betsy, anxiously pacing the hallway, saw the two men beside the elevator. Dr. Waterman's strict visiting rules this week had allowed her into Lorene's presence only five minutes daily, but her sister-loyalty compelled her to spend all her daylight hours on the premises, usually in some waiting room. She spent her nights with a widow who attended North Metro Church. It was lodging that Jason had arranged; he felt it was wrong for he and Betsy to be alone together in the Faircloth house at night.

Betsy had come straight to the hospital from Hannah's gravesite earlier in the afternoon, and she had been present when Lorene's condition abruptly worsened. Now she walked over to learn more about what was happening.

"The symptoms are bio-psychological factors," Dr. Waterman was explaining. "In other words, to make it very simple: Reverend Faircloth, your wife wants to die." The words were precise, and Jason heard an unmistakable emphasis on the word *wants*. "Somehow," Dr. Waterman continued, "in a strange quirk of nature, her mind—having postulated death—has succeeded in shutting down her immune system. So the ear infection and the fever, which are normally minor disorders, are in her case threatening to be fatal."

"You're saying she can actually kill herself?" Jason asked in disbelief. "That she can actually convince her body to die, just by the sheer power of her will?"

"It's an accepted medical fact that many illnesses are aggravated by negative psychological attitudes. Your wife's case may well be an extreme case. And it may be difficult to understand, but you've got to realize—"

"Then what's the cure?" Jason cut him short.

"There isn't one," Dr. Waterman answered slowly. "She can be cured only if she chooses to be. It's all up to her." His voice tapered off to a whisper.

Jason's head was spinning. "How long does she have to choose before it's too late?" he asked. "Does she have a week? A month? A year?"

"At this stage we can only make progressive assumptions," the doctor explained softly. "About an hour after Dr. Weber made his diagnosis, Lorene lost consciousness and her heart stopped. We thought we were going to lose her then, but we rushed her into intensive care and were able to shock her heart back into life. Right now she's alive. Weak, but alive."

"Could it have been a heart attack?" Jason was trying to find a loophole in fate.

"Our tests showed no signs of a heart attack. More than anything else, the whole incident verified that Dr. Weber's diagnosis is accurate."

"So—you're convinced?"

"For two reasons. Number one, she's pretty much defying all the medication we're giving her. And number two—" He was working at not showing any emotion. "During Dr. Weber's examinations she repeatedly alluded to the fact that she doesn't want to live anymore. She kept saying over and over, 'Don't worry, Hannah; Mommy will be with you soon…'"

The words pierced Jason. He looked briefly at Betsy, into her reddened eyes; for a moment they shared each other's unwanted grief.

He turned to the doctor. "Can I see her?" he asked quietly.

Dr. Waterman selected his words carefully. "You can see her. But there's one more thing you ought to know. A couple of times during Dr. Weber's examinations your wife made a forthright accusation. She blamed you for taking away her will to live."

He ignored an attempt by Jason to interrupt, and continued: "It's possible for that to mean nothing. But Dr. Weber felt you should be warned. If you're in there and she reacts negatively, you'll know to vacate the room immediately."

Jason was stunned, despite his natural skepticism of Dr. Weber's interpretation. Never had it entered his mind that he himself might be responsible for Lorene's illness, and he still hoped there was no truth to that suggestion. But the mere thought of it stripped him of his last remaining stronghold of pride. Suddenly his life—all his attainments, his accomplishments, his position of leadership—seemed like a humorless joke.

Losing heart for further talk, he turned in silence and started down the hall toward the intensive care ward.

His own life, he felt, was now at stake.

≈ ≈ ≈

THE HEAVILY EQUIPPED ROOM was mostly quiet. Beside the bed, a nurse was exchanging the nearly empty IV bottle for a full one. Another nurse, having just given Lorene a serum injection to fight the unrelenting fever, was wiping sweat droplets from her head.

Jason stepped closer. Lorene lay with a breathing machine pumping oxygen into her lungs. Underneath the mask, her cheeks looked emaciated. The white sheet covering her body revealed the outline of her shriveled form. She looked as if death had already captured her.

How can she be so wasted? Jason wanted to refuse the truth of what he saw.

The two nurses stepped out, and he was alone with her. Reaching down, he held her hand and whispered a few pleas for her to revive. If Lorene had any hope at all, he realized instinctively, it was only in God.

He briefly closed his eyes, then felt a gentle squeeze on his right shoulder. He turned to find Betsy at his side.

"You stay here with her," he spoke. "I'm going to make a telephone call and start some people praying."

≈ ≈ ≈

IT WAS AFTER MIDNIGHT. Betsy was dozing in a metal upright chair one of the nurses had brought in earlier. Jason was standing at Lorene's bedside. Since nine o'clock he and Betsy had taken turns beside her, lovingly whispering to her, trying to provoke a response. They were weary, but hope kept them trying.

God is going to respond, Jason kept telling himself. He knew earnest prayers for Lorene had ascended from at least four hundred people in the last few hours, after he had called three of the deacons and asked them to mobilize the prayer chain.

Hoping not to disturb Betsy, Jason spoke quietly to Lorene about the number of people praying for her. Then he began singing softly an old hymn.

A nurse came in quietly to again check Lorene's vital signs. Jason hardly noticed her, until she asked in a startled tone, "Have you seen any change?"

"No," he answered. "Why?"

"Her vital signs have taken quite a turn for the better." She continued her assessment while Jason peered into Lorene's face. He saw her eyes give a slight twitch.

"She blinked!" he nearly shouted. At that moment he felt a resurgence of his old faith.

The nurse stepped out quickly and returned with another nurse. Betsy stirred awake and came to Jason's side.

Soon one of Dr. Waterman's associate physicians also appeared and began directing various attempts to make the most of Lorene's improvement. Fifteen minutes later, her vital signs had stabilized at a new level. The doctor soon removed Lorene's oxygen mask. Eventually he and the nurses left, and Jason and Betsy once again resumed their bedside coaching.

No sooner had they started when Lorene's eyes opened.

"Lorene!" Jason said softly with tears.

"Is that you, Jason?"

"Yes, Lorene," he whispered tenderly, joyfully. "It's me—Jason."

She took his right hand in hers. "Lean over me, Jason."

He wiped the free-flowing tears from his cheeks and lowered his head to hers.

She released his hand, slowly raised her arm, and gently placed a finger on the sewn-shut eye.

"Will you forgive me, Jason?" she asked with a bent smile.

Betsy silently patted Jason's shoulder, then left to find the nurses.

"Lorene, of course I forgive you," Jason chuckled. "Besides, it's okay. It's just a little cut. It's going to be all right."

"I'm glad, Jason."

He leaned closer and embraced her. "I love you, Lorene."

Exhilarated, he felt a sense of victory flush over the room. His faith had been honored. He felt a pang of guilt for having ever doubted God. *I'll never doubt you again, Lord,* he prayed silently. For the first time in a week, his soul enjoyed a moment of relief.

Betsy and the nurses hurried in now, and Jason stepped back to let them talk with her, monitor her signs, and reposition the contour of her bed. All the while he kept his eyes on his wife. *Thank you for keeping her alive,* he found himself praying repeatedly. He was struck with just how much he had grown to love and need her over the years. And now that Hannah was gone, he knew he would need her even more.

When the nurses finished their work and stepped out, Betsy followed to ask them a few detailed questions about Lorene's improving condition. Jason again came over to the bed.

Lorene spoke first, soft and smiling. "Jason..." She again took his hand. "I want to tell you...I'm grateful. I don't know...maybe you'll never understand my feelings, as a woman. But Hannah meant more to me than anything in the whole world. She was the best thing that ever happened to me, Jason. I know you never wanted to be a father, but I cherish the fact that you let me have her. It was a great sacrifice for you—I understand that. I know you did it just for me, because you loved me. I just want you to know I'm grateful. She was—"

"Lorene!" he interrupted automatically. He was feeling under attack. "I admit I didn't want children, but that was years ago! To be honest, I never thought I could love a child as much as I grew to love Hannah. It hurts me just as much as it hurts you to have to lose her. It's going to take me years to get over what's happened. But, Lorene! Right now I'm just counting my blessings that you're still alive."

61

Her eyes flickered. "Anyway, Jason..." Her smile had faded during his self-defense, and her voice was now strained. "I just couldn't leave without letting you know I'm thankful. I wanted to get that off my conscience before I see her..."

Jason squeezed her hand. She smiled once more, her eyes growing distant.

"They're coming...for me, Jason. I've got to go now..." Her whole body flinched, and she gave a look of pain before closing her eyes.

Then she was motionless.

For a moment Jason was paralyzed in horror. Then he lunged forward, grabbed her shoulders, and tried to shake her back to life. "Lorene! Lorene!"

In a moment, alerted by the sound of his shout, a doctor and several nurses had pushed Jason aside and gone into action.

One of the nurses shouted that the electronic monitor was showing no life-signs. The oxygen mask was quickly replaced, and within seconds the doctor had torn away her bed gown and had the defibrillator in place on her chest. "Give me immediate power at two hundred watts," he ordered.

The switch was thrown. Lorene's shoulders jerked as the electric shock surged through her body. Everyone looked at the monitoring screen. It displayed only zeros and flat horizontal lines.

"Again," the doctor shouted to the nurse operating the switch.

The electric shock jerked Lorene's body a second time. Again her body offered no response.

"Increase it to three-fifty," the doctor commanded.

With the wattage increased, the switch was thrown for the third time. And for the third time, Lorene's body defied the wizardry of modern technology.

The doctor breathed out in exasperated defeat. As the nurses stood silently in their places, he turned to Jason.

"I'm sorry, sir. She's gone."

With tears gushing from his eyes, he hurried to Lorene's side.

"Don't leave me, Lorene." he pleaded, bending down and touching his forehead to hers. "For God's sake, don't leave me now!"

9

"BROTHERS AND SISTERS," began Assistant Pastor Steve Mitchell in a radio-quality voice. He delivered his next words slowly, with emotion: "This has been one of the longest and saddest days in the life of our fellowship."

He was addressing a somber Wednesday evening prayer meeting crowd of sixteen hundred, most of whom had been in this same auditorium five hours earlier for Lorene's funeral. Jason was seated on the front row, silent and withdrawn.

"Our hearts are heavy," intoned Steve. Tonight he looked much older than his thirty-four years, obviously burdened for his suffering pastor. "I encourage every one of you, without exception, to pray earnestly for the General. We can only imagine how much he must need God's strength during this time of loss. I'm certain you'll all agree that it's our unquestionable duty to uphold him in our prayers. And I'm completely confident each and every one of you will do your personal best not to fail him in this area."

A solemn "Amen" sounded from a few male voices across the auditorium, speaking for everyone.

"In just a moment," Steve continued, "we're going to break up into small groups around the auditorium and spend about thirty minutes praying for him collectively as a church. But before we do that I need to share with you an important decision that was made earlier this evening by the pastoral staff and the board of deacons. Due to the burden the General is carrying right now, we felt it would be heartless of us to expect him to immediately carry on as before. So the board is offering him a four-week recess from all his normal church responsibilities, just so he can have some undisturbed time to regroup and to come back stronger than ever, like the unfaltering soldier he truly is."

The board's decision was news to Jason. He was grateful for time off, but thought to himself angrily, *How can they expect me to recover in only four weeks?* Then he got upset with himself for being critical. Deep down he knew the church's effort to show sensitivity was genuine and well-meant. But his entire life had collapsed; how could he reconstruct it in just a month? He didn't even know who he was anymore, or what he actually believed.

"Now—to make the decision official," Steve continued, "We want to take a church vote. So please show by the uplifting of your right hand if you support the resolution." The vote was unanimous.

Jason, meanwhile, decided it didn't really matter; if he needed more than four weeks, he would take it. That's all there was to it.

Then he wondered: What if he never recovered? What then? *In that case I'll just quit,* he determined, hoping God was somehow hurt by the blatant thought. It came close to being a wish of vengeance.

While the congregation broke up into groups to pray for him, Jason wanted desperately to feel consoled, but the feeling escaped him. For the first time in his life his future was unclear, unclear to the point of being blank. The strong sense of assurance that had always been like concrete under his feet had ceased to exist.

After the service, several individuals approached Jason to offer him meals and other amenities for the upcoming days and throughout his four-week recess. Jason turned down all the invitations and offers, explaining that he just needed to be alone.

He walked by himself to his car, sensing again the loss of direction. That was the way it had been for days. He had found himself spontaneously driving around Atlanta to Lorene and Hannah's favorite shopping malls and restaurants, just to sit and rub in the hurt. Bereavement, he discovered, had a strange way of trying to comfort itself.

With an acute sense of fear he drove out of the brightly lit church parking lot and into the cold darkness. Forty minutes later he was in the cemetery, walking in a circle around the side-by-side graves of Hannah and Lorene. Having cried so much in the last two weeks, he was now beyond the point of tears.

He just circled.

≈ ≈ ≈

THE FIRE ALARM was blaring. He was trying to flee the burning building, but could only move in slow motion. The sound of the alarm was relentless.

Above him, a falling crossbeam dressed in fire collapsed. It started rushing down to crush him. He panicked.

With his heart hammering, Jason bolted upright and stared wide-eyed at his bedroom before him. It had all been a dream. Breathing heavily, he jerked out his hand to slam the off button on his alarm.

He sat still, trying to relax. He looked again at the clock. It was 8:30. Then, without warning, he was ambushed by his real pain. Instinctively he wanted to reenter the dream and die in the blazing inferno.

The dream, fresh and full of impact, sparked seriously within him the unprecedented thought of taking his own life. Never before had he understood the depth of emptiness and loneliness that a suicide candidate reaches, but now he knew. He was there. At the bottom. And in a merciful kind of way, death seemed truly the only sure escape.

Listlessly making his way into the shower, he solemnly contemplated whether or not his life was worth living. As the steamy hot water poured over his tired chest and shoulders, he leaned passively with his hands outstretched against the white tiles of the shower wall. Leaning there, staring down at his feet, he felt like a foreigner alone in a strange land. He was an island. No longer was he a husband or a father. And for the next four weeks, neither would he be a pastor.

If he did decide to keep living, how should he spend those four weeks? What course of activity could possibly restore any meaning to his life?

If only, he thought for the thousandth time, *if only I had one more chance to be a husband to Lorene and a father to Hannah...*

Then, like a full moon suddenly revealed by an opening in the dark, wind-tossed clouds, he remembered: He still had the active status of grandfather. Somewhere in Miami he had a granddaughter who was alive. Could he find her?

It would definitely cost some money and effort, and it would not be easy. But to his obvious advantage was the fact that he had the time.

The musing gave him a tiny spark of hope. Feeling the touch of life coming back to him, he knew he had found his answer, his reason for living. Perhaps he could somehow redeem himself as a grandfather and make up for his miserable failures as a father and husband.

Then and there, standing in the shower, he made up his mind. He knew exactly how he was going to spend the next four weeks.

10

ON HIS WAY OUT of Atlanta, Jason stopped to keep an early afternoon doctor's appointment to have the eye stitches removed. Then he headed south on Interstate 75, opting to split the thirteen-hour drive to Miami into two days. He estimated he would arrive in Orlando—the over-halfway point—by 11:00 P.M. He would spend the night there and, barring difficulties, complete the trip the following day.

Before leaving his house he had telephoned Steve at the church office to say he would be driving to Miami to stay an indefinite number of days. He explained that he wanted to see where Hannah had lived and to visit the site of her accident. He left it at that.

Steve was not surprised, but the news aroused his curiosity. He and others who made up the church's nucleus were aware that the General was withholding specific details about Hannah. They knew only that she had been living in Miami during the last eighteen months, and that she had bled to death due to a freak automobile mishap. That was all Jason had divulged. Out of respect for his privacy, no one probed for more information.

As Jason followed the expressway through Macon, he thought of Betsy. After Lorene's funeral she had graciously offered to stay in Atlanta a few more days to help in any way she could. He had politely turned her down, thanking her for the support she had already given so freely. He also asked her to keep in confidence all the details of Slade Wakefield's report. She assured him that she had not said anything to anyone, and would keep it that way.

For the rest of the afternoon and evening drive, Jason spent his mental energies solidifying his game-plan for Miami. He decided to first try contacting Slade Wakefield, preferably in person. He would play on Slade's sympathy by telling him about Lorene's death, and by explaining that the surviving grandchild was his only living link to Hannah and Lorene. He hoped Slade would feel sorry enough for him to open up and tell him his son-in-law's name and location, so Jason could make a friendly contact. If Slade refused, plan B would be to bribe him with money. Jason was satisfied Slade would somehow make a concession.

At 10:20 P.M. he pulled off the freeway in Orlando and checked into a no-frills motel. Having no interest in being entertained by television, he showered and prepared for bed.

Before lying down he stood at the bathroom mirror for a few minutes, relieved to be able to use his eye again. He closely examined his scar before dabbing it with an ointment prescribed by the doctor. Still in the healing stage, it wasn't pretty and probably never would be. He realized he now had a lifelong physical reminder of his husbandly failures.

As he turned out the lights and crawled under the covers, his thoughts turned again to his granddaughter. What was her name? How was she doing without her mother? Was she suffering any problems caused by the difficult birth? He wanted to pray for her, but doubted it would make a difference. After all, prayers in the hundreds had not delivered either Hannah or Lorene.

He fell asleep reflecting on the confusion that now darkened the beliefs he had held sacred for so long—such as his trust in the power of prayer. His Christianity was rapidly unraveling.

That night he dreamed he became an atheist.

≈ ≈ ≈

INSTEAD OF WAKING ABRUPTLY the next morning, as was his habit, Jason found himself returning slowly to life through intermittent phases of awareness and sleep. It seemed hours before his body finally decided it had been compensated with enough rest.

Even then he lay only numbly awake, listening to the noise of the freeway. The traffic sounded heavy. He reached for his watch, but it appeared to have stopped during the night, so he called the motel office to ask for the time. It was 11:03. He could not remember having ever slept this late.

He was on the road by 11:35. He made the expressway connection onto the Florida turnpike, and headed toward Miami.

Driving south, he lowered the car windows an inch or two and enjoyed the fresh warm air. He had always enjoyed trips to Florida, taking pleasure in its sand, palm trees, sunshine, and even the flash thunderstorms.

An awkward excitement grew within him as he came closer to Miami. How long would it be before he held his granddaughter in his arms? Hours? Days? What was he going to say when he first saw his son-in-law?

He was in Miami by six o'clock, and drove straight into the heart of downtown. He could not find a hotel he liked that was in his price range, so he followed signs and drove out to Miami Beach, where the vast majority of the area's overnight lodgings were lined up along the Atlantic. They stretched endlessly, it seemed, down the mega-lighted strip. Most had lighted "No Vacancy" signs. Their rooms were no doubt packed with thousands of middle- and upper-class Northerners, here for a few days of fun in the sun.

Before long, on the side of the street opposite the beach, he found a reasonably priced and clean-looking motel that actually had a vacancy. He wasted no time checking in.

After carrying his luggage to his room, he immediately found the telephone directory in the drawer of the nightstand, sat down on the bed, and began looking for Slade Wakefield's home number. When his search failed to find the name, he looked in the yellow pages under "Attorneys" for his business number. He gave an audible sigh of relief when his eyes eventually spotted the seven digits in bold print.

Then it hit him that this was Friday night. Business offices were closed for the weekend. Why hadn't he remembered that earlier? What had he been thinking of? How could he possibly postpone his contact with Slade until Monday?

It was already 8:10, but he decided against the odds to call the office number anyway. He quickly picked up the phone on top of the nightstand and dialed the numbers.

He started counting the rings. Three. Four. Five. Six. Seven.

Exasperated, he finally hung up. Now what? He had the entire weekend before him with nothing to do but wait.

With his hope temporarily deterred and with no activity to occupy him, the next several hours passed with excruciating slowness. The powerful sensations of loneliness and grief returned with renewed force. He tried to contend with them, but was gradually overtaken.

Time held him suspended in his pain, without any mercy.

≈ ≈ ≈

THE BREAKING POINT came early Saturday afternoon. The closed curtains blocked out the sunshine. He had neither left his room nor eaten, and had slept only restlessly.

His feelings had pushed him beyond reason. He tried to fight their pull, but absolutely everything in life now seemed bland, meaningless, vain—overpoweringly vain. He had tried to fight back, but at some point in this emotional twilight zone he concluded that resisting was beyond his capability.

Hopelessness swallowed him up.

He did not want to live. There was simply no way to find release, he felt, other than taking his life.

He walked to the bathroom and picked up the razor he had earlier unpacked and set out on the sink counter. He stood for a moment in his underwear, looking in the mirror. With his matted hair and unshaved stubble he resembled a homeless street dweller.

Jason's mind was racing with a million and one thoughts, mostly abstract. He wondered if his head was going to explode.

He slowly removed the double-edged blade from the shaver, and looked in the mirror once more. There were sweat drops on his forehead.

Looking down, he gently laid his left arm, wrist up, over the edge of the sink. He gripped the blade firmly with the fingers in his right hand.

Inch by slow inch he moved his right hand closer to his left, till the blade's edge was suspended only millimeters from the veins.

He made a fist with his left hand, squeezing tightly. He saw the veins bulging beneath the blade.

It would be easy. In a matter of minutes, he would be free.

At the exact moment that the razor slit the surface of the skin and brought blood, there was a sudden loud knock on the outside door. Jason jerked his head in confusion, and stood frozen. Blood was dripping on the floor.

The knock persisted. *Go away*, Jason thought. But the knocking continued.

He dropped the blade in the sink. He awkwardly wrapped his wrist in a towel, slipped on his housecoat, and went to the door. He released the chain lock and opened the door halfway. Hot sunlight flooded the room and momentarily blinded him.

It was the maid. "Excuse me, sir, for waking you," said the young woman in a Spanish accent. "The front office needs to know if you're staying another night."

Her question passed over him. Jason felt the sun shining on his face. Was he really going to kill himself?

"Are you okay, sir?" the woman asked.

He raised his right hand and squeezed his forehead. "Yeah," he whispered. "Uh...I'm okay."

"Well, will you be staying another day or not?" the maid asked gently.

"I'll be staying another day, yeah," he passively replied.

"Well, if you need any more room supplies, just notify the front desk. All right?"

"Sure...I'll do that."

She turned and walked out of sight.

Jason stayed in the doorway, standing in the sunshine that still hurt his eyes. For a moment he lost himself in abstract wonderment at his regression from dynamic leader to pathetic loser. What was happening to him?

All he knew was that death seemed infinitely better than trying to wrestle with reality.

Why did she have to knock? he questioned fate.

He started to close the door and force himself back into the bathroom, when he caught sight of an old man strolling hand in hand with a little girl across the blacktop parking lot. They were in bathing suits, apparently headed for the beach across the road. They looked like grandfather and granddaughter.

He watched as the old man led the little girl in a short-stepped skip. Jason heard the little girl erupt with laughter.

He leaned backward against the door frame, slid slowly down to the floor, and stretched out his legs. The hope of finding his own granddaughter resurrected in full force. Sitting there in the doorway, the towel around his wrist now soaked with blood, he looked up into the sunny sky. A lone tear rolled down his cheek, the first since he'd left Atlanta.

"O God," he whispered, "I'm so confused. All I know is that if I'm going to live, I can't do it without you. But I don't understand you. I even have feelings of hate for you right now. I'm disillusioned with you. I'm angry with you. But I can't live without you. Please...just help me somehow. Enlighten me. I know I don't deserve it, but help me find my grandbaby so I can try to redeem myself."

≈ ≈ ≈

FOR THE REST OF THE WEEKEND, Jason spent all of his waking hours in public places and surrounded by people, as a precaution against another relapse. He went to his room only late at night when he was so sleepy he could manage to do nothing else but collapse in bed.

When 8:30 Monday morning finally rolled around, he was wide awake and punching out the phone number to Slade's office.

"Attorney Slade Wakefield's office," the voice answered quickly.

"Yes, can I speak to Mr. Wakefield please? This is Reverend Jason Faircloth, a personal friend of his."

"I'm sorry, Reverend Faircloth, but Mr. Wakefield is busy with a client right now. Can I take a message?" Her voice was hurried.

"No—I need to talk to him privately. Is there any possible way

I can maybe see him sometime this morning for about fifteen minutes? It's quite urgent."

"Unfortunately, his day is booked solid right up until five o'clock. Maybe he can manage to see you then, right before he leaves. Shall I tell him you'd like to meet with him at that time?"

"Five o'clock? Are you *sure* that's the earliest?"

"Pardon me if I sound rude, Reverend Faircloth, but I've already had a bad morning. Yes, I'm sure five o'clock is the earliest. Knowing that information is what I get paid for."

"I...I apologize for seeming to question your competence, Miss..."

"Miss Chapman."

"Miss Chapman. Well, like I was saying, I'm sorry for questioning your competence. I'm just overly anxious to talk with Mr. Wakefield, that's all."

"Shall I tell him, then, that you'd like to see him at five?"

"Sure. That'll be fine. This afternoon at five."

"Okay. Rev-er-end...Ja-son...Fair-cloth. I've written it down for five o'clock. Mr. Wakefield will be expecting you then."

Jason hung up the phone, disturbed at the thought of wasting another eight hours after already having lost so much valuable time. He was into the fifth day already of his allotted four weeks. But he felt there was nothing he could do until he first got information from Slade. Otherwise, he had no clue as to how or where to begin his search.

He did decide that, since five o'clock was a heavy traffic time, he would go plenty early and locate Slade's downtown office.

At three o'clock he was sitting on a stunted marble wall that surrounded a fountain, right outside the downtown building that housed Slade's law firm.

By 4:45 he was impatiently pacing the hallway outside Slade's office, and at 4:55 he almost knocked the office door off its hinges going in.

"Don't tell me," Slade's secretary said doggedly, without any sign of embarrassment. "You must be the Reverend Jason Faircloth."

"That's right," Jason replied, without being intimidated.

"Well, you're five minutes early, Reverend, so you'll just have to sit there and endure the abuse of a mean old secretary." She smiled.

Jason responded with a volley of his own. "Don't tell me. Let me guess. You not only had a bad morning, but your whole day has been bad."

Her smile was momentarily disrupted by a playful attempt at looking hateful. "Yeah! How did you ever guess?"

"It was real difficult," he said dryly.

"Oh? Next time I'll have to make it easier for you. So watch out!" Miss Chapman hissed and put her hands in the air, imitating claws. They both laughed.

Contrary to his earlier impression, Jason decided he liked her, curly red hair and all.

At 5:05, immediately after an older woman stepped out of Slade's inner office, Miss Chapman ushered him in. Slade was standing just inside the door, and greeted him with an irresistible smile and a solid handshake. "Well, what brings you all the way from Atlanta, Reverend Faircloth?"

"I have a strong suspicion you already know the answer to that question," Jason answered solemnly.

"Yes, I suppose I do," Slade conceded. "No doubt you've come to put yourself through the tedious process of trying to extract confidential information from me, such as the identity and location of your granddaughter and son-in-law."

"Exactly," Jason replied. He could not have said the word more seriously.

"Sit down, and we'll talk," Slade motioned, offering him a seat.

Jason's eyes took in the open and spacious office as he walked over to a brown leather couch which Slade had gestured toward. Every item in the room, from the two potted miniature orange trees to a glistening, gold-framed portrait of some law patriarch, meshed tastefully with the decor. Slade's work sanctuary was in character with his style—immaculate.

Slade seated himself in a businesslike posture behind his large mahogany desk. After he saw Jason was seated and ready to listen, he spoke with resolution.

"Reverend Faircloth, I'll be up front and honest with you. Irrespective of the corruption that may or may not exist in my profession, I will not imprudently violate the promises of confidentiality that I've made to others. And I've promised my FBI colleagues, at their request, that I would not reveal your son-in-law's identity or location to either you or your wife."

"Mr. Wakefield," Jason responded emphatically, "Lorene died nine days ago. She never recovered from the shock of Hannah's death. You've got to understand that my grandchild is now the only living link I have in this world to Hannah and Lorene. I've got to find her."

Slade was noticeably touched by the news, sensing fully Jason's desperation and hurt. He paused for a moment to think, then spoke slowly, with genuine sympathy.

"My heart goes out to you, and my feelings are on your side. But you must try to understand my position as well. To intentionally betray the trust that others have placed in me as a professional is to undermine my entire practice. If I could with a clear conscience give you the information you're asking for, I would gladly do it. But I can't."

Hearing the steadfastness in Slade's words, Jason knew it was time for an approach on a different level. "I'll pay you for the information. Just name the price."

"Bribery? I'm afraid not, Reverend Faircloth." His voice was not lighthearted.

Jason started to feel sick. "So—it's settled then?"

"I'm afraid so."

"There's absolutely nothing I can do to change your mind?"

"Nothing," Slade said concretely.

Jason refused to accept "no" as a final answer. He kept up the fight, begging Slade to put himself in his shoes and reconsider. This case was a legitimate exception to the rule, Jason argued, and a breach of promise could be morally justified.

The attorney refused to yield, and when Jason became somewhat heated and irrational, Slade stood and explained in the most professional way he could that he had no more time to debate the issue. He tactfully escorted Jason out.

Jason was smoldering as he left the building. He had forced himself earlier not to even think about the possibility of Slade's outright refusal. But the refusal had happened.

How was he ever going to find his granddaughter now? He had no clues, no leads, no contacts, no sources. All he knew was that he could not return to Atlanta and continue in his life and ministry without first establishing some kind of functional relationship with his grandchild. He'd already proven to himself that he had to have at least that much to keep on living.

He sat down again on the fountain's marble wall and tried to collect his thoughts. In the midst of his irritation, he concluded that he had no choice but to play private investigator himself. If nobody would supply him with information, he would just have to track it down on his own. He had no investigative know-how or experience; raw determination, he concluded, would simply have to suffice.

Locked on to the new direction, he walked back to his car.

That evening in his room he took out the telephone directory and began compiling a list of addresses and telephone numbers of potential information sources, including police stations, hospitals, city offices, and the Miami branch of the FBI.

≈ ≈ ≈

HIS OBSESSION carried him through the next few days at a feverish pace. With a newly purchased Miami city map, he plunged into the task of accumulating information and looking for a trail.

But his momentum quickly started to subside. There seemed to be an invisible force working against him. A few people were sympathetic with his pursuit, but they had no information or ideas to offer. Time after time, the people who might logically have been the most help to him were ill, or on vacation, or completely tied up with other business. And as for the others, if any of them had a lead or suggestion, they kept it to themselves.

Jason couldn't figure it out. By late Friday, the results he had managed to turn up were absolutely zilch. Why? Why was he always in the wrong place, or in the right place but talking to the wrong people?

Tossing questions about in his mind, he was on his way to

making another hospital inquiry when he stopped at a diner for a quick bite to eat. It was after four o'clock, and he hadn't eaten all day. Inside, he sat down at the counter and quickly ordered a soft drink while he took more time to look over the menu.

He slumped with exhaustion. The week of fruitless hunting had taken its toll.

Two seats down from him, a man was reading the *Miami Herald*. The man soon finished, put the sections back together in a rough approximation of their original arrangement, and slapped the paper down on the counter. He walked out just as Jason's iced drink was placed in front of him.

It was the first newspaper Jason had noticed in weeks. A bold headline caught his eye: "4 Killed, 12 Hurt in I-95 Pileup." Bells suddenly rang in his head. Of course—Hannah's fatality, along with places and names, had probably been reported in the newspaper. A search of the paper's back issues would provide the details.

Forgetting his drink and his empty stomach, he bounded out of the diner and across the parking lot to a telephone booth, where he looked up the *Herald's* address in the directory. In a matter of minutes he was back in his car, and searching his map for the location. It looked to be only about a mile away.

He made it there in six minutes. A male employee, elderly and in uniform, led him from the front reception area to a room downstairs containing the back issues. It was a large room, like a library, with bound volumes of the issues from past years occupying several rows of shelves. On a counter beside tables and chairs were the issues from more recent weeks, arranged in stacks.

Other information seekers were standing at the counter or seated at the tables. Jason ignored them, found a stack of December issues, and quickly located the paper corresponding to the day of Hannah's death—December 15. He began scrutinizing the pages, but saw no mention of the accident. His disappointment was mounting with the turn of every page before he realized the accident would logically have been reported the day *after* it occurred. In a flash he found the issue for the 16th. Again he began his scrutiny, holding his breath page by page as he surveyed the headlines. Then, on page 3, he found it: "**Mother Dies After**

Baby's Roadside Birth." He had only to scan the first few sentences below the headline before he knew the story was about Hannah. He heard himself exhale with emotion.

His eyes went back to the beginning. Carefully he started reading again, digesting each word.

An 18-year-old first-time mother died of delivery complications beside her stranded car late yesterday after giving birth to a healthy baby girl.

Police said the car, driven by the woman's husband, was accidentally forced off the road and became stuck in sand near the intersection of Bird Road and S.W. 87th Avenue.

The couple was reportedly en route to Baptist Hospital at the time of the accident.

The woman was apparently not injured in the single-vehicle mishap.

Bystanders who witnessed the infant's birth said it took place about 6:30 p.m., only ten minutes after the accident. The delivery was assisted by the child's father and others in the crowd.

An emergency medical team arrived on the scene shortly after the birth of the infant and began providing immediate care to the mother. A spokesman for the team said, however, that the woman's blood loss had already exceeded the critical point by the time the team arrived.

As of this morning, the couple's names had not yet been released.

The surviving baby girl was reported in good health at Baptist Hospital.

I still don't have their names, Jason thought with irritation. But at least he knew now where the accident had happened, and bits of other information, too, that might lead to what he wanted. He found a piece of scrap paper on the counter, and copied down the report word for word. When he finished, he reread the article again and again. *Why didn't they give the names?* he thought once more. In sadness and frustration he closed his eyes and tried to rest his mind. He halfheartedly whispered an end-of-the-rope prayer to God, requesting help. It came more as a feeble wish than an expression of faith.

He opened his eyes, then slowly folded the pages and returned the newspaper stack to the counter. He was walking up the stairs when another idea struck him like a lightning bolt. He turned, raced back down to the room, found the stack of December issues, set them on a nearby table, and turned again to the December 16th edition. He began flipping pages slowly, looking for the obituary columns.

He found nothing in the obits for the 16th, but in those for the following day's issue he found the name "Freedman, Hannah Renée." Her age was given as eighteen, and her survivors were listed as her husband, Cody Freedman, and "a newborn daughter." No name for the child was given, but at that particular moment the omission was insignificant. He now knew his son-in-law's name: Cody Freedman. He was certain his reconciliation with both Cody and the baby was imminent.

Out on the street he found a public telephone and searched the Miami phonebook for Cody's number and address. But the search was in vain; it wasn't there. He tried calling the directory assistance number as well, but the the operator said the number was unlisted.

Then another idea came to him. According to Slade's first report in his home, Cody had been a college student—perhaps somewhere in Miami. Jason decided his next step would be to call all the local colleges until he found one that had a former student by the name of Cody Freedman, and then ask for the last address they had on file.

But it was already Friday evening, and after five. The realization jolted him at first. He was in for another weekend wait. But maybe it wouldn't matter now. Things were finally beginning to fall in place. His excitement would carry him through to Monday.

In the meantime, he would drive to the intersection of Bird Road and Southwest 87th Avenue, and soberly try to recapture Hannah's last hour on earth. He would carry out love's strange desire by forcing himself to relive his daughter's moment of greatest agony.

11

"YOU DO REALIZE, Mr. Freedman," came the voice, "that the state of Florida has the power to take you to court if you refuse to cooperate. And if—"

Cody angrily slammed down the phone. Nobody was going to tell him how to be a father, and especially not the government.

He ran through the house in a rage, knocking over a chair in the dining room. "Sophia!" he shouted. Getting no reply, he rushed into the back yard. He saw her there, sitting in a wooden swing in the garden gazebo, feeding Renée from a bottle.

Sophia, a black lady in her late fifties, had been his natural first choice as a fulltime baby-sitter for Renée. She had been his mother's housemaid for eleven years, right up until the time his parents died in the plane crash. Cody had always been fond of her. She was sassy and stubborn, but one of the smartest and most kindhearted women he had ever known.

Fortunately, she had been available right from the start to move in and help out with the baby. Cody knew she would be good for the job, but now—in only four weeks—she had proven to be too good.

Cody had never reopened his business after Hannah's death, even with the baby safe in Sophia's care. Instead, when he wasn't drinking at home, he spent his time in an assortment of local sidestreet bars. During the rare times when he was both at home and sober, he was far from being fatherly.

Sophia soon began preaching to him, insisting that he get his act together and give his daughter a proper upbringing. Then she gave up, seeing that his depression over Hannah's death was greater than his pride as a parent. Instead, she had telephoned the Miami Children's Watchcare Center, an agency of the state welfare division, and told them Cody was an irresponsible alcoholic and an unfit single parent. On a morning early in January, a counselor from the center had paid a visit to Cody's home to investigate his performance as a single father. Recovering from a drunken stupor, Cody had forced her from the house and followed her out to her car, showering her with profanity. Now, in today's telephone call, he had been threatened with court action if he refused again to allow an investigation in his home.

Still fuming, Cody approached Sophia in the gazebo. He knew she had reported him, and he knew she had done it because, in her own way, she cared. But this was not her affair. With the state breathing down his neck, he knew his intention to keep Renée under his own roof was in jeopardy.

He climbed the single step into the gazebo, and loomed over Sophia. He wanted to hurt her bodily, somehow. But he didn't have the nerve for it, not even for an out-of-control slap. He merely stood there, like a riled tiger in a cage.

Sophia knew him well enough. She could tell he was boiling, and she knew why. On her way through the kitchen to the back yard, she had overheard his phone conversation.

Without breaking her slight, rhythmic swing, she continued feeding Renée and waited for Cody to speak first. The wait was only a second.

"Sophia, do you realize what you've done?" His fists were clenched at his side.

"What have I done, Cody?" she answered with equal force, lifting her eyes to squrely meet his.

"You've treaded into somebody else's business where you had no business treading, woman! That's what you've done. And now the state agency you reported me to is threatening to take me to court."

Sophia responded at once: "I did what I did because of Renée." Her voice had the seriousness of someone standing trial.

He shook his fist and swore. "Renée is my responsibility!"

"Then why don't you *be* responsible?" she fired back.

Cody's lower lip trembled, and he raised his fist and shook it in the air. Nearly screaming, he offered his defense: "Because right now I'm a hurting man, Sophia! I'm hurting all the way to the core." He pounded his chest with his fist, punctuating his words: "I can't ignore this agony. I can't pretend it doesn't exist. It *does* exist! And every ounce of me is struggling just to stay alive! Can't you understand that? How can anybody expect me to be responsible about anything right now?"

Again Sophia came back without a pause, but her tone was softer. "You're not trying to beat the pain, Cody. That's obvious, isn't it? In less than a month's time you've become an alcoholic. I know losing someone you love hurts bad, I've been there. I know the hurt. But you can't just give up. You've got to pick up the pieces and keep your life going, just like you did when your mother and daddy were taken from you." She realized she was making bereavement seem like an ordinary foe, but somehow she had to coax Cody back into the fight. She feared he had all but given up.

And it was true. His life had become a nightmare. From whatever angle he replayed the details leading up to Hannah's death, he felt she would still be alive if he had been better prepared and displayed more common sense. Every time he thought about the accident, it drove him crazy.

As an agnostic with no God to blame—Hannah had never pushed her God on him—he could only find room to blame himself. His guilt, mixed with selfishness, was squeezing the life out of him. He knew if he searched forever he would never find another friend to equal Hannah. And besides her friendship, he was convinced she had been every man's dream both visually and sexually. He had known what most men could only fantasize about, and losing it was more than he could stand. It had been a romance envied in heaven, and right in the midst of the ecstasy and passion it had been sent to hell.

The blame was his own. And as he continued pointing the finger at himself, an uncontrollable self-hatred had grown.

"Don't tell me what I've got to do, Sophia. If I want to give up, I'll give up. And there's nobody—not you or anyone else—who can do anything about it!"

"Alright, Mr. Big Man. If you want to trash your life, that's one thing. But you're not going to destroy this little girl's life, not without Sophia doing something about it."

She had pushed him to his limit. He steeled his gaze. "You're fired, Sophia!" he declared abruptly. "Do you hear me? You're fired!"

She should have expected it, but she hadn't. Cody's decision stopped her mind in mid-thought. She had to mentally backtrack. Quickly she gathered her wits, then stood up to confront him face to face. While he waited for her to react, she suddenly shoved Renée and the half-empty bottle into his arms. "Then get used to being a daddy!" she said. With that she stomped off the gazebo and marched across the yard into the house. Within a day or two she figured, he would change his mind and call her back.

The baby felt awkward in Cody's arms. He adjusted his arms, trying to get a more natural position. It had been so long, he realized, since he had held her. Meanwhile, he looked into her tiny red face and was greeted by an inquisitive little stare.

How could he give her up? She was a part of Hannah. If for no other reason than to honor his beloved wife, he decided anew never to give Renée to anyone—*anyone.*

He sat down in the swing and looked across the lawn to the house. It had become a mirror of paradise lost. Since Hannah's death, he knew he would never be able to live a normal enjoyable life here. It was filled with too many memories.

He made the decision that instant. He would sell the house, and he and Renée would move out of the state. That would get everybody off his back.

12

FROM THE MIAMI YELLOW PAGES Jason compiled a list of thirteen different schools of higher education, from major universities to technical schools. His intention was to call the alumni office at each one and ask simply if Cody Freedman was on their list of alumni, or had formerly been listed in the student body directory.

But on his first two calls on Monday morning, the people he spoke with became obviously suspicious of his point-blank question. Jason decided quickly that without a convincing story to back his request, he would get nowhere.

On the third call he told in detail his fatherly story about Hannah and Cody and the baby, hoping his honesty would clinch some cooperation. The woman on the other end of the line listened patiently to his tale, but then tersely denied him any help. Jason wondered if she had misconstrued his motive for wanting to find Cody as being vindictive. He wished his story was somehow more positive and less threatening.

After struggling with—and overcoming—his conscience, he decided to concoct a lie. It didn't take long to contrive, once he was able to ignore the guilt that first accompanied the decision.

"Good afternoon," he said in an upbeat voice to the receptionist at each of the next three schools he called. "This is Reverend Jeremy Fisher. I'm a missionary to Peru, South America, and I've just returned home on furlough." He went on to say he had once been the pastor of a former student in their school—Cody Freedman—and that Mr. Freedman had recently lost his wife in a car accident. Then he explained that he was trying to track him down to offer some moral support.

There was no doubt the fabricated story carried leverage. In each office, the person Jason spoke with had searched the files at length, only to come back with, "I'm sorry, but our records don't show that Cody Freedman was ever a student here."

After the same response at the third school, the woman there added that she was a Christian herself and had a strong concern for missions. "Can you tell me more about your ministry, Mr. Fisher?" Put on the spot, Jason replied that his work was with Indians in the Himalayan Mountains. Expressing genuine interest, she asked him to add her name and address to his mailing list. Pretending to write them down, Jason assured her he would.

When he hung up he felt disappointed, but was glad his story was convincing. *Maybe too convincing,* he thought, remembering that the Himalayan Mountains were an ocean and a continent away from Peru, South America.

As quickly as he could, he called the next six schools on the list. None of them had ever heard of Cody Freedman.

He was down to one last school—the Veterinary College of Miami. As he picked up the phone to punch out the number, he strongly suspected Cody had attended one of the three major schools he had called first before refining his approach. If so, he decided he would just have to visit each of the campuses in person and talk to authorities there, forcing himself to tell another lie if necessary.

"Veterinary College of Miami. Good morning, may I help you?"

"Yes," said Jason, launching routinely into his falsified story.

"So," he concluded, "if Cody was a student there, as I've been told, I'd be grateful if you could give me his latest address that you have on file."

"Just a moment, please, Reverend. I'll see what I can do."

During the four- or five-minute pause, Jason almost yielded to a renewed urge to confess his deceitful behavior to God. But he knew he would probably have to invent even more deceptions before his search ended, and he would not hesitate to do so if necessary. So rather than confess his lying as a sin, he tried to appease his conscience by pretending the delinquent feelings didn't exist. If God wanted to punish him for his foolish thinking, so be it. He honestly figured there wasn't much God could do to hurt him any worse than he already had.

Jason knew by this strange attitude that his turbulent circumstances were starting to recast him. He still acknowledged a personal need for God, but at the same time he was losing his fear of him. And he did not even care.

"Reverend Fisher," the female voice returned. "I have that address for you, if you're ready."

Bingo! Jason could hardly contain himself. "Yes, I'm ready." He nearly flipped his pen across the room as he grabbed for it on the night stand. On a piece of motel stationery he scribbled the address, repeating it aloud slowly so she could correct him if he had misunderstood: "One-four-eight Buzzway Drive. Thanks. I'm extremely appreciative for the information. You've been more than helpful."

"You're welcome. And when you find Cody, please tell him that we here at the school send our condolences."

"I'll do it."

Finally, there in writing, on the butter-colored stationery in his hand, he had Cody Freedman's address.

He looked at his watch. It was 10:40 A.M. With an awesome sense of relief, he headed immediately for the car.

Using his Miami city map as a guide, he navigated his Buick to the neighborhood where he had pinpointed Cody's address. His initial reaction as he got closer was shock. Every house in sight, he speculated, had a market value at least five times that of the average home in his Atlanta neighborhood. Could he have the wrong Buzzway Drive? There was no way a young man right out of college could afford to live in such a posh neighborhood. Or was there? Could Hannah have lived in surroundings such as these?

By the time Jason turned onto Buzzway Drive, his thoughts had shifted from appraising the area's houses to his encounter with Cody. He felt his stomach knot with anticipation. In light of Cody's expressed desire to remain anonymous, he knew his unexpected appearance would most likely provoke a negative response, perhaps even an ugly scene. He tried to mentally prepare himself for such a reaction. He knew that in Cody's eyes he would be the uninvited intruder. But Cody was hiding, and with him he was hiding a part of Lorene and Hannah. No matter how Cody viewed the situation, Jason felt he had a clear case for interfering.

He would just have to be diplomatic in his approach, handle the situation the best he could, then hope somehow a peace treaty could be established between them.

He was almost there. He passed house 140, then 144. And then, there it was: 148.

As his heartbeat quickened, he slowly turned his Buick onto the white-graveled circle driveway. The house, forty yards from the road, was a two-story chipped-rock structure with an unusual strain of vine clinging to its walls. There was a certain harmony between the house and the shrub-trimmed lawn that gave the place a distinctive charm. It was serene, picturesque, and obviously very costly. If this was the right place, Cody was definitely not the typical just-out-of-college young man.

As he neared the home's entrance, a German shepherd next door ran out to the fence that divided the two yards, and began a vicious barking. Jason was glad the fence was there, and hoped there was no way the dog could get around or over it.

By the time Jason stopped at the front door and stepped out of his car, the dog's behavior had drawn his owner's attention. The old man came around the corner of his home and calmly called, "Whoa, boy." He had to repeat the order only once before the dog relaxed.

Before Jason had a chance to ring the front doorbell, the old man spoke up from his side of the fence. "Sir, is there anything I can do to help you?" For some reason he was obviously making Jason's visit to the chipped-rock house his business.

Jason lifted his voice and half-shouted his answer. "I'm looking for a young man by the name of Cody Freedman. I was told he lives here."

"He *did* live there," the old man called.

Jason cleared his throat, then walked across the grass in the man's direction. "I'm sorry, I don't understand."

The man waited to reply until Jason was almost at the fence. "Cody sold the house on Friday. By yesterday afternoon he was already moved out. So I'm afraid you've just missed him."

"Just missed him," Jason said softly. He was in shock.

"Pardon?" the old man replied. With his neatly combed white

hair glimmering in the sunlight, his black-rimmed glasses, and his mustache, he looked like a seasoned scientist.

"Are we talking about the same Cody Freedman?" Jason asked, not bothering to repeat his previous statement. "I'm looking for a young man whose wife just died about four and a half weeks ago after giving birth to a baby girl."

"That's the same Cody Freedman," the man answered, with tenderness in his voice.

"Well, uh...can you tell me where I might be able to find him?"

"I'm sorry, but I have no idea. I've been his neighbor and friend for twenty-five years, and practically a dad to him ever since his own father and mother were killed three years ago in a plane crash, and I couldn't even get out of him where he was going. All he said was that he was leaving Miami."

"He's no longer in the city?" Jason's words were more rhetoric than question. His soaring spirit had been shot down, though he felt a sudden new bond with Cody—the kinship of pain—after hearing he had lost his parents.

"Not as far as I know," the old man answered honestly.

"And the baby?" Jason asked, hoping against hope he would hear a different answer.

"She's with him."

Jason felt himself wanting to cry.

"I don't mean to interfere in your business," the old man continued, "but are you with the Children's Watchcare Center?"

"Children's Watchcare Center?" Jason could only guess what kind of agency that was, but his initial suspicion set off alarms in his head. "No, I'm not," he stated. "But is someone from there supposed to be looking for Cody? I mean, is there some kind of problem with Cody and the baby?"

The old man paused, trying to assess Jason. He wanted to know more about this man before he told him what he knew—information that Sophia in her concern had occasionally come over to tell him. It was obvious to him that the visitor was responding emotionally to the news about Cody, and therefore had some kind of personal interest, maybe genuine. But it did not hurt to be cautious. "Forgive me if I hesitate to answer such a personal question, but I don't know who you are, or why you've come here."

"I'm Cody's father-in-law," Jason stated flatly. "Hannah's dad. Jason Faircloth."

The look of puzzlement on the old man's face was so stark that Jason automatically reached for his wallet and pulled out a small picture of himself with Lorene and Hannah, just to verify his statement.

After the old man studied the photograph at close range, he shook his head. "I don't understand," he said, with surprise in his voice.

"What do you mean?"

"Why would they lie about you? Hannah told us at the dinner table in our home one night that she'd never seen her parents—that they abandoned her at her birth, and that she was raised in a foster home in Orlando."

Jason's mind recoiled at the words. It was another indictment leveled at his performance as a father, and it hurt. But he'd already felt too much pain for the new revelation to cause an extreme reaction. Instead of producing a shock, the deeper look into Hannah's feelings about him simply added to his grief, like a terminally ill patient being told he had only two more months to live instead of three.

"She lied to you," Jason forced himself to say to the old man, "because she was trying to cover up the fact that she was a runaway."

"A runaway?" the old man asked in disbelief.

"She left our home in Atlanta a year and a half ago. And even though she was listed as a missing person with the FBI, we never learned anything of her whereabouts until last month. The FBI contacted us and told us her death had been reported and verified at Baptist Hospital.

"Did Cody know she was a runaway," the old man asked, still in a daze.

"Yeah, he knew," Jason answered without emotion. "He gave the police our Atlanta phone number and address and asked that we be notified. It was because of him that we were able to bury her body in Atlanta."

"Atlanta!" The old man, peering down through his bifocals, spoke the word dejectedly, as if he had just discovered, too late, a major clue in a mystery case. "We were wondering why Cody didn't have a public funeral for her. He told us that for personal reasons he wanted her burial to be a private matter. And we never questioned him. I mean, it never dawned on us that—"

"Don't take it personally," Jason interrupted. "I guess in order to protect their marriage from unwanted intrusions they felt they had to keep a lot of things secret. And when Hannah died, Cody probably felt like he had to keep hiding the truth to save face."

"Maybe you're right..." the old man reflected. He had always had a special liking for Cody. Exceptionally bright, Cody also had a shy disposition, which often worked to his advantage and gave him an added aura of mystery. And now, living up to his character, he had outwitted them all. Yet the old man could not help but take the deception somewhat personally. He had been as close to Cody as an old man could be. *Why,* he wondered, *didn't Cody believe he could be honest with me?* He quickly tried to recall through the years whether he had given Cody any reason to mistrust him.

"I suppose," Jason said, "that when a person's happiness is more important to him than truth, he can be pretty convincing with his lies." The insight came from his fresh experience, and he spoke it from the heart.

He decided to try steering the man back to the subject of Cody and the baby. "But what was it you were going to say earlier about the Children's Watchcare Center? Is there some kind of problem with Cody and the baby? If there is, I want to know. Because of losing Hannah, my wife went into shock two weeks ago and died. I'm all alone now. And the only living link I have in this world to either Hannah or my wife is my little grandgirl. It's of the utmost importance to me that I find her and do what I can to help her."

The old man hung his head for a moment. His heart went out to this middle-aged man who was obviously carrying an untold amount of grief. He could see Jason was desperate.

"Well, as I said before, I honestly don't know where Cody has taken her. But there is a problem I guess I should tell you about. When Hannah died, Cody took it pretty badly. He closed down his business and hired a live-in baby-sitter to take care of the baby, and then he started drinking. It got to the point that he was never sober. A real messy situation. Anyway, to make a long story short, the baby-sitter finally reported him to the Children's Watchcare Center and told them he was an unfit father. I think she was hoping the people there would be able to scare some sense back into him. But the whole thing backfired. When the state agency came down on him, instead of sobering up he chose to run. That's when he sold the house."

As Jason listened, he felt so many mixed emotions that it scared him. He could feel deeply Cody's pain and could even understand his actions. But at the same time, in his grandfather's heart, he felt himself pumped with rage to think that the only parent of his helpless granddaughter was so emotionally incapacitated that he could not properly care for her. It also infuriated him to realize he had missed being able to help the child himself by only one day.

"How in God's name," he asked with the veins in his neck becoming visible, "was he able to sell the house so quickly? I've been here in Miami for two weeks trying to track them down, and now you tell me I missed them by one day! I can't believe it! I just can't believe it!"

In the outburst, the old man saw pain in Jason that was similar to the pain he had seen in Cody. He lowered his voice and sympathetically invited Jason into his house. He decided he would take time to answer, as best he could, all of Jason's heart-starving questions about Hannah's life in Miami. It was the least he could do.

Before letting Jason cross the fence, the old man locked the dog away for his visitor's peace of mind. The dog had been Cody's, he explained, and Cody had asked him to take it right before he left.

Once they were inside and seated, the old man introduced himself as Malcolm Sandberg, and explained that Cody had received many outstanding offers for the house since the death of his parents. "So when he decided to sell, he had a buyer in a matter of hours."

The two men talked more about Cody's grief, then Jason steered the subject back to Hannah. He asked about her and Cody's marriage.

To answer, Malcolm backtracked ten months and started from the beginning. He explained that when Cody first met Hannah, she was living in a ghetto. Cody had rescued her from that existence and given her one of the finest lifestyles Miami could offer, thanks to the money and real estate he inherited from his parents.

Hannah, in return, with her beauty and her bubbling love, had become the life-changing force in Cody's life. Singlehandedly, and almost magically, she had nursed him out of his two-year, self-imposed social withdrawal caused by his grief for his parents. "It was your daughter who gave him back his life," he told Jason proudly.

Believing it would be therapeutic for Jason to hear, Malcolm took most of an hour to recall special incidents lingering in his mind that he had seen or heard about from Cody and Hannah's life together. Their short-lived union had without a doubt been one of the happiest and healthiest he had ever observed. "I must confess," he added, "that I was a little envious myself sometimes."

The consolation Jason felt at that moment was invaluable. Through the long months of no information from Hannah, he had carried doubts and fears about her emotional and physical welfare. Now they immediately dissipated.

"And how about the pregnancy?" he asked.

As the old man described how excited Hannah had acted over the prospects of being a mother, and how glowing and wholesome she appeared in her maternity clothes, Jason could not hold back the tears.

"It's strange, isn't it?" he said. "Here I am hearing all this good news of how happy my girl was, and even though it makes me grateful to no end, I can't help but take it as a slap in the face. I feel like such a failure."

Malcolm replied tenderly, "Well, I don't know much about you, but to your credit let me just say that it's obvious you loved your daughter. It's written all over you. And whatever Hannah's reasons for leaving home, I'm sure she never doubted that love."

Jason was moved. And for some reason—maybe to be fair to Hannah—he wanted to let Malcolm know that though he loved Hannah, he was not without guilt as a father. He had been wanting now for weeks to spill his heart in a public confession of his failures, but there had been no one whom he felt he could be honest with. Now there was. And he could hold back no longer.

He cleared his throat. "Yeah, I loved her," he said, "but I wasn't very mindful of her feelings. My intentions were honorable—I think I can say that—but I'm afraid that in many ways I was just outright blind and too demanding. I was so naive that I actually believed I was an authority on raising teenagers. So whenever Hannah tried to share her feelings with me, especially about my performance as a father, I refused to listen." He paused, then pulled Hannah's runaway letter from his wallet and asked the old man to read it.

The old man adjusted his glasses and slowly read the words on the wrinkled and nearly worn-out sheet of paper. It was the first time anyone other than Jason or Lorene had seen it.

When he finished, he lifted his head in silence.

"So, you see," Jason continued, "I honestly thought at the time that her feelings were childish, and irrelevant to the protective way I was trying to raise her. I guess a teenager can handle only so much of that kind of parental attitude. If I could do it over again, I assure you I would go about it in a different way."

Malcolm felt for Jason. He wanted to be positive. "Well," he said, "at least it sounds like you've learned something valuable from the whole thing. And that's admirable. That's more than could be said for most people."

Finally Jason asked about the baby. The old man described her, as far as he knew.

"And her name?" Jason asked.

"He called her Renée," the old man told him. Jason wasn't surprised. It was Hannah's middle name.

Hearing about the baby made Jason want even more to find her and make sure she was okay. He began to brood again, angry at having missed being united with her by just one lousy day. He was the child's only surviving grandparent, and he had failed to find her—all because of the stupid, unnecessary delays that had plagued his search and wasted so much time. The four days last week he spent spinning his wheels now proved to be crucial time that had tipped the balance against him.

Checking the plunge in his mood, Jason forced himself to be grateful for the information he had learned. Yet it was as if every morsel of information the old man had so graciously shared had been laced with some kind of secret drug that had played mercilessly with his emotions—taking him high, then quickly letting him down.

Jason finally stood to say goodbye after a lengthy stay. They exchanged addresses and phone numbers, and Malcolm also gave him Sophia's address and number. Jason decided to visit her that very evening.

Offering profuse thanks to Malcolm for his generous, unexpected help, Jason walked outside alone.

His heart and mind had been stretched so far and in so many different directions that he didn't know whether to laugh or cry or curse. As a father, he felt that gaining today's information had been a victory over fate. He had been able to steal back much of his daughter's eighteen months of silence that the past had robbed from him. He felt partially vindicated, though there was not much joy in it.

As a grandfather, however, he could not ignore the pounding frustration caused by the narrow defeat. Where could he look for his granddaughter now? Knowing she could easily become a victim of abuse, due to Cody's condition, he dared not entertain the thought of calling off the search. Somehow he had to find their trail leading out of Miami.

The late afternoon sun was spilling golden light on the chipped-rock house. Before getting back into his car, Jason felt compelled to take a stroll around the place where Hannah had spent most of her final year on earth. He wanted to see and remember the home where his daughter had found loving refuge from a tyrannical and hard-hearted dad.

Walking slowly around the yard, peeking through the ground-floor windows of the house, he could almost feel Hannah's presence. A couple of times he even found himself about to talk with her.

In the back yard he found a professionally made business sign leaning upside down against the base of a garden gazebo. It was painted black, and shaped like the silhouette of a large dog. The words were lettered in white:

COE'S ANIMAL CLINIC
For Those Who Care About Their Pets
HOURS: 8 to 4 M-F — 9 to 1 Sat. — Closed Sun.

The bottom of the sign—the lower half of the big dog's legs—were stained with dirt from having been staked in the front yard at the clinic.

Jason thought to himself that the uprooted sign, with all its unknown ramifications, symbolized a desperate man. He feared for Cody. But he feared far more for Renée. He still had two weeks to search for them, and he needed to make the most of the time. As hard as it would be, he would now try to forget the past and set his mind on the future.

He walked back around to the front of the house. As he opened the Buick's door, he lifted his hand and waved toward the house.

"Goodbye, Hannah," he whispered, fighting to hold back the tears.

Driving out the driveway, he refused to look back.

13

SOPHIA GAVE HIM a true southerner's welcome to her home that evening, then listened as Jason explained his ties to Hannah, Cody, and the baby. She found herself caught up in both curiosity and pity as he shared his plight.

This was a man, Sophia decided, who would listen and take action. She therefore felt a personal calling to state frankly her pessimism about Renée's immediate welfare. "For the little girl's sake," she said bluntly, "you need to find her and Cody as soon as possible." By the tone of her voice and the look on her face, she may as well have added, "Or else she's doomed..."

Jason left unnerved. He could only imagine the worse.

His mind raced all night to conjure up a way of finding Cody's trail.

The next morning, against his initial intentions, he called on Malcolm again. Acting on ideas that had come to him during the night, he asked Malcolm for a list of names and addresses— Cody's Miami bank, his real estate agent, some of his business clientele, his local relatives, and the closest Post Office.

Caught up in the urgency of finding Renée and ensuring her safety, Malcolm gladly supplied as much information as he could. And since he was a retiree with a free schedule, and since almost everybody on the list knew him personally and also knew of his relationship to the Freedmans, he suggested that he go along to help add legitimacy to Jason's inquiries.

With thankfulness Jason accepted his offer. Still fresh on his mind were the problems a stranger could face when trying to procure information about someone he didn't know.

The tactic paid off. For the rest of the week, thanks to Malcolm's presence, they encountered no problems making the contacts and getting cooperative treatment. But unfortunately, no one they questioned could offer any useful information. Cody's new location was a mystery to everyone.

The bank reported that Cody, on the Saturday morning after he sold his house, had closed out all of his accounts and redeemed all of his capital, with the exception of money locked in a trust fund set up for him by his parents years earlier, and not available for his use for another four years. The teller who had personally handed over Cody's money could not remember any particular remarks of his that gave a clue to his plans.

The realtor remembered asking Cody if he needed assistance in buying a new house, and Cody had answered simply, "I'm not buying another house." The subject wasn't discussed any further.

The cousin who bought the house said Cody had refused to talk about future plans. Most of Cody's other local relatives knew of his selling the home only through talking with the cousin. Cody hadn't told any of them what he was up to.

Most of the animal owners whom Jason and Malcolm tracked down did not even know Cody had shut down his practice. They responded with total surprise.

The only answer the postal authorities would give was, "I'm sorry, but Mr. Freedman did not leave a forwarding address."

After five days of effort, Jason had run out of ideas. He was running out of momentum as well. From every angle it appeared Cody had simply vanished.

On Saturday afternoon, Jason and Malcolm said their good-byes, resolutely agreeing to contact one another in the event that either learned of Cody and Renée's whereabouts.

Jason returned to the motel. This was his third Saturday night in Miami, and his granddaughter apparently was now further away from him than ever. He felt himself being pulled into another fit of depression.

Why couldn't his life be sure and settled and serene as it had been in the past? *If only Lorene and Hannah were still alive*, he thought once more.

In the last two weeks, the all-consuming pursuit of Renée had successfully distracted him from any death-wishing. But now that the search had reached a dead end, there was nothing on the immediate horizon to divert his emotions. He was once again the prisoner of grief and emptiness. Once again, the thought of killing himself became attractive.

He was convinced these low points in his life represented the most awful state a person could ever be trapped in. It was an emotional abyss that could not be willfully shaken. It could only be endured.

He likened his situation to that of someone whose limbs had all been amputated and the stumps sewn up, and who was then left alone to lie on barren ground in a cold, hard rain.

It was hell on earth.

He knew he could not spend the night alone without risking something desperate. As a protective measure, solely for Renée's sake, he forced himself to sit, think, eat, drink, and doze the night away in a 24-hour grill, a warm, noisy place where he was surrounded by people. It was misery amplified, but at least it kept him alive for one more day.

≈ ≈ ≈

BY 6 A.M. SUNDAY, he had wearily decided to attend a worship service somewhere that morning, if for no other reason than to restore some routine to his life.

He had not attended church for the last three Sundays, a record for him. Since his years in seminary, in fact, he had missed only one service, and that was because of a tough bout with the flu during his third year of pastoring. Even during family vacations he and Lorene and Hannah had always attended church somewhere nearby. The practice had become an ingrained personal habit with him, but he thoroughly believed God expected it to be so and would have argued adamantly with anyone who disagreed. Only in the last three weeks had he lost his heart for going, but now, though his bitterness toward God was still intact, he felt again that he needed it. He needed the comfort, the encouragement. And he needed the security of the past.

At a public phone in the entry to the grill, he checked the yellow pages for churches listed under his own denomination. He saw the name of one he had often heard about at denominational conventions and pastors' meetings. He scribbled down the address on a paper napkin, then headed back to the motel to shower and shave.

Inside his room he flipped on the television to fill up the silence and continue diverting his mind from his depression. A Sunday morning talk show lured his attention: The guest was one of those "rich reverends" who preached that it was never God's will for a Christian to be poor.

Jason listened while shaving at the sink, and heard the man bragging about his three mansions, his four Rolls Royces, and other luxuries God had given him in response to his faith. Jason stepped out of the bathroom to take a look at the man. He was flashing a diamond ring on every finger.

A lady in the audience stood and presented a bold question: "I'm curious as to how you justify your prosperity doctrine for all Christians, when Jesus himself clearly stated that it's harder for a rich man to enter into the kingdom of God than it is for a camel to go through the eye of a needle."

"Lady," the reverend smiled, "I don't have to 'justify my doctrine,' as you call it. It justifies itself. Think with me for a moment: If it's as hard as Jesus said it is for a rich man to enter the kingdom of God, and I believe it is, then just imagine how much harder it's going to be for a poor man!"

Jason groaned. *The idiot,* he thought. *How can he pretend to be a messenger of God's truth, when he massacres the Scriptures like that? With a teaching like that he's either a theological bozo, or a hardened deceiver who preys on the simple.* He switched off the set and went back to his shaving, but couldn't lay aside his irritation. Berating the TV reverend for taking the Scriptures out of context, he started to congratulate himself for his own personal history of being a pastor who always honored the Bible. But his heightened sensitivity brought on by the introspection of the past few weeks ignited an explosive question within him.

He washed the remnants of shaving cream from his face, looked in the mirror, and wondered: *Am I really any less guilty than that brazen fool? Come on, who are you pretending to be, Jason?*

He reached for a towel to dry his face, and started mumbling to himself. "All these years you've acted as if you had a monopoly on biblical truth. All along you've stubbornly—proudly—closed your ears to your critics, such as your own daughter, when they accused you of preaching standards that just aren't taught in the Bible. And they were right. You've deceived yourself, Jason. You've been preaching extreme ideas that were probably fabricated by fanatics like that jerk on TV."

The articulated self-admission led him to ask whether his entire profession was a mockery to God. Was there a preacher alive who treated the Bible objectively, who refused to interpret it in the light of personal experiences and preferences, who preached nothing more and nothing less than the Bible preached?

He thought again of the church he planned to attend this morning, and of the settings where he had heard about it: those state and national gatherings in which pastors convened for mutual encouragement, but inevitably ended up gloating about their ministries, and callously belittling those of others. *Pastors,* he concluded, *are proud, presumptuous, and pathetic little jackasses.*

As he finished dressing, he wrestled with his thoughts: With the feelings he had now, feelings that had been slowly mounting over the last three weeks, how could he go nonchalantly back to Atlanta and proceed in his pastorate?

He wondered if these feelings would pass. Was he just temporarily shaken beyond reason? Would he think differently in a few days, after he had perhaps found his granddaughter and things had settled down? Would his newly risen bitterness eventually die away?

Or did he now know too much to ever be able to pick up the past and be the same?

He grabbed his car keys from the top of the television set, walked out the door, and headed for church.

≈   ≈   ≈

BY THE TIME HE ARRIVED, the church service had already started. But that was fine. He would not be forced to socialize while waiting for things to begin.

In the auditorium, all heads were bowed as the speaker prayed. Jason walked in inconspicuously and slid into an empty space on a pew in the back row.

He longed for the atmosphere of worship to revive his faith and blanket him with a sense of inner peace. But he had already become too cynical. Instead of sitting there with a normal churchgoer's frame of mind—either absorbing the service or deflecting it with wandering thoughts—he found himself attacking it with malice.

Absolutely nothing that was said or sung from the pulpit seemed to be relevant to anyone's real, down-to-earth needs—like his own. The prayers, the hymns, the testimony, even the announcements all seemed part of a heartless, impersonal mechanism that had been activated by a flip of a switch for the one-hour Sunday morning time slot. It all seemed so ineffective, so useless.

Then, with a gushing stream of superlatives, the pastor was introduced. Middle-aged like Jason, he strode to the podium, announced his text, and opened with this statement: "Ladies and gentlemen, music in its proper form is the masterful creation of God Almighty. But in its distorted form it is the damnable work of the enemy. And we're living in a generation that has been infiltrated by the enemy's music.

"How do we identify the enemy's music? That's simple. It's music that is syncopated. It's called 'pop,' or 'rock.'"

Instead of explaining the Bible verses he had announced as his text, and teaching them in their context, the pastor launched into a dissertation of his personal biases—just as the rich reverend did on the TV talk show, and just as Jason himself had done a thousand times before.

Jason started to feel sick. He was seeing an ugly reflection of himself that was coming more and more into focus by the minute. Repulsed as he was, however, he was held to his seat out of morbid curiosity.

The pastor was underscoring the dangers of rock music with a close-at-home example: "I want you to pray for the McAndrews family," he told his audience. "Several months ago Ralph called me aside and told me that his son, Terry, had knowingly violated the family rules and had begun listening to a steady diet of rock music. I asked him if he knew that to be a fact. He said there was no doubt about it, that he had found six or seven unmarked tapes that he didn't recognize in one of Terry's desk drawers. Being curious about their content, he played bits and pieces of them, and found every one filled with modern rock.

"When he later confronted Terry about it, the boy admitted he had been using earphones to listen to the tapes every night in the privacy of his room.

"Ralph said that before he carried out any kind of disciplinary action, he first wanted to seek my advice. Now, the reason Ralph was so concerned is because he knows rock music in all of its variations, without exception, is born in hell, perpetrated by communism, and aimed at destroying morality.

"I told Ralph that if I were Terry's father, I would first of all make Terry destroy the tapes and watch him as he did it. Secondly, I would take away his tape player. By the way, folks, I have two teenagers, as most of you know, and I refuse to let either one of them have his own tape player. To give teenagers their own tape player is like giving them fire. Nine times out of ten they can't control it, and they end up getting burned.

"I mean, let's be honest about it: If they are listening to the right kind of music, they won't mind listening to it on the family stereo in the presence of everybody else. Privacy won't be necessary."

With outbursts of "Amen," several people in the audience rallied behind his remarks. Jason hoped the ameners were not the parents of teenagers, but he knew they probably were. They were parents, he concluded, just like the parents in his own congregation who for years had pledged their blind allegiance to his blind leadership. Here, too, was another case of the blind following the blind.

Jason was finding it almost impossible to remain seated, but he fought himself to hear the rest of the story.

"Well, anyway," the pastor continued after acknowledging the amens, "Ralph took my advice and did as I suggested.

"Nevertheless, he found out a few weeks later that Terry had defied him and had traded a baseball glove for a transistor radio and had kept right on listening to the devil's music. At that stage Ralph asked me if I would talk to Terry.

"I did talk to him. And Terry assured me up and down that there was nothing wrong with rock music, and that he didn't intend to give it up—not for his parents, not for me, not for the church.

"*Are you listening to what I'm saying, folks?* I'm talking about a seventeen-year-old boy. As a result of his constant exposure to that kind of music, just for a period of a few months, he became *defiant* and *disrespectful* toward his *God-given authorities.*

"To make a long story short, when it became obvious that Terry wasn't going to obey God in the matter, Ralph and I agreed that as his father and spiritual leader he should give Terry an ultimatum: to either remove rock music from his life, or leave home. Terry left home.

"*He left home,* I said! Are you understanding it now? Don't you see the destructive power of rock music? And that's not even the end of the story. Three weeks after Terry left home, he was arrested by the Miami police for possessing hard drugs. He's in jail tonight, people. *A seventeen-year-old kid.* His life is scarred and maybe even ruined, all because of rock music. *Rock music, I said!* Are you listening?

"My God, I'm praying for you parents who are soft and who are weak and can't see the danger. I've told this story this morning with Ralph's permission, and I've told it for your sake, to illustrate the seriousness of what I'm teaching.

"And teenagers, you listen to me! If you play God and think you know it all, then you'll end up just like Terry. You don't want—"

With his outrage spinning out of control—outrage at both himself and his pastoral peers—Jason tuned out the sermon. He stood up to leave. The forgotten hymnal that had been lying in his lap fell against the back of the pew in front of him, then fell with a dull thud to the floor. The movement and noise drew the attention of people around him. He felt as if every eye in the room zoomed in on him, but he did not care.

Heading across the foyer and out the front door, he heard a male voice over his shoulder asking if he was all right. "Everything's fine," he shouted without turning to face the man, and kept walking.

Even before he got to his car, the thoughts of his rude exit were already buried out of reach by something larger. His trauma of losing Lorene and Hannah, and the reasons behind it, were finally registering with full force. His ears had been forced wide open. For the first time in all his years of being a closed-minded legalist, he had heard the pastor's story from the viewpoint of a Terry or a Hannah. How in the name of Bible preaching, he wondered explosively, could he and his peers, all seminary and Bible college graduates, preach so authoritatively and so hard—hard enough to divide families—on issues that the Bible was so nondogmatic about? How could they find it so imperative to label every human practice either black or white, acting as if they and they alone knew the absolute mind of God on every issue?

His earlier conclusion about preachers trumpeted in his brain: *proud, presumptuous, pathetic little jackasses*. For all his years of ministry he, too, had practiced a cheap deception.

Jason got in his car and slammed the door. He found himself cursing himself, his peers, his seminary, and his professors. He was confused and uncertain about a great host of things, but there was one thing he was now sure of: He no longer wanted to preach. The decision was final. His heart for the ministry had died. His lifelong beliefs, his do-or-die convictions, his authoritative preaching, his bustling church—all of it was unrecoverable now, unreachable, as if it were fifty centuries in the past.

He steered the car from the parking lot, his bitter frustration escalating. He was fighting mad at the universe and at the one who made it.

Out on the road, he felt like he was suffocating. His nerves and lungs cried out for relief. As if his body had suddenly hijacked the control system of his brain, his foot stomped the accelerator and pinned it to the floor. The tires screamed, and Jason screamed with them.

In a residential zone with a thirty-mile-per-hour speed limit, he was traveling sixty. Heading for a stop sign, he almost decided to speed through, hopefully forcing an accident and killing himself. But at the last moment his reason reclaimed control. He slammed on the brakes. The sound of rubber squealing on asphalt erupted beneath him. He was thrown backward into the seat as the car ended its slide in an abrupt halt.

He sat motionless for a few seconds. His fast, heavy breathing echoed through the car's interior. The temporary outburst had released some tightly wound tension, but he was still mad. He could feel it from his head to his toes.

It was then that he noticed people standing in their nearby front yards, watching him. They looked upset. He slowly drove through the intersection as if nothing out of the ordinary had happened.

In the motel room he locked the door and pulled the shades. In this darkened chamber, alienated from all human contact, he abandoned the little self-control he had left, responding fully and freely to all his emotional turmoil. He yielded gladly—pacing, yelling, punching, crying, cursing.

Like Job, he cursed the day he was born. But unlike Job, he cursed God as well. He cursed him for killing Hannah. He cursed him for killing Lorene. He cursed him for hiding Renée. He cursed him for killing his own self-dignity. And while cursing him, he dared him—even begged him—to retaliate and kill him, too. And when God did not, Jason cursed him for letting him live.

His energy eventually spent, Jason lay across the bed and dozed out of physical exhaustion. But his mind would not rest. It kept battling, throwing him into nightmares.

He awoke, fully aware—and the entire cycle started over again in full swing: the punching and pacing; the crying and cursing; and then, when he was unable to fight anymore, the restless sleeping and the nightmares. He felt every punch that loneliness, grief, and disillusionment could deliver. He suffered as he had never suffered before.

Finally his survival instinct overruled his emotional standoff. He broke his wall to the outside world by lifting the window shade, letting in afternoon light.

He called the motel office and asked for the time. It was 5:30.

"And...what day is it?" he added.

"Tuesday. It's Tuesday, sir."

He had been locked away, engaged in his struggle with God, himself, and life for two and a half days.

He looked around the room. The bed sheets were crumpled into a disfigured pile on the mattress. The bedspread and pillows were thrown on the floor near the closet. The nightstand lamp was overturned, the lampshade off and the bulb broken. The only chair in the room was upside-down against the wall-mounted air conditioner. Its cushion was on the opposite side of the bed. The room smelled of body odor.

He opened the outside door to let the evening air and sun come in, then sat down in the doorway. He felt as if he'd been to hell and back. But for all he'd been through, he did not feel the slightest bit relieved. He still hurt, but was incapable of any further active expression of it. It was like having the emotional dry heaves; there was nothing more that could be thrown up.

After fifteen minutes of sitting silently in the sunlight, he got up to pack his bags.

There was nothing to hold him in Miami any longer.

14

CODY HAD BEEN ALONE with Renée for only forty minutes, and already his nerves were frayed. She would not stop crying.

The babysitter had promised Cody she would be back in no more than thirty minutes. She had run out to buy food and diapers at a grocery store two blocks away from Cody and Renée's efficiency apartment. He was staying in New York City while waiting for the British consulate to process his application for a residence permit. They were moving to England.

During a hot, lazy summer ten years earlier, when the dollar was strong against the British pound, the teenaged Cody and his parents had taken a two-week family vacation in London. Cody's dad enjoyed the English culture so immensely that he later joked half-seriously about moving the family there for a few years while he worked at the European office of his international contracting company. He faithfully mentioned the wishful dream at least once a year, and had spoken of it again just before he and Cody's mother were killed in the plane crash.

Since then, Cody had many times contemplated the idea of living out his father's dream. In fact, only two days before meeting Hannah, he had written "Get a passport" on his weekly planner. But then Hannah came into his life, the sparks flew—and the dream was forgotten.

Now it had returned, and Cody had decided impulsively to make it a reality as soon as the house sold. The consequences and inevitable difficulties of such a radical move were lost on him; he was too busy trying to escape his hurt by staying drunk. Here in New York he was constantly in and out of the city's bars.

As he embarked alone with Renée on a long-distance journey into the unknown, the only thing in his favor was money. Before the sale of the house was finalized he already had more than $100,000 in a savings account inherited from his parents. The sale of the real estate added just over $200,000 to that. And his trust fund, continuing to accrue interest, was nearing $50,000.

To his credit, even in his loose-headedness he was somehow thoughtfully determined to protect his fortune. Besides the rent and paying the baby-sitter, the only other thing he was spending money on was alcohol. That amount was increasing daily—as was the intensity of his inebriation, and the fierceness of his temper.

"Shut up!" he shouted again to Renée, turning to glare at her tiny form lying in the middle of the double bed. Her tiny tongue was trembling in her open mouth. Her face was flushed red. He knew she had been fed and changed before the babysitter left, but the more he yelled at her, the louder and more high-pitched her wail became.

"Shut up!" he screamed again. Her crying was continuous, interrupted only by quick gasps for air.

He was more than half-drunk. For the first time in his life, he felt no inhibition about expressing his loss of temper through physical exertion. He reached over the bed, gripped the baby's waist in his two hands, and jerked her into the air. Her tiny head flopped backward and rolled sideways.

He was yelling while he did it: "Shut your mouth or I'll make you shut it!"

Her screaming became only more hysterical. Her thin arms and legs contracted stiffly into a human ball.

Cody slammed her to the mattress, picked up a pillow, and pressed it over her head, his angry momentum refusing all restraint.

"Shut up!" His voice was a shriek. He held the pillow tightly in place.

The baby girl's legs kicked instinctively. Her muted cries lessened, and then stopped. Finally, her limbs became motionless.

But the sought-after silence was broken by the loud thumps of Cody's racing heartbeat. His mental reflexes were so stupefied that he was heedless of what his hands were doing. He froze in position and listened to the pounding beats.

From the city street six floors below, a sudden blast from a fire truck siren jerked Cody back to his senses. He threw off the pillow from Renée's face. For a second or two he watched with numbness. *She's dead*, his shocked mind told him.

When she abruptly gasped for breath, then again launched into a full-scale scream, Cody cringed in horror.

He backed away, leaving Renée on the bed to cry. He walked over to the window and peered unseeing over the metropolitan bustle. What had he nearly done? What was wrong with him? Was he going crazy?

Barely audible above the baby's screams, Cody heard the apartment's door open and the voice of the baby-sitter calling out, "I'm back!"

Within seconds he had rushed to her, shouting at her for taking so long. Almost before she had time to get the groceries out of her arms, he was marching out the door to get away.

He jogged down the stairway instead of taking the elevator, then hustled out of the building and down the snow-dusted sidewalk.

He did not want to admit to himself that his life was crumbling. Somehow he had to stay positive and pretend there was hope. But could he simply forget and put behind him the fact that he had nearly murdered his own daughter? He convinced himself that he could, as long as he vowed never to touch Renée in anger again. *I'll make it*, he told himself, as he battled a gusty wind that was hitting him head-on.

A few minutes later he was out of the cold and seated on a bar stool. "What can I round up for you, mister?" the bartender asked.

"A Jägermeister," Cody answered, adding, "Make that two."

15

THE LADIES' TRIO was in the middle of their second song about the love of God. The same theme had been sounded throughout the hymns and choruses already sung by the congregation at tonight's midweek prayer meeting, and it was the announced topic of Steve Mitchell's message as well.

With their strong and confident voices, the ladies on the platform were one of the favorite singing groups in the church, and the crowd enjoyed the music. But the overall mood tonight was one of nonchalant sobriety. Steve's leadership as Jason's temporary replacement was appreciated, but nearly every person in the auditorium, each in his own way, was keenly concerned for the

General. No one here, not even the church staff, had heard a single report from him in three weeks. He had been totally silent—something quite unlike his usual style. In their eagerness to understand his grief, however, they attributed his silence to his personal need for privacy and spiritual renewal. No one doubted that within a week or so the General would be back at the reins, more determined than ever.

Suddenly, whispers and nudges swept through the congregation like a fire through a dry brush field. Behind the ladies, Jason had walked out onto the platform through the choir loft door, and was walking unassumingly toward his designated chair on the opposite side of the pulpit. With his slumped shoulders and distant gaze, he looked void of life.

He crossed behind the podium and sat down. There was no smile, no gesture. If anyone present hadn't known him, they might have guessed he was a mentally sick stranger who had wandered in by mistake.

The ladies in the trio glanced over their shoulders at him, trying with difficulty to carry on their singing as if nothing out of the ordinary had happened.

Jason looked down, not hearing their song. His mind and heart felt like thousand-pound weights. What he was about to do was going to change the course of his life, and of the church's life as well. But he felt it was impossible to not go through with it. Beyond his understanding, his heart for the ministry had been slain. Along with that death, his motivation, vision, and concern had been launched into the unknown, far beyond his reach. Cold disillusionment and bitterness had forcefully taken their place.

He used to sit in this very chair with unimaginable pride—as if he were a king, and the chair his throne, and the church his kingdom. But now he felt it had all been a meaningless one-man circus act. To think in such terms about his once-sacred ministerial position disturbed him, but he could not change his feelings, no matter how hard he tried.

With his mind set like steel, he looked up. He could not help seeing everything now in a different light. The ladies' trio, for example. Only a few short weeks ago he had seen each of these women as an exemplary model of godly living. They represented Christianity's finest, the cream of the crop. But now he saw them as nothing more than decorative shells, pathetically hollow and empty of substance, and thus cheap and even fraudulent, as they expressed so easily their particular brand of Christianity. He blamed himself for this, for he was the one who had spiritually fathered and groomed them. He saw them as he had now come to see himself: bold, obnoxious, divisive believers in the rigid do's and don'ts he had always preached. They honestly believed—as their General himself had believed, and taught them to believe—that those standards somehow encapsulated true spirituality.

Though he could not put a finger on it exactly, since he was still groping for understanding, Jason somehow felt that the Christianity in his church—his and countless others—had been pathetically built from the outside while the inside was forgotten. In this church, the tragedy was due to his own inflexible and misguided leadership. But aggravating his frustration was the realization that he and his people were representative of a nationwide camp of Christianity, a camp that was large and loud, a camp that he had always believed possessed a monopoly on spiritual understanding.

The ladies were finishing their song. Oblivious to them, Jason pulled out his billfold and stared at a picture of Hannah. It was all so paradoxical, he thought. He had considered her a rebel because she hadn't passively accepted his philosophy of things. But it was she, he now realized, who was levelheaded, and the one to be admired. She had the character that would not be pushed around by an extreme, out-of-touch religious fanatic. She would not just blindly believe everything the great General had taught. Instead she possessed enough sense to dare rise up and challenge him.

He started to cry. At that moment he missed her more than he ever had. More than anything else in the world right now he needed someone like Hannah to help set him straight.

Lost in these thoughts, Jason suddenly perceived someone kneeling at his side. It was Steve. The ladies had stepped down from the platform. "I'll publicly welcome you back," Steve was saying in an excited whisper, "then you can take the floor." Then he was up and standing, and turning back to address the crowd. Jason had no chance to clue him in on what the next few minutes had in store.

"For eleven years," Steve spoke forthrightly into the microphone, "this church has been blessed with the leadership of a dynamic preacher. And I want to say publicly tonight that of all the pastors I've ever known, I've met no one with the leadership qualities to match those of the General. He's my all-time favorite preacher, undoubtedly one of the greatest preachers in our generation. We've all missed him, and I know we all want to hear from him." Still leaning his head toward the microphone, he turned to Jason. "And I just want to say, it's great to have you back!"

On the third row, the chairman of the deacons jumped to his feet and began to applaud. In a second the whole church was following suit. The applause was thunderous, and there were tears.

Jason, still sitting, knew that he should be awed by the impressive show of support. He should be reveling in this devoted attention. But it was too late. He was already numb.

Sluggishly he looked to Steve, who was giving him a grand gesture toward the microphone.

Jason stood. As he solemnly walked forward, he sensed the excited anticipation among the still-clapping crowd. Suddenly he felt tremendously alone.

He stepped to the pulpit and looked at the microphone. It was the same mike he had approached well over a thousand times before. And at each one of those times he had been a proud, self-assured, indestructible leader, absolutely convinced that he was one of God's personally chosen ambassadors who could do and say no wrong. But now he was broken. His beliefs were shattered. Now he knew all the questions, but not a single answer.

He looked beyond the mike and peered over the sea of faces. He stood motionless and silent as the applause subsided, and the admiring congregation took their seats.

He cleared his throat and began speaking slowly and in a low tone, making no acknowledgment of their standing ovation.

"As most of you know, it has been almost six weeks since Hannah died, and three-and-a-half weeks since Lorene died. In that time I have learned, as many of you have learned through the years, that bereavement has a strange way of upheaving forgotten memories. One day last week, for example, when I was sitting on the warm sand in Miami, I remembered a little incident that happened between me and Hannah just about thirteen years ago.

"Hannah was five at the time. She came to my study one evening while I was reading, and in her little hands she was holding a secondhand blouse that Mrs. Cassidy, one of the ladies in the church back then, had passed on to her earlier that day. Hannah asked me if I would like to see it on her. I said 'Sure.' So she disappeared, and in a few minutes she came back into the room buttoning it up.

"I remember that she looked me right in the eye and said, 'Daddy, I need to tell you something.'

"I said, 'What is it, darling?'

"She said, 'I've already tried the blouse on one time before, and I think I know now why Mrs. Cassidy gave it to me.'

"I asked her why, and with all the seriousness possible for a five-year-old she said, 'The button hole at the top doesn't have a button. And that's not all. The button at the bottom doesn't have a hole.' And then as I tried to keep from laughing, she said, 'Those are the kind of things that get on my nerves.'"

A ripple of smiles and quiet laughter came over the congregation.

"Of course," Jason continued in an almost dead delivery, "the discrepancies were not in the buttons and the holes. They were only in Hannah's understanding.

"I've told that story to help you understand where I am right now. In the last few weeks I've discovered I'm not as strong as I had always assumed. The grief I've encountered has just about beaten me down to nothing. And in that beating I have discovered some major discrepancies between what I have always believed to be true, and what reality says is true."

He paused, cleared his throat, then continued. "At first I was convinced those discrepancies really existed. But then I realized they are only in my immature understanding." He had decided to blame all the confusion on himself, simply to keep from yielding to the temptation to discredit Christianity altogether. "However, though the contradictions are only in my head, they're just as burdensome as if they really existed. And to be honest with you, I'm not handling the situation very well."

He paused. His listeners were deathly quiet.

"It's not necessary for me to try to explain the particular confusions running around in my head right now. It wouldn't do you any good. Besides, they're probably not relevant to your lives anyway." He lied, for convenience' sake.

"Of course, I want you to pray for me. But there is something else I want you to do. I want you to try, and I want you to try very hard, to understand a certain decision I've made. Unlike the battles going on inside my head, this decision *is* relevant to you."

He tightened his grip on the corners of the podium. "I've decided...I've decided to resign. The decision—" The stir of surprise sweeping over the auditorium stopped him in mid-sentence, while a sharp ache ran the length of his spine. "The decision," he continued, trying to show no emotion, "is final. What I'm trying to say is that it's settled. It's settled beyond negotiation. It's over. I've reached rock bottom. I can't go on as your spiritual leader. And as terrible as it might sound, I don't even want to try.

"It's such a certain thing with me, that I'm going to be so bold as to ask you to let me violate the church constitution. As you know, it requires that a pastor give a three-month notice prior to resignation. I'm going to ask that you let me leave within the next two weeks.

"I know you might not be able to fully understand. And I can't blame you if you accuse me of making a hasty and irresponsible decision. I'm sure I'd probably think the same if I were in your shoes. But if you can't find it within you to understand, will you at least try somehow to forgive me?"

Tears came to his eyes. Almost reflexively, others began crying with him. He was sure he could feel their pain increasing simultaneously with his own. Each succeeding word he spoke seemed only to twist the knife he had already driven in.

"I love you people. This church has been my life for eleven years. The church and all who have ever been a part of it have been nothing but good to me. And consequently you deserve better treatment from me. But somehow you've got to believe me when I say that even though this is the toughest decision I've ever made in my life, it's absolutely best for everybody involved. It's what I've got to do."

With tired and heavy eyes he stared out into the audience. He had finished. It had been quick and cold, but now it was behind him.

Everyone thought he was going to say more. Men and women alike in the auditorium were wiping their teary eyes with damp handkerchiefs, while waiting for still more heart-moving details. But none came forth.

Looking out on their faces, Jason saw that nearly every pair of eyes was asking a hundred questions. To avoid a possible outburst of those questions now, he asked everyone to bow their heads, then turned to Steve and motioned for him to take over the meeting. Steve stepped forward. With his heart in a state of shock like everyone else's, and unsure of what else to do, he said a prayer of dismissal.

Jason returned to his chair, and soon heard Steve say, "Amen." For a brief second, beneath all the hurt that held him captive, he thought he felt a faint but refreshing summer shower somewhere in the back corners of his soul.

16

THE NEXT EVENING at six-thirty, the church's twenty-one deacons, three assistant pastors, and thirteen members of the board of trustees held an emergency meeting with the General. At stake, they felt, was the fate of the church. They all hoped in this meeting to persuade Jason to abandon his crazy notion of leaving the ministry. They were not untouched by Jason's disclosure of his inner struggles, but they all agreed his decision was too impulsive. In their discussions with one another late last night and throughout today, the consensus was that Jason should wait at least a month or two before even entertaining the thought of resigning.

The men were packed into a Sunday school room, sitting mostly on metal chairs. Jason was seated on the front row. There was a table placed beside each of the four walls in the room, and a few of the men were sitting or leaning on these. Leaning against the table in front was Eugene Seagers. He was a 59-year-old, hardworking printshop foreman. He had been an outspoken and faithful deacon at North Metro for nine years, and was now their chairman.

Eugene opened the assembly with prayer, begging God to exercise his will during the course of the meeting. Immediately after the "Amen," in keeping with his simple and unpretentious style, Eugene launched into the business at hand. "On behalf of the deacons, the pastoral staff, and the trustees," he said, looking straight at the General, "I would seriously like to ask you not to leave."

The remark drew confirming amens from all around the room.

"I understand your request, Eugene," Jason answered wearily. "But I've already made up my mind, and the decision is definite and final. I simply can't reconsider." To drive home his steadfastness, he added softly but firmly, "I *will not* reconsider."

"Okay," responded Eugene. "It's obvious you're serious, and because I care so much about you, I'll be serious too. Don't you think you owe it to us to at least let us try to help you? I'd never forgive myself if we just let you walk out of here without so much as a try. I admit there may not be much we can do. We're not professional counselors. But at least give us a chance."

"Eugene," Jason came back, "I apologize for perhaps sounding coldhearted." He lowered his head in a humble gesture. "There's no doubt in my mind that every one of you men sitting here in this room would do whatever you could to help. I'm certain of that. But the inner struggles I'm battling now don't have any quick and easy solutions. I don't think anybody's counsel, not even a professional's, can help me right now. I just need time, that's all. Time to get away and time to think."

Eugene quickly replied in his strong, gravelly voice. "I'll be the first to admit I don't understand what you're going through, General. But for the last ten years, ever since I've been a member of this church, I've heard you tell us it's never God's will that we should quit. I could understand," he went on, "if you were changing ministries. But to turn your back on everything and just walk away doesn't make any sense. That's contrary to everything you've ever taught."

Jason found himself wondering about Eugene's thinking behind these remarks. Did he simply want Jason to feel bad about the decision, or did he really feel Jason was being disobedient to God's teaching? He decided the latter was probably true, and had he been filled with his old pride he would have most definitely defended himself to Eugene, whether right or wrong. But now he had no desire to make an issue of it.

"You're right, Eugene," he stated slowly. "My decision is contrary to everything I've ever taught. And I assure you I've reminded myself of that several times already. But to be perfectly honest with you, I've been forced to question the credibility of all my teachings—including those about quitting."

The impact of this last statement drove deeply into every man there. The General, a man whom they knew would proudly die for his convictions, was surely the last person in Christendom who would ever question his faith. It was almost as if they'd heard an admission of self-doubt from God himself.

The awkward silence that followed was broken by Steve Mitchell, who was sitting beside Jason. "What do you mean?" he said in a voice that revealed his hurt.

As Jason answered, those who knew him best could detect a surprising anger in his voice and eyes. "Ever since I graduated from seminary, and even before, I've held to a theology that put God in a box. My beliefs have never allowed God to work outside of my narrow-minded perception of him. It's like this: I've acted as if God gave my seminary and Bible college professors a neat little package of instructions about himself, a package they then passed on to me so I could pass it on to you. And I did—dogmatically, all these years. But I'm discovering that inside that little package is nothing more than pointless matters that strip God of his mystery and his bigness. It tries to make God completely predictable. That package allows God no flexibility—and it allows us no flexibility. It puts every possible aspect of life into one of only two categories: spotless white or sinful black. And of course I've always known the correct category for everything.

"I thought I had God all figured out. I knew how he was supposed to act and react in any and every situation. I knew exactly what he believed on every subject from the Second Coming to hair length and clothing styles, of all things.

"But suddenly I'm realizing that while I've pretended to know all the answers, the Bible plainly states that in this life we only see through a glass darkly, and we only know in part. So I can't kid myself any longer. I can't assume I know the mind of God about every facet of life.

"So that's what I mean, Steve. I'm not convinced any longer that this God-in-a-box theology is without error."

A voice boomed out from the back: "But you're *supposed* to know the mind of God! You're the *pastor!*" It was Rory Vaughan, a deacon and cabinet-maker who was leaning against the back table.

Jason turned in his chair to face him. "I'm only supposed to know the part of him that he's revealed, Rory, and not everything else. But for the past fifteen years I've pretended to know the 'everything else'—and it's not only foolish, it's destructive." He let his eyes roam to other faces in the room, and said slowly, "I mean it when I say this: I'm convinced now that it was my God-in-a-box theology that caused Lorene and Hannah's deaths."

The men's faces contorted in bewilderment. "You're going to have to explain that one," demanded one of them.

"It's simple," Jason began. "If you have all the answers, there's nothing more to learn. You know it all. You become an authority with an authoritarian attitude. With my God-in-a-box theology, that's the attitude I had all these years, without any idea how dangerous it was. It didn't destroy my *ability* to learn from others, but it did destroy my *willingness* to learn, especially when other people challenged my beliefs or convictions. I was unbendable, like cold steel. Not just as a pastor, but as a father and a husband too.

"So when Hannah, in her high-spirited teenage years, needed an understanding father to listen to her and try to understand her, and to give her a little freedom to make her own decisions and mistakes, all she got was a dad who constantly preached to her that he was right and she was wrong. I wasn't on her team, I was on her back. I persistently condemned her. I simply did not give her room to live and unfold. I made her life miserable to the point that she decided she couldn't take my abuse any longer. It was me and my know-it-all attitude that forced her away to her death."

Not giving up, even in the face of such shattering confessions, Eugene quietly spoke up from the front: "But a strong leader has to stand up for what he knows is right. He can't compromise the truth, irrespective of the consequences. You've said that yourself, over and over."

Jason was getting upset. It seemed to him the men were not listening. He wished they would simply be open enough to accept and understand something beyond their own experience.

"You're right again, Eugene; I *have* said it over and over. But right now, as I just explained a few minutes ago, I'm questioning the credibility of the things I've always believed were right. And as far as truth is concerned, I'm not even sure what truth is anymore. As an example—and I could give plenty of others—take the issue of ladies wearing pants. That's one of those areas of so-called truth where I pushed Hannah. She wanted to wear them. I made it plain to her that she would never wear them as long as she lived under my roof, and I criticized her for even wanting to wear them. *And I pushed her right out of our home and to her death over absurd issues like that.*

"Eugene, I'm questioning a lot these days, but there's one thing I know for sure: If I could have her back, I'd gladly let her wear pants. I'd even let her go to the movies and listen to whatever music she liked and a lot of other things, if that's what she wanted. And I would love her more than ever."

There was a moment of stunned silence again. Finally, in the center of the room, Bruce Pearson leaned forward with his elbows on his knees, and managed a smile while he asked, "Well, until you work your way through those confusions, why don't you just stay here as our pastor and simply teach those things directly out of the Bible that you know are true?" Bruce was an accountant, more educated than most of the other men in the room, and considered by some in the church to be too much of a moderate thinker.

Jason responded frankly. "Because I've just let God out of the box, Bruce, and right now I don't feel I know anything about him. He's a complete mystery to me. So you see, I'm questioning everything, even my lifelong interpretations of the things in the Bible that are supposed to be clear. So—hypothetically speaking—if I were to stay, you'd only have a confused preacher on your hands who couldn't preach anything with any certainty. I just don't know what I believe about anything anymore."

Jason could tell that these men scarcely believed what they were hearing. It was like a wild dream to them. He wanted to ease their anxiety, but he figured the best thing to do at this point was to be perfectly honest. At least there would be no doubt in anybody's mind why he was leaving.

"But have you considered," said Bruce Pearson, "that if you feel you were too extreme before, maybe now you're swinging too far to the other extreme, and leaving yourself wide open for attack?"

Rory bellowed again from the back, this time to Bruce. "I don't like the implication of what you just said. It sounds like you're agreeing with the General and saying that to be a right-wing extremist is bad. Of course the other extreme is bad, just as you said. Absolutely. But being a right-wing extremist is neither bad nor destructive. It doesn't matter if the General is questioning that; it's something he's personally struggling with because of his grief. But the rest of us must not be shaken. In order to be pure and spotless from the world, we've got to be extremists. Right-wing extremism is not an option for the serious Christian. It's just plain outright vital. And—"

Jason turned to Bruce, ignoring Rory's fiery outbreak. "To answer your question, Bruce, whether or not I've put myself in a vulnerable position, I've got to have time to think through these matters. But I can see your point. Maybe I am making a mistake." He looked again around the room, searching each face. "I can understand that it's hard for you to accept, but whether you can accept it or not, I've got to start over, from the beginning. As far as I'm concerned I have no choice in the matter."

He looked back at Rory, who was still breathing flames. "And as for what you were saying, Rory, do you mind if I ask you an on-the-spot question?" He was going to ask it whether Rory minded or not.

"Sure, go ahead."

The question was one Jason would have shot down with disgust only a few months earlier. "Is an ironclad rule against ladies wearing pants so vital to Christianity that a father should provoke his sixteen-year-old daughter to leave home over the matter?"

Rory stammered. "Well...uh...it...it's obvious you're referring to your personal experience with Hannah. And in that particular situation it wasn't the rule against pants that was the issue. It was Hannah's attitude, and I say that respectfully. I mean, let's be scriptural about it. God tells children to obey their parents, and he doesn't make any exceptions to the rule."

Jason's temper was rising. "Rory, you don't even have children, and you know nothing from personal experience about being a father. You—"

"When it comes down to it," Rory broke in, "even God himself is an extremist when it comes to being a father. Look what he did to Adam and Eve. They disobeyed, and he kicked them out of the garden. Forever. And under the Mosaic Law he told parents to stone to death any child who was defiant. So as far as I'm concerned, General, you're innocent in your treatment of Hannah. There's no reason in the world why you should be questioning the practices that you and I both know are the will of God."

Jason let out a sigh of exasperation.

Deflecting further argument, Bruce Pearson looked up at Eugene and said, "Maybe it's time we took the vote on the General's request to resign. By now I think we all know pretty clearly what his desires are and how strong he is about them, whether we understand them or not."

Eugene reluctantly agreed, and the group proceeded through the formalities of voting, convinced now there was no changing the General's mind. A few of the men abstained from voting, but the majority decided both to accept Jason's resignation and to let it take effect in only two weeks.

Having made that decision, the men clearly wanted only to leave and find a place for reflection and healing. But there was more business to deal with. Someone had to be appointed to fill Jason's shoes. The church was a million-dollar-a-year ministry, and Jason had been firmly in control of it all: the weekly services, the daily radio broadcast, the school, the church newspaper, the bus ministry, the jail ministry, the nursing home ministry. Finding new leadership for it all would not be a short and simple task. Jason felt guilty for putting that burden on the church, but offered all the suggestions he could during the two-hour business session that followed.

When it was over, Steve Mitchell stood and placed his hand on Jason's shoulder and asked all the men in the room to commit themselves in the coming days to concentrated prayer for the General's uncertain future. Then he asked them all to bow their heads as he led the group in a closing prayer.

With his head down and eyes closed, Jason again detected a slight, refreshing sense of relief. He had just turned his back on eleven years of ministry here, and now had no earthly idea where he was going or what he would do. In a way, it all seemed insane.

He was being set free—but to do what, he did not know.

≈ ≈ ≈

THE NEXT TWO WEEKS raced by, with Jason engaged in constant activity. On the first Wednesday night in February, as he stood in the church's fellowship hall for his farewell reception, he could look back on a long list of details taken care of.

His church-owned home was spotless and ready for new tenants. Everything from the house that he wanted to keep, other than the five suitcases he had packed to take with him, was now boxed and stored in Betsy's attic in Macon. Most of the furniture was staying in the house; at Jason's suggestion, the church leaders had agreed to buy it from him.

He donated his entire library—a twenty-three-year collection of books—to the church. The decision evoked amazement, but Jason said he wanted to learn to think for himself for a while, apart from the predigested ideas and interpretations found in his books.

Over the years, he and Lorene had purchased twenty acres of country land several miles out from the city, while dreaming of someday building their own house there. Jason was able to sell the parcel to a developer for $100,000, providing a substantial profit above their purchase price.

All the church affairs had been settled, at least from his end. Steve Mitchell had been chosen senior pastor on an interim basis only, after he insisted he did not have the necessary gifts and experience to take the job permanently. To the pulpit committee selected by the deacons and trustees, Jason volunteered the names of several pastors at other churches in the denomination who might be candidates for the job at North Metro.

Now, on his last night in Atlanta, Jason was experiencing a twist of various emotions as he waited to say goodbye to the congregation. On one hand he felt as guilty as a thoughtless mother who had rushed selfishly through an unwarranted abortion. On the other, he felt as exhilarated as an adventurer setting out to conquer the ultimate challenge. He felt equally confident, irresponsible, excited, and deranged.

Steve Mitchell and Eugene Seagers each made public remarks to the assembled group, then Eugene presented Jason with a $5,000 check as a token of the church's love and concern. A final prayer was prayed, then the people started filing by Jason in a line. Tears from both male and female, young and old, flowed freely.

I'm really causing a lot of pain for everybody, Jason harassed himself. With a lump in his throat, he was able to speak in only a stop-and-go voice. These were people to whom he had given the prime of his life. Now it seemed he was abandoning them.

When the last person finally passed through the line, Jason noticed that apparently no one had left the room. They were waiting around in mournful silence, wanting to hear more and to say more—but what was there to say?

Past the silent faces, Jason walked toward the door. Eugene met him halfway there, held him in a lingering embrace, and whispered one last proposal in Jason's ear: On behalf of all the church leaders, the senior pastor's position could be kept open for at least six months if Jason thought he might want to return.

With kindness, Jason refused the offer. He had come too far to leave one foot behind. The cord had to be cut.

At the door, he took one final look around the fellowship hall with its bountiful memories, and one final look at the teary-eyed faces gazing back at him.

He was free now to go. Every point of business and protocol had been completed. With nothing to stop him, he turned his back to the room and to his former flock, and walked out to his suit-case-laden car.

≈　≈　≈

BEFORE LEAVING the city that night, he made two stops.

The first was at their former house. As he pulled into the drive-way, the array of sentiments he'd felt throughout the evening suddenly shifted to one side, the side of guilt and loneliness.

He stopped the car, got out, and quickly undertook the errand he had come for. He made his way by moonlight across the back yard and under the pine trees to Hannah's playhouse. He reached inside it, where he could barely make out the tiny stack of red plastic plates he had seen there a few weeks earlier. He picked up one of them, knocked off the dirt, and put the plate in his coat pocket.

He walked away, fighting the urge to lie down in the pine straw and die.

Standing beside the Buick, he took a long, last look at the house where for eleven years he had utterly failed as both a husband and a father. The evening moonlight and midweek quietness highlighted its every detail, bringing to life a thousand-and-one bittersweet memories. The warmth of new tears trickled slowly down his face. He whispered a final goodbye under his breath, got in the car, and drove away.

The tears flowed all the way to the cemetery.

Standing alone at the site of Hannah and Lorene's graves, he tried in halting words to explain what he was doing, and to give them his farewell.

In a heart-wrenching daze, he noticed that a vase of flowers he had put on Lorene's grave earlier in the week had now fallen over. He reached down to prop it up—then fell on his knees in utter abandonment to his feelings of worthlessness as a husband and father. Again and again, he begged Lorene and Hannah to forgive him.

In the cold night air and the cold darkness of grief, he lost track of consciousness and time.

The next thing he remembered was a brightly lit overhead highway sign directing him out of Atlanta. He was heading west on I-20.

PART
TWO

1975-1987

17

IT WAS A THURSDAY MORNING in early November. Jason was sitting in London's Heathrow Airport, waiting somewhat impatiently to board a flight to the island of Cyprus in the Mediterranean.

Over the last four years he had drifted on impulse, searching for truth and a new identity while running from grief and disillusionment. He had spent time in Dallas, El Paso, San Francisco, Las Vegas, St. Louis, St. Paul, Chicago, Indianapolis, and Boston. Along the way he had supplemented his cash fund with a variety of odd jobs—as a salesman in a men's clothing store, a clerk in a convenience store, a school bus driver for a summer school session, a security guard for a chemical processing plant, a truck driver for a health food wholesale company, and a car salesman twice.

From money made in the sale of the twenty-acre parcel near Atlanta, he had initially invested more than $80,000 in various blue-chip stocks. In four years the investment had grown to a paper profit of more than $148,000. The monetary accumulation in itself had not supplied him with any great happiness, but it had allowed him the freedom to carry out the search for himself and his beliefs.

He had maintained an insatiable desire to find Renée. If she needed him, and he had a constant and uneasy feeling that she did, then he wanted to find her at all costs. During his four years of wandering he had stayed faithfully in touch with Malcolm Sandberg, feverishly hoping Cody would eventually break silence and make contact with his former nextdoor neighbor.

Until six days ago, his dozens of long-distance phone calls to Miami through the years had all been in vain. And then, unexpectedly, luck smiled on him. From his Boston apartment he had called Malcolm one evening, and been greeted by the old man's ecstatic voice giving him the good news. Cody had called from

London three weeks earlier. That, of all places, was where he and Renée were living. Cody said they were doing fine, and he had even given Malcolm his London address and telephone number.

The news had refueled Jason's hope. In the next few days he quit his latest job, sold his car, gave up the lease to his apartment, and caught a flight to England, arriving yesterday.

All the way here he prayed the words he had offered up every day for the last four years: "God, let me find my granddaughter. Somehow let me redeem myself." It was his never-dying hope that God would do just that.

He had not contacted Cody in advance. He had chosen, after much deliberation, not to risk having Cody tell him by phone or letter that a meeting would be unwelcomed. He decided Cody would find it far more difficult to say no to his face while he stood there on his doorstep.

Once in London he had struggled for six hours to get from the airport to Cody and Renée's address, located in an outlying borough. A Londoner could have covered the distance in ninety minutes. But Jason, as a first-timer here, took an excessive amount of time figuring out the train trip from Heathrow into London, then finding a hotel and figuring out the Tube—London's underground train system.

Despite the delay in getting to Cody's address, he had been filled with anticipation. After hoping and praying for four years to hold Renée in his arms, the moment seemed near. The excitement helped him enjoy everything he experienced for the first time of the English environment and culture: the accents, the awkward wording on signs, the uniform black taxis and red double-decker buses that filled the streets, and everyone driving on the left instead of the right.

By the time he finally stood in front of Cody's narrow two-story home in a charming neighborhood of row-houses, he was euphoric. He had even been entirely unaware of any jet-lag—that is, until he was told by a neighbor that Cody and Renée had flown two weeks earlier to Cyprus for a three-month escape in the sun from the wet and bleak British winter. It was then that he suddenly noticed his extreme fatigue and physical numbness. And from that moment, all his excitement of being in England vanished for him. Even Cody's neighborhood looked drab.

It was only a momentary setback, however. He knew he could not be content hanging around dreary London for three months, especially knowing Renée's whereabouts. He felt compelled to move quickly. Without much mental debate, he quickly decided to follow their trail to Cyprus.

Now, sitting refreshed in the airport waiting area, surrounded by a myriad of duty-free shops, he was half-anxious again. With nothing to occupy him but his thoughts, he sat and stared at his reflection in a bookstore window.

He felt better about his appearance than he had in the last twenty years. He was fifteen pounds lighter than when he left Atlanta, having dropped from 175 to 160. With a less pressured lifestyle, he had begun jogging regularly, an average of five miles every other day. His diet now consisted mostly of fruits, vegetables, and high-fiber breads and cereals. His arm and leg muscles had definition for the first time since he was in high school. His hair had grown long, and he was sporting a closely cropped beard. He looked more like someone in the pop music industry than the former pastor of a prominent ultra-conservative church.

Emotionally, he was just now coming alive again. Separated from peers, friends, and relatives for the past four years, he had traveled alone, an absolute stranger wherever he ventured. He had kept his past and his Christianity to himself. Only occasionally had he attended church, and then never the same one twice. Being an unknown drifter had given him the welcomed freedom to discover the real "him," and to evolve according to his heart's impulse into his own person. For the first time in his life he was free from the moral expectations of others—and the freedom had changed him drastically.

Philosophically he had not lost his heart for God, but he had long since lost his heart for his traditional Christianity and all its manmade disciplines. With cynicism he had renounced it altogether. It was too out of touch with reality, with what could actually be seen with the eyes and perceived with the mind. It just did not mesh with what he now felt was obvious about life and about God.

He had come to the steadfast conclusion that his old brand of extreme Christianity was utterly unnecessary and pitifully superficial. In its place he was subconsciously, on his own, trying to build a Christian philosophy that was more biblical, more basic, more realistic, more in tune with life around him.

To go about it, he had become a self-motivated wisdom hunter. He was diligently searching for what he called the secrets of life, those insightful truths where life and the Bible come together, where truth is naturally obvious and not fabricated by one's whimsical fancies. He was trying to cut through everything man teaches and assumes, and learn what God reveals about life.

He had even begun putting together what he called his Wisdom Book, in which he wrote down special insights discovered through personal experience, honest observation, and open-minded thinking. As he recorded his discoveries, the bitterness that had simmered in his heart was duly registered in ink.

Thus far the volume contained four entries:

1. STUDENT ATTITUDE *vs.* AUTHORITARIAN ATTITUDE

All my Christian life I was taught, both directly and indirectly, both professionally and nonprofessionally, that a preacher should be an authority, and that he should clearly, and forcefully if necessary, display the attitude of an authority. "No one," I was told, "should ever develop the idea that the preacher is weak or doesn't know the answers."

After having succumbed to that philosophy and being driven by it for fifteen years, I am now convinced that there are few things more counterproductive, self-defeating, and utterly destructive than a mortal preacher with an authoritarian attitude.

I realize now that my attitude was the cause of countless and uncalled-for offenses. The number of people who left my ministry because of it was almost equal to the number of people who joined it for other reasons. For the first time I now understand that those who could not tolerate my attitude, and thus decided to leave, were people who had more

130

potential for dynamic Christian growth than those who stayed. The ones who stayed were the simple-minded "yes" people. The ones who left were the "thinkers," the people whose active, creative, and hungry minds were being suffocated by my style of leadership.

Never again will I be characterized as one who has an authoritarian attitude. For as long as need be, I will purposely work at suppressing that kind of flagrant attitude and will work at cultivating a student attitude in its place.

It's now clear that I actually know very little. Therefore I've resolved to open my mind and let the world be my classroom. So that I don't swing to the other extreme and become a philosophical anarchist, I'll let the Bible, objectively interpreted, be the filter that governs what I soak up in my quest for true wisdom, understanding, knowledge, and insight.

Though I am no longer in the ministry, and have no desire to be, I am somehow convinced that God takes sides with me and is maybe even the one who helped me learn this lesson. After all, the only group of people whom Jesus could not and would not tolerate were the self-righteous and know-it-all Pharisees. Even Jesus, God-in-the-flesh, could not enlighten them and expose to them their extreme and distorted beliefs. Their authoritarian attitude prevented him from penetrating their minds with the facts. Fed up with their foolish know-it-all attitude, Jesus told them outright that they had discarded knowledge. They had locked up the room where real learning takes place, and thrown away the key. And both they and their followers were on the outside of that room. They had closed their minds to learning because they already "knew it all."

Never again will I be pharisaical and lock myself and those I influence out of that room. From this day forward, I will have an open mind and a student attitude.

2. HONEST QUESTIONING *vs.* BLIND BELIEVING

I have discovered that my thinking was naive during the duration of my ministry, and this has left me feeling completely humiliated. In retrospect, I must shamefully admit that I blindly believed everything my older peers and my right-wing Bible college and seminary professors fed me. I never honestly questioned the validity of anything they said. Why was I so gullible?

The more I've thought about it, the more I've realized that at least one reason for my gullibility was the fact that I was never asked, encouraged, or taught to learn by the process of questioning, disagreeing, challenging, or thinking. Rather I was left to assume (whether intentionally or unintentionally I still am not sure) that all my teachers were masters of their subjects and could neither teach nor believe anything wrong. Consequently I learned by being programmed like a computer. I was not taught <u>how</u> to think. I was taught <u>what</u> to think. As a result I became a pathetic little parrot who all his life simply repeats what he hears.

Convinced that I was preaching the inflexible truth, I expected all my followers to blindly believe what I was passing down to them. I carried out a pastoral crusade of "Believe exactly the way I believe or be damned." The real tragedy is that my peers, thousands of them, were of the same mold, and still are.

My heart now shudders. Like the Catholic hierarchy of old, we indirectly asked our followers to blindly believe us, and then socially punished them in the name of "church discipline" if they did not.

I now understand that to blindly believe any teaching is treacherously wrong. The Pharisees blindly believed the manmade and traditional teachings of their forefathers, equated them with the Scriptures, and guarded them with tenacity. Jesus told them that their blind adherence to those impotent teachings, and their insistence upon revering them, made their worship of God utterly vain (Mark 7:1-13).

Instead of blindly believing, we must honestly question every so-called Christian teaching. We must do it to weed out the irrelevant and wasteful manmade teachings from that which truly has eternal value. In Acts 17:10-11, the Bereans even tested Paul's teaching against the Scriptures, and were considered noble for their wise approach.

During my state of disillusionment over the Christian faith following Lorene and Hannah's deaths, I began in my desperation to question everything, even such fundamentals of the faith as the deity of Christ, his virgin birth, his resurrection, the Bible's credibility, etc. I've put on trial each of these dogmas that for so many years I just assumed were right. And I've done so without the slightest bit of mercy. I have tested them as thoroughly as I could, and they have refused to fall. This objective investigation has done nothing less than substantially reinforce my basic faith. I am convinced now more than ever that Jesus was God in the flesh, virgin-born, without sin yet the scapegoat for sin, resurrected from the dead, and the exclusive Savior of mankind, freely accessible to anyone who accepts him in repentance and faith. And I am now persuaded to a greater depth than ever that the Bible is the preserved Word of God, irrefutable and trustworthy.

Of course, a lot of other beliefs and ideas, especially extra-biblical ones, have had to go.

The honest questioning of my old beliefs has proven to be extremely educational, and it is still only in the infancy stage. I've learned that questioning is good, and that not one dogma, theory, or interpretation should be exempted from its demolishing attempt.

Truth, I've discovered, will not be destroyed by questioning or scrutiny. It will always stand unbeatable. Questioning only confirms truth and makes it visibly stronger; it never crumbles it.

On the other hand, the manmade distortions of truth—those that we sometimes hold to be so valuable, and use as a criteria for fellowship, and are even sometimes willing to die for—will fall apart under such honest questioning. And anything that is destroyed by honest questioning is obviously spurious and deserves to be junked. By crumbling and falling apart, it proves to be vain.

From this day forward I will never again blindly believe

anything. I will honestly question everything first. Likewise, if I ever, in any situation, try to share my beliefs with others, I will neither ask nor expect them to blindly believe me. I will encourage them to honestly question and challenge everything I say.

One who learns through the process of honest questioning, objective thinking, and respectful challenging is more apt to know in the end what is really true. And he will also know "why" he believes it.

3. BIBLE TEACHINGS *vs.* BELIEVERS' TRADITIONS

The premise of the Christian faith is the Bible, not passed-down provincial traditions.

It is clear to me now that many beliefs in the Christian community are held to be valuable not because there is any inherent biblical value in them, but simply because the former generation held them to be valuable.

We must give these "traditions" their lesser place. We should not be guilty of equating these provincial traditions with the teachings of Scripture. Jesus refused to tolerate this gross error among the Pharisees. And he refuses to tolerate it today among the hard-core legalists, despite the fact that most of them have hearts that are hardened to that notion, just as was the Pharisee's heart.

I personally have made a resolution to separate Bible teachings from believers' provincial traditions. And I'm just as resolved not to give the latter any universal value, if any value at all.

And never again will I be guilty of misinterpreting the Bible because of looking at it through the filter of believers' provincial traditions. From this day forward, I will endeavor to the best of my ability to strip away all traditions and look objectively at the Bible—the raw and naked Word of God.

4. SPIRIT PRESSURE *vs.* PEER PRESSURE

Another weakness that contributed to my miserable performance as a husband, father, and pastor was my failure to yield to the pressure of God's Spirit. I yielded to peer pressure instead. As a matter of fact, and I now see this clearly in retrospect, I was so calloused to the pressure of God's Spirit that the only pressure I felt in any real, effective, and decisive way was the sly but powerful pressure of my peers.

At the time, I misunderstood the peer pressure. I felt God was using it to keep me on track. I was obviously confusing pressure from my peers with God's inner guidance.

It never dawned on me at the time that anything such as pastoral peer pressure even existed. I had to get out of the trees to see the forest.

Of course, pastoral peer pressure does exist, and in a mighty way. I am now convinced that pastoral peer pressure can be just as harmful and destructive as worldly peer pressure. It can be rightly argued that pastoral peer pressure can be a positive motivational factor, but it can also be argued with just as much evidence that pastoral peer pressure can be a motivational factor in the "wrong direction," especially if all your peers are going in the wrong direction.

If each of the peers is fearful of changing directions because of the risk of being condemned and ostracized by the others, the whole group is locked into an unchecked path.

If one dares break free to question the legitimacy of the group's direction, he is quickly classified as a liberal, and thus ceases to wield any inside influence. None of the other pastors—again because of peer pressure—will give the guy a sympathetic or attentive ear. None of them will listen to his reasons or arguments. They will refuse to be associated with him, lest they, too, lose their acceptance.

As shameful as it is, I honestly believe that most pastors in the legalistic camp are influenced more by peer pressure than Spirit pressure. It's obvious they are not listening to God's Spirit as long as they continue to preach and believe their extreme and senseless traditions of legalism, and with a self-righteous and know-it-all attitude.

They have become the Pharisees of our day, and their inner-circle peer pressure keeps them blinded to that fact.

In spite of Jason's intellectual pursuit of truth, and the discoveries so clearly shown in his Wisdom Book, he still had not regained his heart for the ministry. As far as he was concerned, he would never preach again. And without the feelings of responsibility that go along with the ministry, he had lost all motivation to go out of his way to live right. His life had become a self-contained paradox.

Philosophically he was a zealous hunter of wisdom, and no one could have been more sincere. But in practice he slowly reached the point at which his day-to-day Christian living lost its distinction. More and more he was overruling his once sensitive conscience, and was testing the waters of normal worldly behavior.

He had lived under the discipline of Christianity nearly all his life, and because of those disciplines he had made countless sacrifices of life's carnal pleasures. Now that those disciplines had lost their appeal and their hold, he could not control his feelings any longer. He wanted to run wild, without restraints.

In the face of Scripture's teaching that Jesus fully satisfies his children and never leaves them hungering, Jason had seemingly become an exception. He did not understand why, but the ways of Jesus alone no longer fulfilled him. He now hungered for carnal knowledge.

His four years of living among non-Christians and observing their carefree lifestyles had left him envious of their guiltless pursuit of self-indulgence. More and more he felt cheated for having never splurged in life's selfish pleasures. He was now ready to taste them all.

His loss of appetite for Christian disciplines, however, really did not bother him. What did bother him was his guilt for having indirectly caused Hannah's death by his iron-fisted effort to prevent in her life the same careless attitude that now reigned unchallenged in his own.

But at least, he reasoned, he was not trying to block God out of the picture. Jason might have lost his heart for Christian living, but he had certainly not lost his heart for God.

Here in the airport, as he again turned over in his mind his discoveries and desires, he felt that in an odd way his relationship with God was stronger than ever. It felt more natural. He was a normal human being now who needed his God more than ever. And whether or not God wanted to listen to him, he constantly shared with God his renegade feelings—all with a please-help-me attitude, not a rebellious attitude.

This honest exchange of feelings, Jason concluded, made his relationship with God very intimate. As far as he was concerned, God was his best friend, the one who understood completely his prodigal tendencies.

"Your attention, please." The voice over the public address system jarred Jason from his thoughts. "Passengers for British Caledonian flight two-zero-three to Cyprus can now board at gate twenty-six. I repeat: Passengers for British Caledonian flight two-zero-three to Cyprus can now board at gate twenty-six."

18

BRIEFCASE IN HAND, Jason boarded the Boeing 727-200, and took his window seat in the no-smoking area just in front of the wing. Smoking was one of life's so-called pleasures that he could still resist with no problem.

Within twenty minutes the plane had taxied to the head of the runway behind four others.

Barring accidents or delays, he would be in Cyprus in five hours. The thrill of being so close to seeing his granddaughter came over him again—and this time, he felt certain, he would find her. It was true he had not been able to obtain any specific hotel name or address for Cody and Renée, but it didn't matter. Cyprus was a relatively small island. It would only be a matter of inquiring at all the hotels until he located her.

It looked as if God were finally going to answer his prayer.

Jason looked over the crowded cabin. Every seat seemed to be taken—except, surprisingly, the one next to him.

The pilot announced over the intercom that they were cleared for takeoff. Thirty seconds later the three 16,000-pound-thrust engines revved, followed by the breathtaking acceleration. The plane, with vibrations coursing through the cabin, was suddenly screaming down the runway at a hundred and fifty miles per hour.

I love it, Jason thought. The feeling of faith combined with risk had always made the takeoff his favorite part of a plane ride.

At the critical moment the plane lifted its nose upward. The back wheels quickly left the ground, causing the tail to momentarily fall into the openness until the rushing air caught the plane and gave it complete lift. They were airborne and climbing.

Jason was mesmerized by the dazzling sight of London passing below him. When he flew in yesterday morning the clouds had obstructed the view; now he soaked up the scene for all its worth.

He was suddenly startled by a female voice.

"It's big, isn't it?"

"Huh" he said, caught off guard, as he jerked his head around. He found himself staring into the sparkling green eyes of the most beautiful woman he'd ever seen.

"London. It's big, isn't it?"

She actually took his breath away. "Uh...yeah. It is." He was almost swallowing and choking on his words. "It really is."

He self-consciously straightened himself in his seat and nervously ran his hand lightly over his hair.

"Is it your first time?" she asked.

Jason was fighting to bring his eyes under control. Her shoulder-length, wheat-blonde hair cascaded down and around her slender neck. It was cut stylishly in layers, tapered slightly down and back from the bangs on both sides. It blended perfectly with the high cheekbones in her Nordic face. Her lips, full and shapely, almost begged to be kissed. And her teeth, seemingly perfect in form and whiteness, sparkled as brilliantly as her eyes. Even her blonde eyebrows were tantalizing.

Her beauty was all the more powerful because it was natural; she wore only a shade of makeup, just enough to make a statement of style. She was wearing a high-fashion pink cotton dress that perfectly complemented her tanned complexion. She was an absolute feast for the eyes. Everything about her made a man thirst.

Jason knew he was staring. He was embarrassed, though she seemed oblivious to the battle he was having with his eyes—or else she was only pretending, being used to that kind of male response. "Uh...what do you mean?" he finally replied to her question. *Come on, Jason,* he lectured, *get control of yourself.*

"Seeing London from the air, of course!" she explained chipperly. Her voice sounded fresh and intelligent, and Jason found it as arousing as her appearance.

"Yeah. Actually, it *is* my first time," he managed to answer. "But how did you know?" *She even smells good,* he thought.

"Probably because you were so captivated," she said with a slight grin. "Those who see it more often aren't usually so taken in."

Normally, Jason might have responded to such a statement by sarcastically asking whether the person had ever taken a scientific poll to find that out. But at the moment, being sarcastic never crossed his mind. His manliness took over in full force. Just for the visual excitement alone, he felt himself wanting to stay in this lady's company forever.

He therefore hoped to prolong this conversation indefinitely. "I don't see how anybody could lose interest in such an awesome sight," he said gently.

"Well—you know people. They become calloused to awesome sights rather quickly."

On impulse Jason wanted to say it would take an extremely long time for anyone to grow calloused to the awesome sight of her beauty. But flirting was not coming as easily as he desired.

"How about you?" he responded neutrally. "Have you lost interest?"

"Well, I guess I'm different from most people. I've seen that same sight from the air hundreds of times, and I still find it fascinating."

"Hundreds of times? Sounds like you spend most of your time in the air."

"Yes," she chuckled softly. "I guess you can say I do. It's just part of my work as an international courier. But I love it." Her voice fell off to a whisper, followed by an eye-catching smile.

There was a moment of silence as he once again lost himself in her beauty. He didn't want to admit it might be wrong—but at the moment he could not help fantasizing about being in full physical union with such a goddess.

"By the way," she said, extending her hand. "I'm Corinna. Corinna Nykvist."

"Jason," he replied. The handshake was warm and friendly. He savored the touch of her smooth skin, hating to let go of her hand.

Corinna explained that just before takeoff, seeing the vacant seat beside Jason, she had moved up from the smoking section where she had been assigned by mistake. "I hope it's okay."

Jason assured her—repeatedly—that it was. He began to feel embarrassed as he realized he was overdoing it, but soon forgot how silly it sounded when Corinna showed no signs of taking notice.

In the warm conversation that followed, he learned that she was from Norway. He knew little about the country, but found himself at once having a keen interest to learn. Corinna was equally eager to teach him.

Norway, she said, was Western Europe's northernmost country, and perhaps the best-kept secret in the world. It possessed scenery that was unsurpassed for beauty anywhere. It was a wild and virtually untouched land, ninety-five percent mountainous, with massive glaciers and majestic peaks lying high above the timber line. It was surrounded on three sides by the sea, which cut breathtaking fjords all along the endless wooded coastline. It boasted the cleanest air and water anywhere on the planet.

And the society? Well, it offered one of the highest living standards in the world, with poverty totally eliminated within its borders. All four million residents were materially secure from the cradle to the grave. The unemployment and crime rates were among the lowest in the world. The Norwegians themselves were a strong and stimulating people. With their Viking heritage they were modern-day adventurers who had fashioned on their shores a lively, comfortable, and thoroughly up-to-date culture. They were intelligent, most of them speaking at least three languages and many speaking four or five. They were also among the healthiest people in the world. Without a doubt, Corinna assured him, Norway offered one of the most relaxed and pleasant lifestyles in the twentieth century.

Jason finally asked her jokingly if she were maybe a little prejudiced.

"Not in the least," she joked back.

It was all fascinating information. But then, she was a fascinating lady. Jason speculated that her articulate and colorful style of conversation was a result of her international work. *Then again,* he thought, *maybe I'm so overpowered by her, I'd be impressed no matter what she said.*

As they continued their engaging conversation, Corinna finally asked Jason about himself.

His mind worked quickly to solve a dilemma: Should he lie to her? Impulsively he had second thoughts about telling her the truth. They had enjoyed a positive exchange so far, and he seriously suspected that the religious aspect of his story would put a damper on it—the last thing he wanted to happen. Nevertheless he also felt a strange, powerful urge to be honest.

Honesty won out. To Jason's relief, when Corinna heard that he had been a pastor, she accepted it without any sign of disapproval or unease. She even asked him why he had quit. So, for the next hour, Jason freely described his former ministry, his authoritarian attitude, the deaths of his daughter and wife, his disillusionment, his resignation, his wanderings, his search for wisdom, his search for Renée, and now his consuming indifference toward Christian living.

Corinna listened, showing genuine interest. When Jason reached the end, she asked to read the entries in his Wisdom Book.

As she read, Jason pretended to look out the window. But he kept stealing glances at her out of the corner of his eye. It was as if his eyes were so hungry for her beauty that they refused to be brought under control. His secret gaze dropped to her thighs and legs, their shapely form outlined beneath the pink dress. He found them as provocative as any other part of her.

When she finished reading, she closed the book. "Your insights are thought-provoking, Jason," she said with quiet sincerity. "But I can't help finding it sad that now, after gaining such a balanced perspective of your Christianity, you don't have a heart for living it."

"Why do you find that sad?" he asked, grateful for her interest but surprised by her apparently favorable regard for Christianity.

"I'm not sure. Maybe it's because there are so few good people out there, especially good people who are not naive or self-righteously obnoxious."

"And?"

"And—I think our world would be a better place if there were more of those people around. *And*, it sounds to me that after all you've gone through and all you've learned, you have a strong potential for being one of them. It would be a tragedy to waste all the insights recorded in your book.

"It's your business, of course," she continued. "But why do you want to dismiss all your Christian values and run wild, anyway?"

Thinking it over, Jason answered, "Because for a long time now I've felt cheated."

"Cheated?"

"Yeah. Cheated."

"Cheated of what?"

"Carnal pleasures, I suppose," he answered honestly and somewhat timidly in her presence. "I look at the few people around who have everything, you know—money, good looks, personality, success, no moral restraints—and I get a little envious. Dancing around with smiles on their faces—they look so...fulfilled."

"If they look fulfilled, it's an illusion," Corinna said with certainty. Jason thought she sounded as if she were talking to a younger brother, but he was interested in what she had to say.

"An illusion?"

"Exactly. Over the years my work has brought me into the lives of hundreds of people like those you mentioned—movie stars, rock singers, fashion models, millionaires, ambassadors, prime ministers, playboys. Not one of them is without his own personal struggles, Jason. They're all battling with something, and they all think the grass is greener on the other side of the fence. They're battling with their marriages, or with their lovers, or their self-image, or their finances, or with the law, or with drugs or alcohol; the list goes on and on. There are as many different types of battles as there are people. Nobody is exempt, Jason. Money, good looks, success, and moral freedom can never lift anyone above life's tough circumstances."

"You sound convincing."

"I'm only saying what I know to be true."

"So, in your opinion, I've set my heart on chasing a rainbow that doesn't exist?"

"It sounds to me as if you're on the verge of trading gold for sand."

"I don't know," Jason said with a shrug. "Maybe it's too late for me. Maybe my heart is already too far gone."

With a smile she said softly, "It's never too late to be good." She touched her hand to his arm. "No matter what, Jason—don't ever give up."

He felt a spark of rejuvenation, and a measure of astonishment that a stranger had made it happen.

"I guess you need to forgive me, then," he said. "I've been staring at you this whole trip, and I can't say my mind has been exactly pure. But, you must admit, you are beautiful to look at." *There—I've said it.*

"I do forgive you, Jason. And thank you for the compliment." She spoke with another beautiful smile. "But you know the old adage: Beauty is in the eye of the beholder. Besides, I'm just another typical looking woman compared to all the other Norwegians."

"Typical looking? Don't tell me Norway also has the world's most beautiful people."

"Yes, I guess so." She gave a slight, almost flirtatious grin. "If you prefer tall slim blondes, that is."

Jason could not imagine a whole country full of women as gorgeous as the one sitting next to him. *If it's true*, he thought, *Corinna's right: Norway IS the world's best-kept secret.*

The captain's voice sounded on the intercom, announcing that the plane would be landing in Cyprus in twenty-five minutes—ten minutes ahead of schedule.

"Excuse me," Corinna said politely. She stepped into the aisle and joined a short line of passengers heading toward the restroom in the rear of the plane.

Jason allowed himself to look back at her, for the first time taking in her full five-foot-nine physique.

She was irresistible.

Never in his life had he felt both the liberty and desire to be so open and real with anyone. Meeting this stranger had begun to feel to him like the sweet reunion with a long-lost lover. Corinna and her chemistry had worked incredible magic, striking cords in him that he did not even know existed. Yes, she was irresistible. And it was not only because of her extraordinary looks, keen mind, and magnetic personality, though all these were surely true enough. She had supremely manifested a good heart as well—and that clinched it for him.

I'm in love, he thought, nearly gasping.

Already he was planning his next move. He definitely could not let her walk out of his life. As soon as she came back, he would ask her to have dinner with him tonight.

While he waited, he pulled out the Wisdom Book, and wrote quickly, with inspiration:

5. BATTLEFIELD LIFESTYLE *vs.* BEDROOM LIFESTYLE

This absolute angel appeared out of nowhere and has touched both my heart and my mind in an extremely encouraging way.

Her name, Corinna Nykvist, is as beautiful as she is.

After talking and listening to her for only a few hours, she has helped me better understand myself. For the first time I see my present condition in a more focused perspective. It seems, because of my prolonged inner struggle, that for many months now I have been longing after what I will coin a Bedroom Lifestyle. By that I mean I've been coveting a one-dimensional lifestyle characterized by pleasure, ease, freedom (or unaccountability), and selfishness—characteristics that are associated with the bedroom.

But is it true that such a free and pleasureful lifestyle does not really exist? Is it true, as Corinna said, that it's only an illusion? Is life, because of the fact that it has been cursed, a battlefield for all and a bedroom for none, irrespective of whether one is a spotless Christian or a financially independent playboy?

Maybe Corinna is right. Maybe everyone's life is two-dimensional, and includes struggles, wounds, pains, confusion, and discontentment (characteristics of the battlefield), whether one is rich or poor, good-looking or not, famous or unknown, scholarly or simpleminded.

But if this is true, and the bedroom lifestyle has no more substance than a mirage, why is it that almost everyone is helplessly trying to pursue it? Why is everybody chasing after the rainbow, or at least fantasizing about chasing it?

Could it have something to do with the fact that God has set eternity in the hearts of men (Ecclesiastes 3:11)? Is that the underlying premise of man's longing?

If so, there must be a rainbow somewhere. There must be a bedroom life that is somehow obtainable. And if it is not here, then it must surely be the eternal state of paradise. Is that what we're longing for, by providential design, without our even being aware of it? Is heaven the bedroom, and earth the battlefield? If so, perhaps I should figure that I'm battling my way to the bedroom.

Jason had finished writing when the "Fasten Seat Belt" signs lit up. He wanted Corinna to read what he had written. But where

145

was she? She had been gone for fifteen minutes. He half-stood up from his seat and turned to look down the aisle, but didn't see her.

He sat back down and fastened his seat belt, assuming she would be back any minute. But she was not.

The plane started a noticeable descent, heading for a landing.

Where is she? Jason wondered. *Did she get locked in the restroom?* No, he decided; someone would have come to her aid by now. He wondered if he had offended her with his remarks about his impure thoughts. Thinking about it again, however, he realized she had shown too much sincere concern to be offended by his honesty.

Could she have been lured to sit in the back of the plane—with another man, perhaps? *Maybe a full-maned, good-looking, six-foot-two hunk,* Jason calculated. *Someone more in her league.* At the mere thought of it, he found himself hurting with jealousy. But surely that wasn't her style, he eventually persuaded himself.

Then what happened?

He finally concluded she must have returned to her original seat somewhere in the smoking section, though he had to admit he didn't understand why she would—unless, perhaps, she had carry-on luggage or a coat stored in the overhead compartment above her former seat. The more he thought about it, the more he was sure that was the answer. She simply hadn't had time before the plane started descending to tell him she was changing seats. He could easily imagine her trying to offer some kind of apology when they landed.

Outside his window he saw the blue Mediterranean contrasting with the coastline of Cyprus. They were to land at the international airport in Larnaca, a city on the island's southern coastline. He had a magnificent view. The sky was cloudless, the sun's rays bathing the land and water with gold.

Jason found himself in a party mood. Everything, it seemed, was now going well for him. Besides having good health and plenty of money, he was only days or hours away from ending his four-year search for Renée.

And he was in love. He hoped Corinna would accept his invitation to dinner, and give him a chance during their island stay to get to know her better.

Within minutes the plane's tires squealed as they grabbed the runway. Jason was suddenly aware of the happy chatter inside the cabin. There seemed to be a Look-out-Cyprus-here-we-come spirit among the travelers. Most of them, he supposed, had come here like Cody and Renée for a sunny, relaxing getaway.

The plane rolled to a stop at a designated spot on the pavement about a hundred yards from the terminal. Jason saw a mobile stairway on the back of a truck, whose driver was positioning it underneath the plane's doorway in front of him. He joined the rush of passengers lining up to exit. Standing in the aisle, he turned back to look for Corinna, and noticed that passengers far behind him were moving toward another exit in the rear of the plane. *She'll probably go out that way*, he decided. He determined to get out as quickly as possible through the front exit, then walk outside to the plane's rear to watch for Corinna there.

The doors were open, but the line moved at an agonizingly slow pace. He wanted to push his way to the front, but politeness —and the jam-packed aisle—kept him from it.

Finally the flow of passengers picked up speed, and Jason followed them to the front and out the door. Stepping into the open air he was greeted by the intense warmth of the Middle-East sun, and by the island's distinctive smell—an aroma almost like suntan lotion. He descended the stairway and hurried back to the one in the rear, where a stream of passengers was still coming down. His eyes searched all around, but Corinna apparently was still on board. He looked carefully at every face as it appeared in the plane's doorway. In only a few minutes, no more faces appeared.

With rising anxiety, he glanced toward four oversized buses parked nearby, waiting to transport the passengers the short distance to the terminal. Most of the buses were nearly filled, and one was already slowly pulling away. He nearly panicked. If Corinna was on that bus, he could lose her if he didn't hurry.

He quickly turned and ran for the bus nearest him. He made it just before the driver closed the doors.

The first bus was halfway to the terminal before the bus he was on started rolling. *Come on, move it,* he muttered uselessly to himself. He hoped that when his bus reached the terminal, he would have time enough to run ahead and spot-check everyone getting off the first bus before they had a chance to scatter.

Suddenly his bus stopped. The driver had halted to give way to a couple of luggage trams. Then, as if fate were against him, the bus's engine died. The driver pumped the gas pedal and twisted the ignition key. By the time he was able to get the bus started again, Jason could see that the first vehicle was already completely unloaded.

He was the first one off when they finally made it to the terminal. He moved quickly into the building, straining his eyes all along for Corinna. Once he found her, he would compose himself and pretend not to be acting out of the ordinary. Until then, he was driven madly to find her.

He surveyed the lines at the three different passport-control checkpoints, which passengers had to go through to proceed further. Corinna was not in any of the lines.

Without a second thought, he walked to the head of the line nearest him, spotted a gentle-looking elderly English lady, and successfully played on her sympathies with a hurried story of accidentally getting separated from his ailing wife, and needing to get quickly through to find and help her. She let him in line ahead of her.

As he stepped up to the checkpoint, he asked the passport controller, a middle-aged Greek Cypriot man, if he had seen a tall, beautiful blonde in a pink dress pass through any of the lines. In broken English the controller assured him unsympathetically that he had not, then stamped Jason's passport with a tourist visa and sent him through.

Only a few people from his flight had made it as far as the baggage-claim hall; but Corinna wasn't one of them.

Now Jason felt silly. He had made it to the head of the crowd, and it now seemed certain Corinna hadn't preceded him into the building. He figured she must still be behind him somewhere. He decided his best bet was to simply wait for her there in the baggage-claim hall.

But she never came through.

When all the luggage except his own had been picked up and carried out, Jason was left standing alone and confused. It did not make sense. He was sure he had screened everyone who had gotten off the plane, and Corinna simply wasn't among them.

Frustrated, he picked up his suitcases and walked out of the terminal, unable to shake Corinna from his thoughts. He was already too obsessed with her to simply let the freak separation be dismissed.

He concluded, therefore, that his search on the island would now be for two females.

19

"LOOK AT THE BIG HORSEY, DADDY! Look how big!"

"Shut up!" Cody snapped. "It's not a horse anyway, you little idiot. It's the Sphinx."

"The pinks?" asked Renée, looking up to her father with hurt in her eyes.

"I said the *Sphinx*," Cody snarled. "Why can't you talk right? Are you stupid? Can't you hear? It's the *Sphinx*, I said."

Renée cowered as if Cody might hit her in the face.

She was walking between Cody and a woman. The three of them were strolling in the sand, having distanced themselves from others in their tour group. They were all making their way from the parked charter bus to the ancient Egyptian wonders towering in the distance.

The woman was glaring at Cody. "Don't be so hard with her, Cody," she said in her thick Cockney accent.

"It's not your business, Michelle!" Cody barked. "So keep your mouth shut."

Michelle glared back at him. She found her courage, and stopped in her tracks. "All right. I'll stay out of it. But she's just a sweet little girl, and you treat her like you were her pimp."

The words stung. Cody fired a look at her that could have melted steel.

Michelle said nothing more. She did not want to end up like Renée, who had big bruises on both her legs from Cody's belt buckle, and a three-day-old cut over her left eye inflicted by his fist.

Quietly, the three began walking again through the sand.

Michelle was a London prostitute whom Cody had been visiting regularly for several months. He had invited her to come along to the Mediterranean with them, and was paying all her expenses. She had gladly agreed. She liked Cody, though disturbing questions about him sometimes arose in her mind.

Now the questions came back. She wondered what devastating experience had caused him to develop such disrespect for people's self-dignity, including his own. But she did not dare probe him again. She liked him, and her heart went out to him, but she was afraid. Two weeks ago, on their plane trip from London, she had tried to question him about his past. He had responded with a sharp outflow of foul language, burying the subject at once.

Unlike most of the male friends who came in and out of her life, Cody had the markings of a once normal and respectable existence—a college education, a high-income profession, and a family. That much she knew. But somehow it had all been destroyed, and she had no clue as to how. It must have had something to do with his wife or a lover, she guessed. Whatever it was, it was still a part of him, still eating away at him. He seemed to carry a load of bitterness the size of the Pyramids they now saw looming beside the Sphinx. Perhaps he carried that much guilt as well.

The telltale marks were there: Cody forced himself through life with little, if any, enjoyment. He seemed always to be running, as if trying to escape from something. He was in no way motivated to be productive. He was a capable and educated man who was drinking away his best years.

Something else disturbed Michelle: Cody was obsessed with Renée, almost out of his mind with obsession. Yet it appeared to be for totally selfish reasons, for Michelle never saw him display any real love or affection for Renée.

She could not help but hurt for the girl. Now nearly four years old, she was quiet-tempered and beautiful, with curly blonde hair and ocean-blue eyes. But in those eyes Michelle could see that Renée was being molded by her father's abuse into an insecure and frightened creature.

Michelle reached down and took Renée's hand. The girl looked up with sadness. Michelle tried to give her a reassuring smile.

20

"WHAT DOES THAT ONE cost per day?" Jason asked. He was pointing to one of the 100-cc motorcycles, the next-to-the-smallest rental bikes in the shop. In spite of its smallness, Jason was still a little apprehensive; he had never been on a motorcycle in his life.

"That one? A hundred and eighty-five pounds," said the stubble-face shopkeeper.

Jason quickly calculated: At the present exchange rate, that would be about four and a half dollars.

"I'll take it," he said.

At the man's gesture, Jason sat down at the shop's beat-up, grease-covered wooden desk and started filling out the necessary papers.

The shop, with bare concrete block walls, was just one big

room with a toilet closet in one corner. Motorcycles of all sizes, mostly Japanese makes, were standing in three different rows on one side of the room, along with the desk and an old rusty file cabinet. The other half of the room was used as a mechanic's area for repair work, and scattered around it were various tools, engines, engine parts, and gasoline and oil cans.

After filling out the papers and paying the money, Jason stepped outside to wait while the shopkeeper gave the bike a final check-over and filled it with gas.

Jason had been in Larnaca three days. Using a list of overnight guest quarters—hotels, bungalows, and efficiency apartments— which the desk clerk in his hotel helped him compile, he had criss-crossed the city by foot and by taxi, making inquiries about Cody, Renée, and Corinna. The exhaustive search had left him only with the assurance that none of the three were in Larnaca.

He was now anxious to extend his search to other towns on the island, while keeping his base of operations at Larnaca. Thus, the motorcycle. A rental car would have been a more logical choice, but a bike was more economical and more adventurous. And the adventurous spirit of the island was certainly playing with the boy in him.

In a few minutes the shopkeeper rolled the motorcycle out the front door onto the small cemented front yard. He handed Jason the key, then went back inside.

Since Jason did not know how to activate the clutch or even shift through the gears, he knew he would only create an embarrassing spectacle if he tried to climb on the bike immediately and attempt to start it. He decided to roll it down the hill until he could find a spot safely out of the shopkeeper's view. Straddling the bike, it took him only a few moments to figure out which of the hand levers was the clutch release and which was the front brake. He released the clutch and started coasting toward the street.

He was concentrating so intensely on handling and balancing the bike that he momentarily forgot the left-side-of-the-road driving rule in Cyprus, a former British colony. He rolled out onto the wrong side of the street, and almost immediately found himself face to face with a horn-honking Fiat coming out of a blind curve.

Impulsively he swerved the bike toward the curb. Except that there was no curb—only a three-foot-high concrete wall. Panicking, he forcefully squeezed the front brake. But it was too late. As the car swerved, the front of the bike crashed at an angle into the wall, and Jason felt his right leg scraping painfully against the ragged concrete. Simultaneously the rear of the bike came off the ground; then the entire bike slid several feet on loose gravel before falling over. Jason found himself half-jumping and half-falling onto the asphalt, and rolling off to the side.

He was in pain, but finding himself able to move he quickly got up, made sure no other cars were coming, then moved the bike to the correct side of the street.

He was terrified. His breathing was so hard he could hardly hear himself think. A collision with the Fiat could have been fatal, and he knew it. Fortunately the only injuries he incurred were the scrapes and bruises on his leg, and more on his arm where he had rolled onto the asphalt.

To Jason's pleasure, the driver of the Fiat did not even bother to stop. But the sound of his honking had attracted the attention of the shopkeeper. He was running out toward Jason.

Jason signaled to him that he was okay. But the man kept coming, and said with agitation, "What happened?"

"I...forgot I was supposed to drive on the left," Jason answered a little sheepishly.

The shopkeeper replied only with a look of frustration. Then he examined the bike. There was no major damage—only a few more scratches to add to the dozens already there.

"Stay right here," the man said to Jason, running back toward the shop.

Jason expected him to come back with his four and half dollars, then take the bike and roll it back into his shop. Instead he saw him come running out with a helmet in his hand. He handed it to Jason, saying only, "You'll probably need this."

Jason thanked him, got back on the bike, and coasted it all the way to the bottom of the hill. At the first intersection he pulled into a vacant lot—and began figuring out how to operate this machine.

Half an hour later he was cruising east on the island's two-lane coastal highway. He was heading for Ayia Napa, reputedly the most popular beach resort in Cyprus, and the town recommended to Jason by his hotel clerk in Larnaca as the best place to search next.

Playing it safe, he scooted along at only seventy kilometers an hour. Giving the bike most of his concentration, he was able to relax just enough to enjoy the ocean view as the road wound parallel to the water's edge. As the wind whipped up into his open-face helmet, bringing with it the smell of the sea, he felt a fresh sense of freedom. It was a great feeling, one of those rare moments of ecstasy. He had to shout just to release the built-up exhilaration.

The thought struck him: Here he was, a middle-aged man, bearded, slouchily dressed, cruising along on a motorcycle on a European resort island, doing nothing but enjoying life—while back in his native Bible Belt culture he would quickly be condemned for not conforming to the expected image of a pastor. *My poor Christian peers*, he thought. He could not help but give God thanks for his freedom.

For nearly twenty minutes he stayed high on the excitement. But with his back starting to hurt due to his nervous stiffness as a first-time rider, he decided to take a break. About halfway to Ayia Napa, he stopped at a quaint-looking cafe with outdoor tables.

It felt good to sit in one of the metal-framed chairs with a back-rest. A stout Cypriot woman who could speak no English came out to take his order. At a table next to Jason, a man was drinking a glass of orange juice. Jason ordered one too, by pointing to it and raising one finger.

He laid his head back and let the sun warm his face. After his drink came, he had just taken his first sip when at least a dozen motorcycles rumbled off the road into the cafe's gravel parking lot, raising a dust cloud. The young riders, traveling two to a bike, were yelling like a group of American teenagers at a high school football game. It appeared to be a party on wheels. Jason immediately felt a bond with them. He understood their mood.

The cafe's peaceful atmosphere was instantly transformed into a fiesta, with laughing, hugging, pushing, and loud talking.

Jason took the initiative to join some of the group in conversation. He learned that they were from a city about an hour west of Larnaca, and that they were spending the day circling the Greek side of the island.

When he asked what the "Greek side" meant, he learned for the first time that Cyprus was a divided island, with two peoples and two governments: Turkish Cypriots in the north, and Greek Cypriots in the south. The two sides were not the best of friends, and had a long history of animosity. A heavily guarded border ran between them.

The bikers' next stop was Ayia Napa. When they found Jason was on his way there as well, they invited him to tag along for the fun.

And fun it was. It was another new experience for Jason, and thoroughly stimulating. He had never known people could actually get drunk from excitement, but these young and carefree merrymakers proved it could be done. Horns were blowing and lights were flashing. A few of the girls were dancing on their foot pegs, their hands resting on the driver's shoulders in front of them. Several of the bikers took turns accelerating like dragsters to the head of the pack, then suddenly slowing down and falling to the rear to do it all over again. Two of the drivers had no passengers, and they were doing wheelies. And one driver was deftly zigzagging his way through the pack while reaching out and shaking hands with the other riders.

In a moment of strange exhilaration, Jason had to shout again. All around him, other bikers shouted with him.

As they pulled into Ayia Napa, Jason thought it was a miracle none of them had been either injured or arrested. He regretfully parted company with them, sad that the ride was over. But now he had to get back to the business at hand.

With renewed zest, he spent the afternoon moving from one hotel to the next. After inquiring at the last one at 5:30, he decided to ride back to Larnaca. Canvassing all of Ayia Napa's apartments and bungalows would have to wait till tomorrow.

On the return trip to Larnaca, he reflected on how much he needed a friend with whom he could share life's experiences, like today's motorcycle gala. He had been alone for four years, he reminded himself, and it was becoming less and less endurable. *What I wouldn't give to find Corinna right now...*

Back in Larnaca he dropped off the motorcycle, then jogged his routine five miles, this time along the beach. He capped the day with an exquisite dish of sea trout at a seaside restaurant. Back in his hotel room, he was sound asleep within minutes after his head hit the pillow.

≈ ≈ ≈

VISIONS OF CORINNA were still dancing in his head when he reached Ayia Napa the next morning, once more on the same rented motorcycle. He pulled up to the first vacationers' apartment complex he saw.

The woman in the reception office had never heard of Cody, Renée, or Corinna, but like the hotel clerk in Larnaca she was more than willing to help him by compiling a list of the city's vacation rentals. Jason was becoming more and more impressed with Cypriot kindheartedness. He slipped the woman a few coins and assured her of his gratefulness.

The list paid off. Early in the afternoon he felt as if a million-ton weight had been lifted from his shoulders when he found the apartment where Cody and Renée were staying. But when the manager added that they were on a ten-day excursion to Athens, Tel Aviv, and Cairo, Jason's elation turned to bitter frustration. Why was it, he wondered, that whenever he came close enough to culminate his search for his granddaughter and her father, there was always someone there saying he had just missed them? It was almost as if God were teasing him, like a kid teasing a kitten by pulling a string in front of it.

"When are they scheduled to be back?" Jason asked.

The manager looked at his desk calendar, figuring it up. "Three and a half days," he answered.

Jason knew it might sound like a stupid question, but he asked it anyway: "Did Renée—the little girl—look healthy and normal?"

The manager said he hadn't really noticed.

Jason left the apartment building, then drove down to the beach. For thirty minutes he sat solemnly in the sand, watching the people but thinking about Renée. Being so close to seeing her only intensified his desire and determination. "Let me see her, God," he prayed again, fervently. "Somehow, she needs me. I just know it."

His concern had driven him for four years to find her. *I guess I can wait another three and a half days*, he thought, sifting sand through his fingers.

Soon he had psyched himself back into a cheerful mood. The three days would pass quickly; besides, they would also give him more time to look for Corinna. And if he got tired of searching for her, which he honestly doubted, he could always try his hand at water-skiing or windsurfing or maybe even parasailing.

There were only nine more addresses on his Ayia Napa list, so he spent the rest of the afternoon checking them out. At each one, no one had any knowledge of Corinna Nykvist.

But he had found where Cody and Renée were staying—a fantastic achievement—and on his ride back to Larnaca he decided he would celebrate. Maybe he'd go to a disco or a nightclub.

That evening he trimmed his beard and spruced himself up in the sportiest clothes he had with him. At 9:30, under a brilliant full moon, he was sitting on a beachside bench across the street from what appeared to be Larnaca's most popular discothèque. The flashing neon sign mounted over the front door reflected in the windows of the cars parked tightly out in front. Besides the cars, there were motorcycles parked on the sidewalks, under trees, and anywhere a motorcycle would fit.

Jason started to get up and go in, then hesitated for the dozenth time. Not once in his forty-six years had he ever been inside a dance hall. And though he was by no means the extreme right-wing conservative he once was, his background and the hypersensitive conscience it spawned were putting up a small fight. But he wasn't terribly concerned. He had beaten that resistance a hundred times before on other matters without suffering any dire consequences, and he knew he could beat it again. It was just a matter of building up his nerve to take the first step.

After sitting for thirty minutes, he finally thought to himself, *What the heck. Go for it.* He got up and walked across the street.

As he walked through the bouncer-guarded entrance and paid his cover charge, he was directed to a monstrous cellar now converted into a cozy, low-ceilinged subterranean night spot. As he walked down the stairway and into the room, he was bombarded by smoky haze and loud music.

Just inside the entrance, he stood and stared. He was overtaken by the sudden overload to his senses: the demanding music with a throbbing bass sound so heavy it literally vibrated the room; the gyrating and swaying young bodies crowded onto the slowly revolving dance floor; the flashing, sweeping multicolored strobe lights; the dim background lighting that gave everything a mystical, almost out-of-focus appearance; the shifting, talking mass of bodies that surrounded the dance floor and filled the place nearly from wall to wall; the busy barmaids rushing to and fro delivering drinks; and the overall feeling of sexual heat.

Standing there, he felt as if everybody in the room was checking him over. Doing his best to play it cool, he made his way through the press of bodies to the elevated bar area, acting like he knew what he was doing.

A man was just getting up from a bar stool, so Jason took his place. The bartender approached and asked what he wanted. He ordered an orange juice and tried not to look embarrassed.

From his perch on the bar stool he had an unobstructed view of almost the entire room. As he sipped the juice, he slowly gazed at all that was going on.

Suddenly he made eye contact with a brunette leaning against a round, shiny metal pillar only eight feet away. She was alone. She offered a smile that undeniably meant she was available. For what, Jason did not know. To dance? To drink? To talk? To…?

Jason nervously broke the visual contact and tried to act neutral. He was suddenly reminded of what he used to say when he preached against Christians going to bars and discothèques: They were hives for immoral sexual stirrings.

However, he really did not want to deal with such thoughts right now. He was not in the mood for debating moral issues with himself. Besides, he was beginning to feel good here, and didn't want to leave.

Out of curiosity he looked again in the brunette's direction. Almost simultaneously she returned the look. Again, she smiled.

This time Jason did not break the stare.

She started walking in his direction. She was not great-looking, but not bad either. She looked to be about twenty-six, Jason figured. Her hair as cut short. She was wearing tight jeans and a ruffled-collar white blouse.

"Hi," she said, extending her hand. "Ich bin Elke."

"Pardon?" Jason responded, raising his voice to be heard above the music. He was holding her hand.

She switched to English. "My name is Elke. Are you together with someone?"

"No, I'm alone." He slowly let go of her hand. "My name is Jason."

"You're American?" she said, with interest in her eyes.

"Yeah. I'm from America." He got up from the stool. "Here," he said, "have a seat and we'll talk."

The next three-quarters of an hour quickly slipped by. The talk was shallow, but constant. Due to the loud music they talked mouth-to-ear, occasionally touching.

Elke kept pressing her knee gently against him. He let himself shift his body closer to her.

His mind was running wild, wondering where all this would go.

A particularly wild song began, and Elke reached out, clasped Jason's hand, and held it to her leg.

Jason put his lips to her ear and whispered in a state of surrender, "What are you doing to me?" He let his lips brush against her soft, perfumed skin.

"Anything I can," she answered, turning to him with a penetrating smile. "And you are welcome to whatever you want."

Ignited by passion, his body screamed for a woman, a satisfaction he had not known for four years.

Beyond the point of reason, he told her, "Let's go."

She stood. Jason put his arm around her waist and escorted her to the door. He quickly decided they would go to his hotel room. They would take a taxi.

Before starting up the stairs to the door, she turned to him and said, "Excuse me for a moment. I'll be right back." She disappeared into the ladies' room.

Jason leaned against the wall, waiting for her. He was stunned. Nothing like this had ever happened to him, even during the last four years when he had been more or less available. *Maybe it's the place*, he thought. Did this happen to people all the time in discothèques?

An alluring song started playing over the mammoth speakers that somehow matched his floating-on-a-cloud mood. When Elke came out, he pointed to the air and said to her, "Nice song."

"It's Abba," she said.

"It's what?"

"Abba," she said again, more slowly. They were walking up the stairs.

"Abba? What's that?" He thought it might be a new kind of music.

"Abba. That's the group that's singing." When she saw no look of recognition on his face, she smiled and explained, "It's a new singing group from Sweden. Well, three of them are Swedish. The other one is from Norway. They're one of the hottest groups in Europe right now."

They were at the top of the stairs, but Jason's thoughts had been abruptly sidetracked. The word "Norway" set off a brief chain reaction in his mind. *Corinna. Norway. Corinna. What if Corinna saw me here? What would she say? "It's never too late to be good, Jason." "No matter what, don't ever give up."*

He suddenly felt he wanted to be loyal forever to beautiful Corinna. Not only *wanted* to be, but *could* be. He really did love her, didn't he? No other woman had ever had the kind of impact on him that she had. Only she had been able to touch whatever good was still left in his heart. And there was so much good about Corinna. Divine. Pure. *I've got to see her again. I need her—I need her.*

His new thoughts refused to slide, but instead trumpeted in his head like a sentry blowing a final warning. And they rekindled his conscience and made it feel heavy now with wrongdoing.

They stepped into the night air. Elke was at his side. He wanted to run. He wanted to escape the trap he had so carelessly walked into. But how? Could he just simply tell the lady he had changed his mind? What if she were the sensitive type? What if she screamed aloud with utter embarrassment? What if she became violent and made a scene?

The driver of a taxi parked just outside had seen them, just as he had obviously seen couples in this stage many times before. He started his engine. Elke moved toward the door. Jason opened it for her. She was starting to slide in when she suddenly straightened and looked back. "My purse!" she blurted out. "I left it in the ladies' room." She gave a quick "Just a moment," to Jason, then darted back inside.

Still holding the door open, Jason struggled for twenty seconds, then made his decision. He climbed into the taxi and shut the door behind him. "Go," he ordered the driver.

≈ ≈ ≈

THE NEXT MORNING, feeling exceptionally good, Jason was eager to continue his search for Corinna.

The 100-cc motorbike was beginning to feel small, so today he rented a 250-cc model. Soon he was speeding toward the center of the island along its only stretch of expressway. It led to Nicosia, the capital of the Greek side of Cyprus. Because of Corinna's business, he thought the capital city would be his next best bet for finding her.

In Nicosia he made his way slowly through the heavy traffic, then spotted a hotel. Inside he found that Corinna had not been registered there, but once again the Cypriot clerk behind the desk willingly offered to aid Jason in his quest. This time it was a list of Nicosia's eight most prominent hotels.

He contacted six of them without any luck. The seventh was a smaller and more out-of-the-way hotel, and decidedly drab. He almost decided not to try it; why would Corinna stay in a place like this? But inside he finally heard his first positive word about her whereabouts. The clerk was a young woman who looked about seven months pregnant. She displayed a warm, inviting personality that Jason quickly responded to. It lured conversation out of him. Instead of simply asking if a Corinna Nykvist was registered there, he launched into an extended explanation about her mysterious disappearance and his long search for her. He described her appearance in detail, and made his desperation obvious.

As the young woman listened, Jason waited to see the same I'm-truly-sorry-but-I-can't-help-you look he had seen in so many other faces. Instead she seemed to be deeply in thought, almost as if she were trying to solve a problem of her own. In fact, by the time Jason neared the end of his description of Corinna, he fully expected the clerk to shake out of her daze and apologize for not listening to him.

But then he heard words that elated him. "Just a moment," she said. "You know, maybe I can help you. I'm almost sure another clerk here became friends with a lady fitting that description. Today's her day off, but if you like, I can call her at her home and ask about it."

"Fantastic!" Jason responded. "Yes, please," he almost begged.

She picked up the phone and soon was speaking Greek, of which Jason understood nothing. From her serious expression and the subdued tone of her voice, he wondered if there was a problem. But when she hung up she was smiling. "It seems that your lady friend stayed here for two days. My co-worker remembers her distinctly. She said she has never seen a woman so beautiful. But she says the lady left Nicosia yesterday. It seems she's staying just across the border in the Turkish sector. She'll be there, in Lefkosa, for only a few more days, and then she'll leave the island."

Jason was astounded at his good fortune. "Lefkosa! How do I get there? Is it far?"

"No, not far." The woman smiled a knowing smile, and Jason had the impression that, for his sake, she was enjoying this stroke of luck as much as he was. "It's only about ten minutes. The border, or the green line as we call it, runs through the middle of the city and divides Nicosia from Lefkosa." The woman's smile faded, and became a look of apprehension. "But if you're planning to go after her, you might not find it so easy."

"What do you mean?"

"Tourists vacationing here on the Greek side are not ordinarily allowed to cross the border. The political problems, you know."

"What do you mean by 'ordinarily'?"

"Well, it's not impossible to go across. The authorities on both sides will sometimes grant a foreigner a visa—but only for special business cases."

Jason took in her words. He whispered a profanity, slapping his right fist into his left palm. He didn't mean to be so expressive, but to finally know her whereabouts and yet not be able to see her right away was a cruel blow.

"You must want to be with her real bad," the woman said, her face sympathetic.

"More than you'll ever know," Jason confided.

She smiled again, hesitatingly. With a touch of indecision in her voice she said, "If you'll promise not to tell anyone, maybe I can help you."

Jason's eyes lit up with hope. "You can trust me," he affirmed. "Go ahead. I'm listening."

"Okay. But I'm serious: You've got to promise not to tell this to anybody. Do you understand?"

"I understand. And I promise. You've got my word."

She nodded. "There's a man—I won't give you his name, but I'll tell you where you can find him. For about three hundred American dollars he can stamp your foreign passport with an official Turkish visa and a Greek permit so you can cross the green line." With those hard facts she stopped, offering no further explanation.

"How do I get to him?"

"I'll tell you. But it's going to cost you something for me, too."

"What's that?" he said, wondering if she would require a few hundred dollars as well.

She smiled again, almost apologetically. "I've got a cousin who lives in Lefkosa. She's getting married next week, and I have a wedding gift for her. But because of the political problems, I don't trust the mail over the border, and ordinary citizens aren't allowed to cross. I've been wondering how I was going to get the gift to her. But if you decide to cross over, maybe you can take it to her for me. It wouldn't be a problem. I can give you her name and address. The stop would only take a few minutes."

It seemed to Jason a small price to pay for his ticket to Corinna. Besides, the Cypriots he had encountered had been nothing but kind and helpful toward him. He owed them a favor.

"It's a deal," he said.

The lady smiled.

21

WITHIN TWO HOURS Jason was back at the drab hotel, after having a little trouble finding it again due to his lack of familiarity with Nicosia. He was three hundred dollars poorer, but his passport was newly stamped with a standard seventy-two-hour Turkish visa and a Greek permit to go into the North. Ready now to cross the border, he had stopped here to pick up the wedding gift, as he promised the pregnant clerk he would.

She brought out the gift-wrapped box, thanking him repeatedly for doing the favor. Jason protested that he owed her at least that much for her willingness to share the secret about "the passport man."

As he said goodbye, she gave him one last bit of vital information.

"When you get to the border, remember: That visa you have would normally be granted in an office that's next door to the border police checkpoint. So, to prevent any suspicion, make sure you go first into the visa office and wait around inside for about forty minutes. That's how long it usually takes to get a visa. Then you can go on out to the checkpoint, and the police will check your passport there."

"Gotcha," he said.

"By the way," she added with a secretive smile, "in case you'd like to know, the gift you're carrying includes some perfume and some packets of very exotic bath powders—things they never have on the Turkish side. She's my favorite cousin, and I know she'll love it." She playfully pointed a warning finger at him. "So take good care of it."

Jason smiled back at her. "I'll guard it with my life."

≈≈≈

AS HE HUNG AROUND the visa office, acting as if he were waiting to meet someone, Jason had only one thing on his mind: Corinna. He decided he would have to move quickly once he was in Lefkosa. If he failed to find her in the next three days, he was convinced his chances of ever seeing her again would be zero.

When exactly forty minutes had gone by, he stepped out of the visa office, pulled out his passport from his shirt pocket, and walked across the open pavement to the border checkpoint.

On the near side, the Greek Cypriot border guard did a double-take when he examined his passport. Jason, who hadn't had the slightest anxiety about crossing the border until now, felt himself getting warm.

"You're American?" the guard asked.

Jason was puzzled by the question. Surely the identity of his nationality had to be the least suspicious aspect of his passport. "Yes, of course," he answered, hoping the question wasn't leading up to others he couldn't so easily answer. He was already wondering angrily whether his three hundred dollars had been wasted. But then the guard looked briefly in the direction of the visa office shrugged his shoulders, and allowed him to go ahead.

A moment later, with an uneasiness he couldn't shake, Jason presented his passport to the Turkish police guards on the other side of the green line, who were even more taken aback by his papers. They consulted with one another in Turkish, then asked him to step inside their small office cubicle.

If there was a problem and they wanted to turn him back,

Jason decided he would plead with them and maybe even dare to make a monetary offer.

Somehow he had to get through.

≈ ≈ ≈

AT THE HOTEL, the phone rang at the pregnant clerk's desk.

She answered it, and immediately heard a rough male voice ask urgently, "Has he left already?"

"Yes," she said confidently. "Almost an hour ago. He's probably through the border by now." She heard her caller let out a groan of vexation. "What's wrong?" the clerk asked.

"And he has it?" the man countered heatedly.

"Yes. In the envelopes, like you said. And I told him it was bath powder. Why? What's wrong?"

She heard him swear. "They aren't granting border permits to any Americans today," he said with disgust. "I just heard it on the radio. Something political. They're angry at the U.S. for a public statement yesterday in support of the Turkish state." His voice quickly become keener: "What would he do?"

"I have no idea," she said. "I don't think he's smart. That's why I picked him." The seriousness of the situation was starting to weigh upon her.

"Call your point," the voice ordered, "and tell her what's happened. Make her call you in fifteen minutes to tell you whether he's made it there. Maybe he'll get through anyway. But if he doesn't, you'll both have to hide."

≈ ≈ ≈

WITH THE GIFT BOX in his lap, Jason was carefully watching the policeman's face across the desk that stood between them. He was the senior of the two guards, and was in the middle of an intense telephone conversation. He said nothing Jason understood, except when he read "Jason L. Faircloth" from the passport lying open in front of him. Jason hoped the call wasn't to the visa office.

When the five-minute call was over, the policeman closed the passport and folded his hands on top of it. Then he launched into Jason. "What is your business in the Turkish Federated State of Cyprus, Mr. Faircloth?"

"I'm trying to find a friend," Jason answered. Instantly he wished he had lied and given a more important-sounding reason.

"Where does this friend live?"

"In Lefkosa."

"Where in Lefkosa? Can you be more exact?"

"No, I can't. I don't know exactly. I was going to search for her in the various hotels."

"In the various hotels? Who actually is this friend, Mr. Faircloth? Is she a Turkish Cypriot?"

"No, she's Norwegian. Her name is Corinna Nykvist."

The man glanced at the other policeman, who had been standing behind Jason the entire time. Then he glared back at Jason.

"What's in the box, Mr. Faircloth?"

"Why...it's a gift. For my friend." It was a convenient lie to keep things from becoming any more complicated.

"Mr. Faircloth, is this the same story you gave to the authorities when you applied for your visa?"

"Of course. Why would I tell one story to them and a different one to you?" Jason wondered how much the old eye scar was contributing to his apparent lack of credibility at the moment.

His questioner again looked up at the other policeman, and this time Jason turned to look at him too. The man's deep-set eyes were giving serious signals to the senior officer. Jason turned back around, fidgeting in his chair.

He seriously considered asking for his passport back, then getting up and walking back across to Nicosia. He could try to cross the border at another location, though it would mean further delay.

The senior policeman interrupted his thoughts. "Mr. Faircloth, under the present political circumstances, it is absolutely inconceivable that either the Greek or Turkish authorities have granted you permission to cross the border today for such a personal matter."

Now Jason was mad. He knew it was going to be a long afternoon.

"Mr. Faircloth," the policeman ordered coldly, "please open the box and show us what's inside."

"I told you, it's a gift," Jason snapped. "It's nothing but perfume and bath powder. Why are you—"

167

"I said open the box, Mr. Faircloth."

Jason pulled the box closer to his stomach and placed both hands over it, as if to protect it. "You don't understand," he tried to explain. "I *can't* open it. It's not—"

To the side of him, Jason saw the barrel of the policeman's rifle suddenly pointing at his head.

"The box, Mr. Faircloth." The senior policeman's eyes were colder than ever.

Jason slowly took his hands off the box, then set it on the desk in front of him. The policeman carefully began removing the wrapping paper, then cautiously proceeded to open it.

This is crazy, Jason thought. *They act like it's a bomb or something.*

A moment later a bottle of perfume and six sealed envelopes were lying on the desktop. The policeman first opened the bottle and held it to his nose. Then he set it down and picked up one of the envelopes. He shook down its contents, tore off a corner, and emptied some of the powder in his hand. He licked one of his fingers and dabbed it in the powder. He held it to his nose, then lightly touched it to his tongue. He turned to the other policeman and said, "Cocaine."

"Cocaine?" Jason said queasily to no one in particular. He was stunned.

The policeman tore open the next envelope. He tasted the powder. "The same," he said.

Fear swept through Jason like a fire as the truth sunk in: *I've been set up.*

In the next moment, without taking time to think, he lunged out the door and started running as fast as he could toward the Greek border station. His thoughts were in such a state of terror that the shouts of the policeman never registered with him. His legs had become his brain, forcing him to move frantically back toward Nicosia and safety.

He had covered only fifteen yards when he felt himself being tackled. He fell face-first to the pavement with the weight of a 170-pound man on his back. Pain shot through his body when he smashed against the ground.

He struggled to get free, but once again found himself looking up the nose of the semiautomatic rifle. That, along with the I-dare-you look in the policeman's eyes, jarred him back to his senses.

Within seconds he was handcuffed and surrounded by five other border guards, all with guns aimed his way. Feeling nauseated, he lay motionless on the ground while they frisked him for concealed weapons. He understood without being told that if he tried running again, he would be shot down on the spot.

≈ ≈ ≈

HE WAS SITTING PETRIFIED in a wooden chair in the middle of a dirty room. He had been in the chair for six hours undergoing interrogation by three Turkish policemen. They had explained that since the drugs were in his possession, a severe sentence was already a foregone conclusion. They just wanted to know who he was working for and who his contact was on the Turkish side. If he cooperated by giving them the information, the judge would possibly reduce his sentence by four or five years.

Stuttering with confusion and anger, Jason tried repeatedly to explain what had happened. But he couldn't back up his story. He never knew the name of the pregnant clerk. Nor could he remember the name of the hotel where she worked. After he had been "told" where to find Corinna he had thrown away his list of the eight Nicosia hotels and their addresses. He did, however, have the name and address of the pregnant clerk's "cousin" written down. He quickly handed over the sheet of paper. An hour later the interrogators told him that a search of the state's registry files showed no person in northern Cyprus by that name. And the address on the paper was only that of a drug store. They agreed he was using the name and address only as a distraction or decoy.

"But I'm innocent," Jason pleaded. "You've got to believe me. I was set up!"

"All drug smugglers are innocent and have been set up," one of the police replied sarcastically.

Finally they told him he would continue to be kept in confinement, and would stand trial in a Turkish court within forty-eight hours.

Jason then demanded to see an American government representative—the ambassador, a consul, a lawyer, anybody.

They replied that an official summons had already been prepared on his behalf, and would be sent to the American embassy located on the Greek side in Nicosia. Anyone responding to the summons would be allowed to meet with him in his cell the next morning.

The interrogators left him, while other policemen remained to guard the room's entrance. Jason was left isolated for another hour, then was whisked off in a military jeep to the Lefkosa state prison.

≈ ≈ ≈

"AFTER ALL," Jason said, "she's probably the only hotel clerk in Nicosia who's seven months pregnant. You won't be able to miss her!"

"I'm a lawyer, Mr. Faircloth, not a detective," the man replied, "and I'm not about to go around spying on hotel clerks. But if I locate the place and she's there," he said without enthusiasm, "I'll find out what I can."

The lawyer, introducing himself as Carl Puckett, had come to Jason's cell early this morning. Jason disliked him from the start. He was a short, skinny, bookworm-looking guy who wore glasses that seemed two sizes too big and fifteen years out of fashion. In a high-pitched voice he told Jason coldly that so far the evidence was a hundred percent against him, and that he could expect a ten- to fifteen-year jail sentence, standard punishment in Turkey for drug smuggling.

Not knowing what else to do, Jason was now begging him to do a little footwork and track down the hotel clerk. In last night's sleeplessness Jason had racked his brain to remember more details, but he could offer Puckett only a vague idea of the hotel's location, plus a few scanty impressions of its drab appearance.

"If I discover anything of value," the lawyer said, "I'll be back."

It was a small hope, but it was all Jason had.

Puckett left. Feeling pressure in his bowels, Jason decided to ask the warden for some toilet paper. He had already figured out that the sunken porcelain basin in the cell floor was his toilet; it had corrugated porcelain footpads on both sides so one could squat over the top of it without slipping, and it had a gaping drain hole in the middle, stained with human waste.

The warden knew almost no English, and at first couldn't

make out what Jason wanted. When Jason finally made him understand by way of a visual illustration, the man broke into uncontrolled laughter. When he was able to calm himself, he indicated to Jason with an equally graphic gesture that around here, people did not use toilet paper; they used their left hand.

Jason's next thought was, *Ten years in a Turkish prison with no toilet paper!*

For some crazy reason it made him laugh too.

≈ ≈ ≈

LATE IN THE AFTERNOON the warden awakened Jason to give him a handwritten, unsealed note. Jason sat up on his thin-mattressed, metal-framed bed, rubbed his eyes, and read it:

> Mr. Faircloth:
> I've found the hotel that seems to fit the description. However, the manager insists there are no pregnant women on his staff of clerks.
> There is nothing more I can do.
>   Carl Puckett

Jason crumpled up the note and threw it down the toilet drain. He decided it wasn't even worth saving to use in the place of toilet paper.

He had never felt so abandoned and so hopeless in his life. When Lorene had died, at least he had been surrounded by familiar people who tried to care, and by familiar territory that offered some sense of emotional security. Despite the uncertainty looming ahead of him in those days, he at least had the liberty to chart his own course for the most part. Now he was sitting in a filthy prison cell on an island in the middle of the Mediterranean, with no friends, no freedom, and no future.

He wanted to pray and ask God for a miraculous delivery. He wanted to believe God would hear and intervene. But his confidence in prayer had never been fully restored. He talked to God all the time, maybe even more than when he was a pastor, but his prayers now were more a sharing of feelings than a presentation of requests. About the only thing he ever petitioned God for anymore was his continual prayer for help in finding Renée—and it now appeared God didn't intend to grant that request.

Nevertheless, whether he had strong faith or not, he now had to ask God for divine help. If there was even the slightest of chances that prayer could make a difference, it was stupid not to attempt it.

Besides—by the look of things, there was nothing else to try.

So he prayed. He prayed hard.

≈ ≈ ≈

FORTY HOURS LATER he was stepping through the broken sliding door of a rusty military van. Handcuffed, he sat alone in the back.

Two armed military policemen were in the van's front seat, one driving and the other keeping his head turned toward Jason. They were transporting him across Lefkosa to the court hall where he was to be tried and sentenced.

At the trial he sat in the presence of six men. One was the judge. One was a translator who would explain to him in English all that was happening. One was the prosecutor. One was the court secretary. And the other two were the policemen from the border checkpoint.

From the translator's explanation, Jason learned that the envelopes in the gift box had contained one hundred and eighty grams of cocaine.

When the time came, Jason explained to the judge his side of the story in careful detail. He begged his honor to believe him.

A few minutes later, the trial was over. The judge pronounced him guilty and sentenced him to twelve years.

Engulfed in shock, Jason went silent.

Riding in the military van on the way back to the prison, his indignation at distorted justice and deprived freedom began to consume him. How could he let these people steal twelve years of his life? They had flayed him of all human dignity, and now were going to imprison him like a deranged and dangerous animal.

And what about Renée? he asked himself. He was still persuaded that she desperately needed him. He could not afford to submit her to twelve more years of his silence. It was just that simple.

He felt he was going to explode.

And then, without forethought, he did.

The van had stopped at a traffic light in the heart of downtown Lefkosa. Both the military policemen were momentarily absorbed in watching the lunch-hour crowds that filled the streets around them.

With all the power his lungs could spend, Jason leaned out of his seat toward the side door and shouted, "NOOOOOO...!"

Before the guards had a chance to recover from their unexpected fright, he had thrown open the broken door and hit the street running. *I'll die,* he vowed, *before I'll be caught again.*

Powered by his instinct for freedom, his initial thrust into the sidewalk crowd was so strong that he knocked four or five people off their feet.

He kept bulldozing, ignoring the policeman's cry of "Dur! Dur!" He started a zigzag pattern to create more confusion. The moment he ducked behind a cluster of people he heard a gun shot. He flinched in mid-stride, then heard a scream. In his swirling mind it sounded like a woman. He felt a rushing desire to want to stop and help—but he couldn't.

He cut across the street. Due to the handcuffs that linked his arms in front of him, he had to battle a lack of balance. But he kept up his zigzagging sprint through the heavy traffic, and stayed on his feet.

Following a twisted pattern through another packed intersection, Jason caught one quick glimpse far behind of a policeman still coming hard.

He knew he could run all day. He was thankful for his training during the past years that had conditioned him for endurance. But he knew also that simple running could in no way compete with the police vehicles which would soon be after him. He had to somehow lose the policeman now pursuing him, and then, possibly, he could hide.

After taking sudden turns and weaving back and forth through several crowded streets, he suddenly found himself in a narrow back alley, alone. It was long and straight, and bounded by concrete walls on both sides. Intuitively he knew he would be an easy target if he continued down it, but it was too late to reverse his direction.

He was about forty yards into the alley when he heard the policeman shout. Once again the shout was followed by the heart-stopping sound of gunfire, but this time it was not just one shot, but several. Jason cut as sharply and unpredictably as he could in different directions. Suddenly he saw an opening in the wall, ten yards ahead. He aimed for it, made the turn, and discovered it was an enclosed, dead-end lot. Strewn with debris, it looked like the local junkyard.

His eyes fell immediately on a two-by-four board, about three feet in length. He picked it up, and took a position against the corner wall, next to the entrance from the alleyway. Gulping air, he stood still and waited.

The policeman's steps were coming fast and getting louder. Jason gripped the board like a baseball bat, cocking it over his shoulder. He took one last breath.

When the policeman rounded the corner, only barely breaking his stride, Jason swung with all his might. He planted the plank squarely into the man's midsection.

The policeman was knocked off his feet, falling backward with the upper part of his body lying in the alley. He was clutching his lower rib cage with pain.

Jason grabbed his left foot and jerked him out of the open alley and into the cover of the lot. When the man tried to reach for his pistol that had dropped on the ground, Jason kicked him in the groin. The man's eyes rolled back in his head, and he started throwing up.

Jason quickly tried to search the policeman for keys to unlock the handcuffs. But between his own nervousness and the man's squirming, the effort proved a fiasco. When he heard voices in the alley, he knew he could not waste another second.

He quickly picked up the pistol. He held the handle backwards, so the barrel pointed toward him, then awkwardly rotated and aimed the pistol so it would fire into the left bracelet of the cuffs, without shooting his arm or any other part of him. He squinted, then fired. The metal bracelet popped free, but the percussion of the blast at such a close range burned the surface flesh off his left wrist. He tried to ignore the screaming pain.

He stepped on the loose-hanging end of the cuffs with his left foot, stretched it out tightly, and then with the gun in his left hand, shot off the other bracelet. He incurred the same excruciating wrist burns.

Just then two young men came cautiously snooping around the corner from the alley—curiosity seekers, no doubt, who had heard the shots and perhaps earlier witnessed part of the chase. Judging by the surprise on their faces, they must have assumed the policeman had already shot "the bad guy" into pieces.

Not knowing their intentions, Jason aimed the pistol at their heads, slowly sweeping the gun from one to the other. He motioned them farther into the lot, where they froze in their places. They looked down at the wounded policeman, but said nothing.

Jason slowly backed away, then darted off down the alley with gun in hand. He looked once over his shoulder and saw no one following him. He was off in a full sprint.

He eventually found a place to hide and regroup, crouching between two cars in a graveled, eight-car parking lot. He could now hear sirens in the distance. He knew then that to try to hide in the city would be a lost cause. He had to get out. But how? He still had the gun. Maybe he could waylay a car.

Then he heard the rumbling noises of a down-shifting motorcycle. He raised himself slowly and peered through the windows of one of the cars. When he saw the bike pull into the lot he almost panicked, though he was relieved to see it wasn't a policeman. Should he crawl beneath one of the cars? He forced himself not to let fear dictate his actions, not while he still had a chance. Fighting for a decision, he suddenly saw it. The motorcycle. His way out of the city.

Not taking another second to debate the issue, he ripped off his outer shirt and draped it over his face below his eyes. He took the two long sleeves and quickly tied them around the back of his head. With his mask in place, he started easing toward the bike.

The driver had just killed the engine when Jason stepped out in front of him with his pistol drawn. Aiming the gun into the man's fear-stricken face, Jason waved him face-first to the ground. He then took the man's open-face helmet. Quickly he removed the hanging shirt from his face, threw it behind a car, and slipped on the helmet. He then straddled the bike. *My gosh*, he thought, *it's heavy.* It was a 900-cc. He cranked it. Brown dirt and pieces of rock spewed into the air as he accelerated out of the lot.

If he was going to ride openly through the town on a bike, he was glad he didn't have the shirt, since it was undoubtedly part of the description that the soldiers and police would have their eyes peeled for. He hoped a man dressed simply in jeans and a white T-shirt would not draw suspicious attention.

After a ten-minute drive, he found himself heading northeast out of the city. He had passed two police jeeps without incident.

He threw open the throttle now. He knew the bike's owner would waste no time reporting the theft.

He soon found himself traveling on a less-than-mediocre two-lane road running parallel to the foot of a mountain ridge. If necessary, he figured, he could use the mountains as a place of refuge, so he kept going northeast on the same road, though he had no idea where it led.

By mid-afternoon he reached the sea, and entered what appeared to be a fishing village with several docks. He had driven more than seventy miles. The bike's gas gauge showed an empty tank, but since all of his money had been confiscated along with his passport, purchasing more gasoline was out of the question.

Bystanders in the village were glancing at him. He was thankful the helmet prevented anyone from getting a good look at his face.

He drove a mile and a half back down the coast and away from the village, following a rutted, unpaved road that came out on a lonely strip of rocky beach. It was time to disassociate himself from the motorcycle, and it became clear to him now how to do it. After making sure he was alone and unobserved, he drove the motorcycle into the ocean, up to its handlebars, and left it. The tide seemed low, so he thought the graveyard would be secure for some time. *I hope the owner has insurance,* he thought as he waded out of the waves.

He went back to the gun he had left lying on the beach, picked it up, and decided to see how many bullets it had left. To his amazement he found the cylinder empty. He started to throw the gun out into the water with the motorcycle, but changed his mind and decided to keep it for a while. If it became necessary, he hoped he could use it as convincingly as the two times before.

After kicking away the motorcycle tracks in the sand, he sat down behind a boulder about seven or eight feet high, with a base that was being sloshed by the surf. It put him out of sight of anyone who might come strolling along the beach from the village.

For the moment he was as free as a man could be. But unless he could think of a way to get off the island soon, he knew his freedom wouldn't last much longer.

Finding an airport was out of the question. He didn't know where the airport on the Turkish side was located, but even if he managed to find it, the police would be waiting there. Besides, he had neither money nor a passport.

Crossing the border was probably out of the question as well. Lookouts would surely be posted, and though there had to be over a hundred miles of border, and he could attempt a crossing in a desolate area, still the border at its closest could be no less than forty miles from here. He could, he thought, steal a car, disguise himself, drive south along the coast until he reached the border, then abandon the car and slip over the green line under cover of darkness. But what about the Greek police? Would they be looking for him? And if they caught him, wouldn't they extradite him back to Turkey?

The more he thought about the slim possibilities available to him, the more overcome he was with hopelessness.

As he leaned back against the rock and gazed out tiredly over the water, Jason's eyes suddenly caught a glimpse of a small speck on the liquid horizon. It was a boat of some kind. He watched for some time as the vessel drew nearer. Eventually he made it out to be a fishing boat, and it appeared to be heading toward the village. He remembered all the docks he had seen there.

Suddenly a new possibility opened up in his mind: He could escape the island as a stowaway on a fishing boat. It was certainly a more viable option than anything else he could think of. He would at least make an attempt at it.

It meant staying in the vicinity for the rest of the evening and most of the night, for fishing boats would not go back out to sea until the predawn darkness tomorrow. Maybe it was too risky. But then again, so was getting up and moving on. He decided to stay put.

≈   ≈   ≈

A SWEEP OF THE INNER CITY by six Lefkosa police jeeps had failed to apprehend the runaway American, but it did produce a key piece of information: A man had approached one of the jeeps to report the theft of his motorcycle. His description of the thief matched that of the escapee. In a quick search of the theft site, the police even found a discarded American-style blue shirt.

The chief of the state military police force was immediately handed responsibility for a wider manhunt. He ordered blockades at all of the north island's ports of entry, including border stations, the airport, and ferry ports. The suspect was described as a bearded, brown-haired American, 180 centimeters tall and weighing 70 kilos, wearing a white T-shirt and jeans, and possibly riding a Kawasaki KZ 900 motorcycle. He was classified as armed and dangerous, and the soldiers were given authority to shoot to kill if necessary.

As an afterthought, the state police chief also deployed four jeeps to head north out of the capital, each taking one of the four major roadways leading to the various coastal towns.

The strategy paid off. When a police jeep rolled into the fishing village of Zafer later that afternoon, an old man sitting under the shade of a carob tree reported seeing a strange man in a white T-shirt who was riding a motorcycle on a back road that led out of town.

The report was immediately radioed in to police headquarters in the capital. By six o'clock the entire village was crawling with soldiers being organized into search teams to scour the surrounding countryside. Some of the town's fishermen who were in for the evening volunteered to join in the hunt.

Moving outward from the village along the coast, the search teams were to comb the beaches and up to two-hundred yards inland.

≈   ≈   ≈

AS THE TIDE began coming in, Jason moved from the ground to the top of the boulder. Soon its bottom half was under water. Jason was lying on his back, soaking up the last of the evening sun's rays, when he heard voices. He slowly rolled his head and looked up the beach. A hundred yards away he saw two armed policemen; two other men, armed but not uniformed, were with them. He had no doubt who they were looking for.

Quietly he rolled off the opposite side of the rock and disappeared into the water. He was quite sure he had been undetected. If he was wrong, it would be only a matter of minutes before he was either dead or imprisoned again. It was too late to make a run for it now. And there were no city crowds to get lost in this time.

Jason submerged everything but his head under the sea water. He tried to keep himself pressed tightly against the rock, to keep the waves from bouncing him off the giant stone like a yo-yo. But not knowing what was happening on the other side of the boulder made him feel extremely vulnerable. It was as if the rock were not there at all, and he was standing out in the open, waving a six-foot American flag.

He had been frightened before, but never like this.

His eyes were glued to the part of the beach he could still see. He was breathing hard, and his heart was pounding. After a wait that seemed forever, he got a glimpse of human movement only twenty yards away, just a few feet beyond reach of the tide wash. He took a quick breath, then put his head under water. Immediately he realized that his sudden movement had created a distinct splash.

Underwater, he held his breath for nearly two minutes. It seemed like ten. His lungs screamed for air. He was fighting to keep his throat closed, to keep his lungs from belching out their carbon dioxide waste. But he forced himself to stay under.

At some unclear moment, when he thought he was going to pass out, his mind refused any longer to perceive the fear of being shot at, captured, or imprisoned. The need for oxygen was the new and overruling priority. He was literally forced upward.

But the very instant he came up for his lifesaving gulp of air, his thoughts switched back over to the existing man-imposed danger. He hugged the rock like a frightened lizard to make himself as inconspicuous as possible.

Now where are the men? he asked himself. He was almost afraid to move his head, for fear of being spotted. Should he go back down again?

In his peripheral vision, he caught sight of the soldier walking westwardly down the beach, away from him. *The other three— where are they?* He demanded an answer of himself.

He watched the lone soldier walk out of view. Only then did he dare take a peek around the other side of the clump of stone. Carefully he looked. Nobody. Nobody anywhere. Was it a trap to lure him out into the open? No, he was sure; if they had seen him they would have already made their move, especially since he was at such a vulnerable disadvantage.

He suspected they were still in the area somewhere, and might even walk by the beach again. As a precaution, he decided to stay where he was, at least until dusk.

For two hours he ignored his hunger pains, his shivering, and his impatience.

Once the early darkness started to cloak the landscape with shades of gray, Jason felt secure enough to venture out onto the beach. He crawled on his belly across the sand until he reached vegetation. And then, as much as was possible, he collapsed and let the stiffness in his back and shoulders dissipate.

After about thirty minutes, he decided it was time to move. He knew where he had to go, and had already decided the route to take.

It was going to be a cold and sleepless night, probably one of the longest he would ever know. But he was convinced it would be the surest way to guarantee his escape. To get to the fishing boats, he would spend the night in neck-deep water, slowly wading around the tip of the peninsula between himself and the village.

He entered the sea water for the second time that evening, and the chilling bite swamped his body.

Unless they plan to dredge the coastline, he thought, *they're not going to find me.*

22

UNDERNEATH THE OVERHANG of the dock, Jason was standing chest-deep in water on a narrow, submerged ledge of the dock wall. Beside him was the bow of a fishing boat tied to the dock. It was the last vessel, the one closest to the open sea, in the line of several fishing boats moored here.

Above him was a boat tire hanging on the dock wall, used to protect the boat's finish from being scraped by the dock's rough siding. The tire, he knew, would help keep him hidden.

The sky was beginning to lighten. For hours he had been numbed by the chilling effect of the water. He was almost to the point of hypothermia. But he had survived, and the night was almost over. He hoped to God that the misery he had suffered would soon be rewarded with his freedom.

In the emerging light he saw what appeared to be a stable steel ring fastened to the middle board in the boat's bow. It was about a foot above the waterline. That ring, Jason decided, was what he needed.

When he finally heard some stirrings of life on the docks and then on the boat itself, it was like being presented with a long-awaited gift. He wanted to cry.

He heard only one set of footsteps on the boat, and no conversation. When the fisherman cranked his boat engine, Jason made sure once again that the pistol was fitted snugly into his pants. Then he took off his T-shirt and eased his way closer to the bow. The loud knocking of the diesel motor would drown out the slight noise of his gliding through the water.

He tied the undershirt securely through the ring, then placed both of his hurting, flesh-burned wrists through the bottom half of the shirt loop. He slowly twisted himself round and round in the water until the shirt had tightened around his hands. He knew he did not have enough strength in his arms or enough flexibility left in his cold, stiff fingers to simply grab the metal ring and hang there; rather, he would be held up by the strength of the shirt, and be pulled along in the water like a dinghy. As much as possible he would keep wiggling his fingers and flexing his forearm muscles to assist the blood circulation.

When the boat finally started moving, Jason let himself drift to the starboard side of the hull, out of the view of fishermen in nearby boats who might glance in this direction.

A few minutes later, when the boat moved out of the cove and into the open sea, Jason felt that his freedom was actually within grasp. He was cold and miserable, but his survival instinct, strong and determined, kept him alert.

For about an hour he allowed himself to be pulled through the water while he did his best to work his arms and fingers. But they were losing their feeling. Finally he decided he couldn't take it anymore. He knew if he didn't make his move soon, he would risk losing movement in his arms altogether. Besides, he reasoned, the boat was probably in international waters by now and out of Turkish jurisdiction.

He managed to roll his body around a couple of times so the wrist cloth loosened its grip. Then he slowly removed one hand, careful not to lose his hold with the other on the shirt. If he slipped, he could be swept beneath the boat and on through its churning propeller.

His free hand reached inside his pants and removed the pistol. The movement was agonizingly slow because of his stiffness.

Eventually he was holding it by the barrel. He started slowly beating the steel ring with the gun's steel-laced handle.

Soon he heard the engine's throttle cut by half. *He'll probably check the engine first,* Jason reasoned, *and then search the hold.* Jason knew he might have to keep up the noise a long time before the fisherman thought to look down here.

He kept beating, sending up the sound of steel on steel. Finally he saw a weathered face leaning over the railing, wincing at the unexpected.

Minutes later, Jason—minus the gun, which he deposited into the depths of the sea to placate the fisherman—was sitting on the wooden deck, having been hauled out of the water by a rope. He looked tiredly but cheerfully at the old fisherman, who was wearing an expression of unbelief.

"Do you speak English?" Jason finally said, exhaustedly.

"Yes," the fisherman answered. "I speak a little English." He was staring at the pus-covered wounds on Jason's wrists, and at the scar over his eye. No doubt, Jason reasoned, the fisherman had heard about the prison escapee being hunted by the police and had already concluded it was the same man with whom he was now sharing his boat deck in the middle of the Mediterranean. But Jason detected pity in the fisherman's dark eyes and wrinkled face.

"Can I tell you my story?" Jason said. The man paused before he nodded.

For the next half hour, as the welcome sun warmed his numb body, Jason told him the truth about everything—his search for Renée, his discovery about Cody and Renée's temporary excursion, his search for Corinna that led him to Nicosia, the hotel clerk and the set-up, the arrest at the border, the trial, and finally the escape.

Before allowing the fisherman to respond, Jason immediately pleaded for his help.

The old fisherman sat in silence for a few seconds, obviously mulling over Jason's plea.

"You are a lucky man," he finally said. Then he flashed a sympathetic, nearly toothless smile, and shook his head. "I don't like Turks."

Jason almost shouted out his surprised relief.

The old fisherman had a story to tell as well. He was a Greek Cypriot living in the north. A year earlier, when the Turks had undertaken a military buildup on the island, they had taken land from the man's family in the coastal town of Famagusta. They had never offered the family any payment.

He also said he felt indebted to Americans. His brother, who served in the British army in World War II, had been liberated by Americans from a German prison camp.

Still overwhelmed with relief, Jason decided he couldn't have picked a better boat in all of Cyprus to hitch a ride on. The encounter had to be heaven-sent.

Realizing that his even being here was already presumptuous enough, Jason nevertheless spoke up with a gutsy request: "Would it be possible for you to drop me off on the nearest mainland?" He knew it was asking a lot.

The fisherman gave a laugh. "Are you sure you want to go to Turkey?"

Jason grunted. He felt small enough to hide behind a few grains of beach sand. Right then and there he vowed to brush up on his geography if he ever got the chance. "Then I suppose," he said graciously, "I should ask where else we could go?"

The fisherman thought, then suggested Israel, three hundred kilometers to the southeast. Jason would likely find a positive reception among the pro-American Israelis, he said, and he could apply for another passport at the American embassy in Tel Aviv. The trip was too far for his boat's fuel capacity, but they could enter the shipping lanes used by cargo vessels between Israel and Greece, and with luck meet up with a returning Israeli vessel that could take Jason aboard.

"Let's do it," Jason said.

As the fisherman altered the boat's course, Jason chewed on a piece of bread the man had given him, and leaned against the outside of the boat's wheel house.

It occurred to him that Cody and Renée should be back in their Ayia Napa apartment today. The thought left him with a crushed feeling. He had come so far and been so close.

The daring notion pressed within his mind to tell the fisherman to turn the boat around and take him to Ayia Napa. Then he sadly asked himself, *What good would I be to Renée if I were caught and returned to jail for twelve years?* The risk would be too great.

But he wasn't beaten yet. After all, Cody and Renée wouldn't stay on the island forever. In two more months they would return to England. And he could be waiting for them there.

For now, he concluded he should be thankful to God he wasn't marking off day number two in a Turkish jail cell with no toilet paper.

Though he was utterly fatigued and could have fallen asleep instantly, he dared not even lay down until he knew he was absolutely safe. To fight his drowsiness he chatted with the man. Jason learned that his name was Dimitri. He had been a fisherman for forty-five years, a staggering thought to Jason. And like Jason, he was a grandfather; he had a six-year-old granddaughter who loved to ride on the boat with him. Jason found the man to be noble-hearted and easy to talk with.

He was also an excellent seaman. By eleven o'clock, after steering the boat in the middle of the shapeless sea, he was pulling alongside a medium-sized Israeli cargo ship en route from Athens to Tel Aviv.

As Jason started climbing up the rope ladder that led to the larger vessel's deck, he turned to the old fisherman and was overcome with gratefulness for his kindness.

"Dimitri," he said, "I will never forget you. I mean that. One day when I'm sitting down with my granddaughter propped up on my knee, I'll tell her about you. I'll tell her that you did what most people would never have done. I'll tell her you saved my life because of your good-heartedness. And I'll tell her to make sure she passes the name and the story of Dimitri down to her children and her children's children. That's what I'm going to do, my friend."

Dimitri's chest swelled, but he did not speak. He gave Jason a handshake with his thick and calloused hand, a gesture that seemed to say, "I understand the beauty of freedom."

≈ ≈ ≈

AT 3:00 P.M., JASON was awakened by one of the ship's men. They were docking in Tel Aviv.

He had collapsed into sleep right on the open deck, in the direct sunlight. He stood up now and looked out over the city. A slight breeze blowing in from the Mediterranean gently stroked his rested body.

During his years as a pastor he'd planned several times to visit the Holy Land, and had never been able to make it. Now he had come—not as a pastor to further his theological studies in the land where Jesus walked, but as a fugitive fleeing from the Turkish police. *Life is crazy,* he mused.

Leaving the boat, he got directions to the American embassy, and completed the half-hour walk before the offices closed for the day. Once there, he had to explain several times, to several different officials, the chain of events that brought him to Tel Aviv with nothing but what he wore. When they were satisfied they understood his situation, the process of applying for a new passport was put into motion.

He was told there would first have to be an official investigation into his background, which could take several days. To make the work easier, Jason was asked to record in writing all the pertinent information he could remember about himself and his past—everything from his education and employment background to details about his family, his finances, his places of residence, and more. Meanwhile he was given a place to live in the apartments housing the Marines who formed the embassy guard. When he was taken there that evening, the first thing he did was take a hot shower.

Later an embassy staff member drove him to a bank where he was able to have money transferred from his bank account in Boston. In a department store a few blocks away he bought two new complete sets of clothes, some toiletries, and a briefcase.

His billfold that the Turkish border police had confiscated—along with his passport—had contained his money, bank cards, driver's license, and Social Security card, all needing to be replaced. More importantly it had contained Hannah's runaway letter, which was irreplaceable. He brooded over that one.

In Cyprus he had left behind in his Larnaca hotel room his clothes and luggage and his Wisdom Book—and Hannah's little red plastic plate. He brooded over that one too. He had carried it around with him for four years, hoping to give it someday to Renée.

During the next few days, while waiting for the embassy's report, he remade his Wisdom Book, rewriting from memory the five prior entries, and adding a sixth:

6. JUSTICE LATER *vs.* JUSTICE NOW

I have come to understand that one of the most common and basic religious philosophies happens to be a distortion of truth. The philosophy is this: If a Christian willfully sacrifices his selfish dreams and ambitions in order to do God's bidding, and disciplines himself to live his life according to God's rules and regulations, then God in his goodness will reward that person with a life of happiness, fulfillment, peace, health, prosperity, and even recognition. On the other hand, if a person places the crown of authority on his own head and tells God to take a walk, and defiantly chooses to make his own decisions and rule his own life apart from God, God in his justice will render unto that person a life of misery, misfortune, poverty, pain, and disgrace.

An objective and honest look at life around me tells me that real life does not agree with that philosophy. There are many ungodly people dancing around in healthy bodies, with smiles on their faces and money in their pockets, people who are honestly at peace with themselves and with life. Some of these people even live the duration of their lives this way, all the way to the grave.

And there are dedicated Christians who for God's sake have pledged themselves to a life of purity and moral consciousness, yet who are not happy, or fulfilled, or healthy, or prosperous, or publicly recognized.

The truth is that sickness and health, wealth and poverty, unhappiness and joyfulness, peace and misery are found equally among Christians and non-Christians alike. There is no discernible difference.

Does this lack of distinction mean God is not fair? Does it mean God is not especially good to those who choose to follow him?

For years I thought the answer to both questions was Yes. But as I've had time during the last few days to sit and reflect and read, my eyes have been opened—due primarily to a "chance" reading of Psalm 73, which so wondrously intertwines with my personal experiences and brings them to light.

From this psalm I have learned that I must take a long-range view of life in order to remain sane in my Christianity and to retain love and respect for God. The truth is that God has never promised his children a life that's fair. He has never committed himself to complete justice and fairness here and now, to me or to any other Christian. He has, however, committed himself to complete justice and fairness at the final judgment in the future.

If a Christian is not rewarded here in a significant way for his devotion to God, then one day he will be. The rewards due him will be forthcoming at the Judgment.

Likewise, the ungodly who curse, deny, or ignore God and who are having one big party in their selfish and immoral ways, and are seemingly getting away with it, will also face ultimate justice.

So it does matter if I live for God or not.

God has not promised that this life will be fair, but that he will be with me in the midst of all the unfairness, and give me counsel and guidance to survive it.

I can live with that.

As a matter of fact, for the first time in months I feel a new love for God rising in my heart.

≈ ≈ ≈

FIVE DAYS AFTER his arrival in Tel Aviv, Jason was called into the senior consul's office at the embassy. The consul pointed to a stack of papers on his desk. "These are the reports from our investigation. You've been through a lot. Quite an amazing story.

"From the American side," he continued, "you're clean, and I'm glad we can help you. All we need now is a couple of new photographs, and we can provide you immediately with a new passport. Then you're free to go.

"But let me stress that you're on your own. And of course I need not remind you that your life is at risk if you go back to Cyprus. You should stay out of Turkey and Greece as well. And England."

"England?" Jason asked, his face suddenly tightening.

"That's right. The Turkish authorities—if they followed normal procedures, and I'm sure they would have in your case—have already contacted the British police through Interpol, the international police network. Since you traveled to Cyprus from England, it will be suspected that you might return via that route.

"Unless and until you're proven innocent and have your name cleared from the police files," said the consul with earnest warning, "I suggest you don't put a foot anywhere in Great Britain."

≈ ≈ ≈

IN THE APARTMENT, Jason fell on the bed and cried. He was a lonely man who felt he could no longer cope with defeat.

Renée would now be living where he could no longer safely travel. Only ten days ago his granddaughter was within reach, but the harrowing events since then had essentially pushed her further away than ever.

Today was November 20th. On December 15th, just a few weeks away, Renée would be four years old. Already four years of her life had gone by, and he had not shared a single second of it with her.

"Why, God?" he prayed in a fit of anguish. "Why are you keeping her from me?"

He tried to reflect on his recent Wisdom Book entry, but depression stayed with him anyway.

What was he going to do now? He had toyed earlier with the idea of staying in Israel and touring the ancient places of the Bible, but that thought had now lost its savor.

He thought of Corinna. He needed Corinna. He needed her badly.

Now, as always before when he needed it, there seemed to be a new rope to grasp: Corinna was probably back in Norway by now. He could go to Norway. He would go to Norway and somehow find Corinna.

≈ ≈ ≈

THE NEXT MORNING, on board a connecting KLM flight to Oslo, Norway, Jason pulled out a sheet of paper from his new briefcase, and wrote a letter.

> Dear God,
> Right now, in spite of all I have learned about
> you in the last four years, you are as mysterious to
> me as on the day I walked out of the ministry. And

I am mad. It seems to me that you have no sympathy for my cause or for my feelings. If I was big enough, I would threaten you somehow. I would try to hurt you in return for all the pain you've put me through, pain that never seems to let up.

There's a part of me that wants to forget you even exist. But if I turn my back on you and walk away in anger, where will I go? You are the consummation of wisdom, of truth, of knowledge, of insight, of power, of friendship, of love, and of life. Outside of you there is nothing. I am not so blind that I don't see that.

So—am I going to run from you in my anger? NO! I'm going to run to you in my anger. I'm going to cling to you, pester you, bother you, trouble you, chase you, pursue you, seek you, wrestle you, love you, worship you, and extol you...until you decide to help me.

23

"TAKE ME TO A NICE HOTEL in the center of town," he told the driver at the airport as he climbed inside the taxi. Jason was carrying only a briefcase and a small duffel bag, which contained his one extra set of clothes.

The plane had landed at Oslo's airport only minutes ago. With his few belongings, Jason had quickly passed through customs. Then he stopped at the small bank located in the airport lobby and exchanged five hundred American dollars for just over twenty-six hundred Norwegian *kroner*. He couldn't pronounce it, but it was colorful and it would spend.

The motorway from the airport to the city ran parallel to a beautiful fjord. On the city's south side the fjord led to a harbor that seemed to be a nest of ships of every imaginable kind and size. The city streets were bustling with people, fair-skinned and mostly tall, all dressed in their heavy winter coats. Jason realized that if he hung around this place for long he would definitely need to buy warmer clothing.

Everything—streets, trees, buildings, housetops—was covered in a thick blanket of fresh snow. Jason had never seen so much snow in his life, but it didn't seem to hamper the city's life in the least.

After a twelve-minute drive the taxi delivered him to the twenty-two-story SAS Hotel. For the fare Jason had to fork out a frightening fifty kroner—$11.50. It was his first taste of the cost of living in one of the world's most expensive cities. Corinna had failed to mention that aspect of her country to him.

After grudgingly paying the fare, he sought refuge in the hotel's inner warmth.

The lobby was clean, modern, and huge. In the middle was a large open fireplace of an almost futuristic design, surrounded by dark leather couches draped with reindeer skins.

As Corinna had said, the Norwegian people were tall, slim,

blonde, and beautiful. The three female clerks behind the central desk, Jason noticed, were absolute knockouts. *If they're typical of their kind,* he joked to himself, *I'm going to end up with neck problems.*

Learning that a room cost ninety dollars per night, he registered for one night only. After getting his room key, he asked one of the desk clerks how he could go about finding someone in Norway for whom he had no address or phone number.

Without any attempted friendliness, she said his only option was to go the the national *Folkeregister,* the central registry where names, addresses, birthdays, and personal ID numbers for every resident in Norway are filed. In light of that information, Jason wondered for a moment if he was in a free country. He started to joke with her about it, but her serious manner changed his mind. He wrote down the address she gave him for the Registry.

He went up to his eighth-floor room, threw his bag and briefcase inside, then returned to the lobby and exited the building.

It was late afternoon, and he made it inside the Registry just before it closed. He found his way to the main desk, where an elderly woman asked if she could help him. Jason told her he had come from America to find his second cousin, Corinna Nykvist. When she asked for more details, he said he had heard about her through sketchy family records, and knew only her name and her approximate age, which was thirty-five. The woman hurried back to a row of at least thirty file cabinets, pulled out a drawer, and began looking. In twenty minutes she was back. She had retrieved the addresses and phone numbers of eleven different Corinna Nykvists between the ages of twenty-eight and forty-five. Two were in Oslo; the other nine were spread out over the rest of Norway. Jason thanked her, and departed.

At the hotel he immediately got down to business. He obtained a street map of Oslo from the front desk, pinpointed the addresses of the two Corinnas in Oslo, then found out that both could be reached by public transportation.

The first address was on the north side of town. He reached it by T-ban, the newly built Oslo subway system. The address was a hilltop apartment building sitting in a complex of fifty or so others just like it.

He checked the names on the mailboxes mounted just inside the main entrance to the building. Nykvist was on the sixth floor. He took the stairway instead of the elevator. It would give him extra time to relax and compose himself.

On the sixth floor he found the door with the name "Nykvist" on it, and nervously rang the bell.

When the door opened, Jason was frozen speechless by the unexpected. The person answering the door was a man.

"Ja, hva er det?" the man asked.

The man was at least forty-five. Could he be Corinna's husband? Jason had never even asked if she was married.

"Uh...yes," Jason finally said. "Do you speak English?"

"Yes, I can speak a little English. What do you want?"

"I'm looking for a Corinna Nykvist, a young woman about thirty-five years old. She works as an international courier. Can you tell me if this is where she lives?"

"The only Corinna here," the man said coldly, "is my wife. She is forty-four, and she is not an international cour...or whatever you said."

"Okay, then pardon me, please. I've come to the wrong address." Jason left as fast as he could.

Jason, you're an idiot, he told himself as he made his way back along the snowy path to the T-ban station. It had never crossed his mind that Corinna might be married.

What if this really *had* been the home of the Corinna he was looking for, and that had been her husband answering the door? It was clear how explosive the situation could have been. From now on, he decided, he would always telephone first.

Back at the hotel again, he marked off the first Corinna from the list of eleven, and started calling the other ten. He got an answer at only two of the remaining numbers. Neither was the home of "his" Corinna. He called the other eight numbers three more times each, but no one answered at any of them. It was Friday evening, he reminded himself—universal party night.

With nothing else to do, he went to the lobby newsstand and bought copies of *Newsweek* and *U.S. News & World Report*. He went back to his room and read himself to sleep.

The next morning he checked out of the hotel and headed for the downtown department stores. He bought a long winter coat he liked, along with snow boots, gloves, and a pair of thermal underwear. With a smile and a greeting, he set them down on the cashier's counter. After she totaled up the prices, Jason thought he heard her say in English, "That will be nineteen-hundred crowns and seventy-five ears."

He asked her to please repeat the total.

She said more slowly, "Nineteen-hundred crowns and seventy-five ears."

When she saw his perplexity, she explained that "crowns" and "ears" were the direct English translations of *kroner* and *øre*, the Norwegian dollars and cents. He handed over the money with amusement, until he calculated that he had just spent the equivalent of almost four hundred American dollars. *It might as well be seventy-five ears*, he thought.

"You're the kindest thief I've ever met," he joked with the cashier. "You just took all my money, and you didn't even use a gun."

He checked into another hotel forty minutes later, and had to pay with traveler's checks. The hotel was old and far below the standards of the SAS, but it still cost fifty-five dollars a night. *If I stay in this country long*, Jason thought, *I'm going to have to get a job.*

That afternoon he was on the phone again. When he called the other Oslo number, an elderly woman answered. She could understand English slightly better than she could speak it, which wasn't much. "Yes, I have a girl thirty years," she said. "Corinna is her name. She is jobbing with Internationale Forretning."

"Does she reside with you?" Jason asked.

"Jeg forstår ikke hva du mener," she replied.

Jason decided he would make an exception and go to this address in person. If his Corinna lived there, and if she was indeed married—well, he would think of something.

This time he took a bus. The address was a thirty-minute ride from the center of Oslo, in the more well-to-do west side.

Once off the bus, he spent twenty minutes walking around on the snow-covered streets and sidewalks, trying to find the right home. He was thankful for the thermal underwear, the coat, and the boots and gloves.

He finally found it. Sitting behind a larger house, it was nearly hidden from view from the street.

The old woman answered the door; Jason recognized her voice from his phone call. He tried to explain that he was the American who had called a couple of hours earlier. After a minute or two she finally acted as if that much had registered. Jason wasn't sure he had the patience for this. Then an idea came to him.

"Do you have a picture of Corinna?" he asked, enunciating his words carefully.

"Picture?"

"Yes. Picture." He pointed to a landscape painting hanging on the wall in her entryway. "Picture. Do you have a picture of Corinna?"

The light of understanding shown in her eyes. "Ett oyeblikk," she said, then disappeared into another room. Reappearing a few seconds later, she was holding a framed portrait. "My Corinna," she said.

Jason looked at the picture, and his heart sank. He had never seen this woman before in his life.

When he finally talked himself out of the house, he marked that address off his list. *Only seven more*, he thought. At least he was getting closer.

Riding the bus back to the center of town, he was more relaxed than on the trip out. He gazed out the window with an empty mind. At one point along the way the bus passed an old wooden meeting-house. He noticed the big red letters on a sign in front: "INTERNATIONAL COMMUNITY CHURCH—English Speaking." He made a mental note of it.

Back at the hotel he spent the rest of the afternoon calling the other numbers on the list. By late afternoon, after repeated dialings, he had reached someone at six of the numbers. None of them had heard of Corinna Nykvist, the international courier who had flown from England to Cyprus two and half weeks earlier.

He got no answer at the only number left on his piece of paper. It was to an address in Bodo. On the chance that Bodo might be an

Oslo suburb he couldn't find on his map, Jason called the front desk and discovered it was a small town north of the Arctic Circle. He was pessimistic. He felt his Corinna was too cosmopolitan and refined for such an out-of-the-way place. But he decided to keep calling until he knew for sure.

He went for a walk down one of the major pedestrian walkways cutting through the heart of the city. Like an unloved derelict he moped through the snow with his head half hung. He envied the people he saw passing him. He figured they all had families, friends, lovers. Lucky people, he thought.

He looked into the northern winter sky, already dark at four-thirty. He silently prayed: "Well, God, at least I've got you."

The thought of the international church came to his mind. It had been months since he had attended a worship service anywhere. Suddenly he found himself missing it.

By the time he returned to the hotel, he had decided to visit the church at least once. Today was Saturday; he would go the next morning.

≈ ≈ ≈

HIS CRITICAL TENDENCIES were strung like an arrow to a bowstring when he stepped off the bus. He immediately thought the meeting-house looked old and uninviting.

Inside, however, the environment was so in contrast to all he had experienced before that he didn't know whether to belittle it or chalk it up as a pleasant surprise.

Whatever this church was, it was certainly not pretentious. The interior walls were painted dull green, and looked even duller due to the poor lighting. Five rows of folding chairs were arranged in a semicircle. The speaker's homemade portable podium was sitting on a folding table in the center.

But it was the people themselves who presented the greatest contrast. Numbering about a hundred and fifty, they were the most hodgepodge gathering he had ever seen under a church roof. Every race and color of skin was represented, all mingling together easily. Some of the men wore suits; others were in casual dress clothes, jeans, or attire unique to their native homeland. The women's clothing was just as varied—expensive dresses, casual dresses, pants, jeans, a nurse's uniform, Indian saris, even a kimono.

He could somehow feel the acceptance in the room. It seemed obvious that everyone here, regardless of ethnic origin, economic status or educational background, was respected and appreciated. It seemed almost...well, spiritual.

Soon, however, he was disappointed. As Jason found the only empty seat in the back row, a middle-aged man with an English accent stood in front to begin the service. He was nervous and obviously unsure of himself. His shakiness made Jason tense, though he couldn't tell whether it affected anyone else. Jason just hoped the man wasn't the pastor. He really couldn't tell; there was no designated pastor's chair up front, as he was used to seeing in American churches.

After leading a few contemporary choruses from a spiral-bound book, the man said in his quavering voice that he wanted to recognize the visitors. Jason sat tight, but a few others were introduced, including a Swedish woman, a Filipino businessman, and a West African from Ghana. A man who spoke with a German accent introduced a family of five from Romania for whom he was providing temporary lodging. He said they were Christians who had escaped from their country four days earlier, and who were seeking political asylum in Norway. He said they did not speak English but wanted to come to the church anyway. He asked the congregation to remember them in prayer.

The man with the English accent led them in another song, then made a few announcements. This was followed by a special solo sung by a young woman introduced as an American student at the University of Oslo. She also seemed to Jason to be jittery in the public eye.

Jason's assessment of the church so far was mixed. It definitely seemed to have potential, but in his opinion it lacked the professionalism and expertise he had come to expect in successful American churches.

The meeting was then turned over to the pastor, an Oriental man who stood up from his seat on the second row and walked the eight or nine steps to the center. Though his face revealed him to be elderly, he moved with agility, and his hair was still the color of coal. He was short—only about five-foot-five—and his skin was a light brown. He was dressed in a bland pair of trousers and a colorful wool sweater that seemed to clash with his Asian face. On the whole, he looked a little unconventional.

As he stood for a few moments in silence behind the podium, there was something regal about him. He reflected neither the aura of obvious self-confidence nor the tense vibrations of nervousness. He simply stood, as if he were a nameless messenger divinely appointed by the Supreme Being himself. In that unspoken selflessness there was something powerful about him, yet unintimidating.

Under his leadership the atmosphere of the service now seemed to come together as something solid and strong. The man was definitely the church's spiritual leader; his presence alone said that. Jason sensed God himself radiating his royalty through the old man.

After the moment of silence, the pastor smiled kindly and nodded toward the first row, where the American soloist and the man with the English accent were sitting. "I wish to thank two people," he said with a heavy accent. "Thank you, Graham, for leading in our worship service for the first time. And thank you, Sandra, for your gracious song, your first song ever in public."

He then lowered his head and was silent for several seconds, as if waiting for God to settle something for him. Then he spoke. "My sermon this morning is not important. What is important is that this family needs God's special intervention." He was pointing to the visiting Romanian family.

"This family no longer has a home. No longer has a country. No longer has feelings of security. And they do not speak English. But in their new freedom, God has brought them here to us this morning. Therefore we must now be their home...must be their country...must help them feel secure.

"In the royal blood of Christ we are their brothers, we are their sisters. It is our duty to let God love them through us."

With that introduction he put his planned sermon aside. He asked the German man to tell the Romanian family that the congregation was truly sympathetic with their present situation, and that they wanted to pray now for the family's needs.

With that done, the old pastor asked everyone to stand, and to encircle the family with clasped hands. Without any awkwardness they responded. For all of them, it seemed the right thing to do.

When the family was completely surrounded by the people, the old leader asked them all to bow their heads. Jason sensed a feeling of sacredness and reverence permeating the meeting hall.

A man with an Australian accent prayed first. When he stopped, another soon began, then another, and another.

An hour and twenty minutes later, the praying was over. They had bombarded God with prayers of supplication for their new friends.

The Romanian family was in tears, and so were lots of others.

As the pastor dismissed the group, he asked if anyone had anything to say.

Jason saw someone whispering into the ear of the German, who then stood and said, "Above and beyond our giving to world missions, our treasurer informs me we have a surplus of a hundred thousand kroner in our account. This family," he continued, putting his hand on the Romanian father's shoulders, "no longer has a source of income. Most likely it will be a few months until they can get a residence permit and a work permit, and those will come only if Norway grants them political asylum. Therefore I propose that we give them one-third of what's in the account: thirty-three thousand kroner." In quick succession, a dozen or so people in the group stood to agree. A vote was quickly taken, and the decision was unanimous.

The church treasurer was already writing out the check while the German next to him was explaining to the Romanians what had happened. The Romanian father, his wife, and their three teenage daughters seemed dumbfounded.

Jason was awestruck as well. He quickly calculated that the church had just given away well over six thousand dollars.

The service had ended. Jason noticed the pastor had taken an inconspicuous position in a corner of the room. His old, thin brown face was beaming with joy.

Before Jason left the meeting hall, his hand had been shaken by forty or fifty people, all offering a sincere welcome and showing a genuine interest in him. He even received a few invitations to dinner, but courteously turned them down.

During the bus ride back to the hotel, Jason was in deep thought. Without a doubt he had been touched. Never in his life had he been in a church service so authentically Christian, so loving, so moving. He felt as if he had been transported back in time to a New Testament church led by one of the apostles. He did not know another pastor alive who would have spontaneously sacrificed his showcase Sunday morning sermon in order to pray for an hour and twenty minutes for a strange, lonely, poor family, much less give away a third of the church's money to them. He was certain the transcendent display of unadulterated Christianity he had witnessed was more than a rarity; it was a manifestation of something he thought was practically extinct, surviving only in New Testament stories and in preachers' idealistic sermons.

He was so attracted to the church that after an afternoon nap he felt compelled to go back for the evening service.

Before leaving to catch the bus, he tried once more to call the Corinna Nykvist in Bodo. Again there was no answer.

In the meeting that evening about a hundred people were present, sitting in a double circle. The Asian pastor passed out blank sheets of paper to them, and asked them to draw a vertical line down the middle of the page, forming two columns. He asked them to label one column "External" and one column "Internal."

"And now," he said in his gentle, disarming old voice, "everybody here has an image floating in their head of the ideal Christian. Describe that image in words. What does that ideal Christian look like on the outside? And what does he look like on the inside?"

For the ten minutes allotted them, the people wrote. When they finished, the pastor asked them to each take twenty or thirty seconds and read aloud what they had written. Starting at one end of the outer circle and continuing around to the last person in the inner circle, they all read from their sheets of paper.

When the reading was over, one man stood and said, "I need

to ask the Americans something. As most of you know, I became a convert to Christianity at home in France only five months ago. Now my greatest desire in life is to please my God. Several of you from America said the ideal Christian on the outside should be clean and well-groomed, neatly dressed, and things to that effect. This concept of the Christian testimony is foreign to me. But if it is really what God expects, then I want to know so I can make the necessary changes in my life. I need to be taught. So—what Scriptures must I read to learn of this idea that I should always look clean and neat?" His question was posed with obvious sincerity.

The pastor sat in silence, listening and waiting.

A woman with a Southern accent responded first. "Well, I can't pinpoint the exact Scripture for you, but it must be there. Every church in America teaches it."

Several others spoke up, and the discussion continued in a lively exchange of ideas, feelings, questions, opinions, and Bible verses.

The spontaneous interaction appeared to be something this group was used to, but Jason had never seen anything like it in a church service. It was as foreign to him as the concept of the "well-groomed Christian" was to the Frenchman. Jason found it, though, to be thought-provoking, invigorating. As a matter of fact, he downright liked it.

One of the Americans, a middle-aged man, conceded that the "clean-cut" idea was perhaps culturally influenced. He then nodded to a few of the Europeans, Africans, and Asians, and asked them to read again what they had written. "Hands that are willing to work hard," said one. "A tongue that speaks kind words," said another. And another said, "Ears that listen to things of worthwhile substance."

Soon the old pastor spoke again, his first words since the discussion started. "I want all of us to ask ourselves a question: If Christianity is present in a country for a long time, and becomes tightly intertwined with the culture, is it possible that Christianity in that country could become more defined by the culture's qualities than by the actual teachings of the Bible?"

Jason was thinking, *Yes—yes it is possible. I've even recorded that in my Wisdom Book.*

The pastor opened his Bible and read a passage from the book of Mark. Then he showed from the passage how the Pharisees sincerely but destructively passed off manmade traditions as the word of God.

That was all. He did not attempt to draw any conclusions, but simply ended the service with prayer.

Jason felt drawn to meet the pastor. When he walked up to him, the old man spoke first.

"I have watched you today," he said with earnestness. "My heart tells me that you have been hurt, that you are a lonely and searching Christian, that you are in a place where God is teaching you with much pain and many tears."

He paused, then added, "You need someone in your life who tells you that God still cares for you, someone to remind you that you will make it. You need a brother who listens and who understands.

"If you want," he said with caring eyes, "I'll be that brother."

There on the spot, Jason choked up and wept. Who was this man who could read his life, and who was willing to love a stranger?

When he could speak, Jason asked, "What's your name?"

"My name is Maung Maung, but that is not important," he answered. "You are important."

Suddenly, awkwardly, Jason felt loved in a way he never had before.

For the next fifteen minutes the old pastor bathed Jason in spiritual reassurances, building him up. And still Jason had not told him any of the details of his life, though he wanted to. He noticed other people still waiting around for some of the pastor's time, so he thanked the old man and said goodbye. He promised himself that he would be back.

As Jason headed for the bus stop, a man getting into his car in the meeting hall parking lot called out and asked if he could give him a ride. Jason accepted.

The guy was typically Norwegian, blond, tall, athletic-looking. He introduced himself as Sven.

Jason got in the car and told him where he was staying. Sven knew the area immediately; the hotel was just a few blocks from his office.

Jason leaned back in the passenger seat and said, "That's some pastor your church has."

"Yes," Sven agreed. "Yoma is one of the wisest and humblest men you'll ever meet. He really lives his Christianity."

"Yoma? He told me his name was Maung Maung."

"His real name is Maung Maung. He's from Burma, and Yoma is his Burmese nickname that everybody calls him. It means main bone."

"Main bone?"

Sven smiled. "The church is made up mostly of international transients who stay in Norway only two or three years. Yoma was the founding pastor, and he's about the only person in the church who's permanent. So we call him Yoma, main bone."

"He's such a discerning and compassionate man. How old is he?"

"Eighty-eight."

"How long ago did he start the church?"

"Twelve years."

"You know," said Jason, "with a pastor like that, and after twelve years, I would expect the congregation to be larger than it is."

"Actually," Sven explained, "when you look back over twelve years, more than two thousand people have been a part of it. Though—as Yoma would be quick to say—'That is not important.'"

They both chuckled.

"And maybe he's right," Sven continued. "But two thousand in twelve years is still impressive to me. And what's even more impressive is that under Yoma's ministry, twenty-nine men from eighteen different countries have become full-time pastors and evangelists and missionaries, all of them giving up their secular careers. And in addition to them, there are hundreds of men and women who were merely 'spectators' when they came into the church, but leaders when they left. They've gone back to their countries and become elders and deacons and teachers and Bible study leaders and so on."

Jason reflected on his own years in the ministry. He'd had more than two thousand people in his church, but they were all "yes" people whom he had beaten into mush. And only one young man from North Metro had decided to go into full-time ministry. He had entered the same Bible school and seminary Jason had attended; by now, Jason thought, he had no doubt been turned into a legalistic rubber stamp.

"So," he asked Sven, "how does all this fruit come about?"

"It's simple," Sven answered. "Yoma gets everybody involved. And when that happens, spiritual gifts start surfacing."

It dawned on Jason that the man who led the morning service and the young woman who sang the special music were some of the "spectators" to whom Yoma was giving a chance to develop. How many other pastors, Jason wondered, would risk the image of their Sunday morning service by letting novices cut their ministry teeth on it?

"So," Sven spoke up with an inviting tone. "What are you doing in Norway?"

"Right now I'm just an unemployed drifter. What about yourself? What do you do?"

Sven kept his eyes on the road. "I'm a police officer here in Oslo, working in narcotics. I follow up on leads, and arrest pushers, dealers, international smugglers—that sort of thing."

24

JASON PLACED ANOTHER CALL from his hotel late Sunday night, and learned that the Corinna Nykvist in Bodo was another stranger to him.

Weary of frustration, he decided to pack his few belongings and return the next day to the United States. He now feared staying in Norway—Sven might somehow discover he was a convicted and wanted "drug smuggler," and turn him in.

I'm so tired of being alone in the world, he thought as he dropped to his bed for the night. Weighed down with the oppressive thought of leaving Norway without finding Corinna, he fell into a fretful sleep.

But the next morning he argued with himself in the bathroom mirror: *Have you exhausted every possible means of locating Corinna? No. Then how can you leave, even if staying in the country is risky?*

And what in the name of life would you do in the States? Drift again? Get a mundane job? Live alone? No, no, no, a thousand times no! I can't endure that way of living anymore, not when I know Renée's whereabouts, and not while I still have a chance of finding Corinna.

So, it was settled: He would stay and face the danger of being caught, at least until he knew he had explored every reasonable avenue to find Corinna.

Besides, he thought, by staying he could continue attending the only church he'd ever known where Christianity didn't seem plastic or prefabbed.

After a breakfast of Norwegian musli and hard-boiled eggs, he put on his coat and snow boots and went jogging. Running through the massive public grounds of the city palace of Norway's king, he breathed in the fresh cold air and juggled ideas in his head for finding Corinna. By the time he was back in his room splashing warm water on his face to melt the frozen clumps of sweat and condensation hanging on his beard, he had chosen his next plan.

≈ ≈ ≈

AT THE MAIN DESK in the central registry he found the same woman who had helped him before. With his list in hand, he explained that he had contacted the eleven names and none of them was his cousin. "Are you sure the list is exhaustive?" he asked.

The woman took his list, marched back to the row of file cabinets, pulled out the same drawer, and began double-checking. Fifteen minutes later she was back at the counter, and assured him the list was complete.

"Is there maybe another way to spell Corinna?" Jason inquired.

"You don't remember how it was spelled in your family records?" she asked.

"No. I'm sorry, but I don't," Jason replied with humble sincerity.

"Well, is it possible the name is actually pronounced *Kar*ina?" she replied, stressing the first syllable. "If so, the name would likely be spelled K-A-R-I-N-A."

Perhaps, Jason speculated, he had misunderstood Corinna's accent when she told him her name. "Yes," he answered. "Perhaps. Let's try it."

Forty minutes later he was stepping out into the fresh air again, carrying a list of thirty-four Karina Nykvists with their addresses and telephone numbers. He took a deep breath. The ball was still rolling; all he could do was to keep trying and keep hoping.

He stayed busy on the phone the next few days, calling at all hours. By late Thursday there were only nine numbers left at which no one had answered. Jason again felt his chances growing slim.

There was a church meeting scheduled at seven that night, so he put away his list and showered.

The now somewhat familiar bus ride to the church's meeting hall gave him a chance to clear his mind. With more ease than usual he was able to put his soul into a mood for worship. As he

206

thought about what he had seen of Yoma's pastoral approach, the depth and freshness of it stirred something positive within him.

During the opening song of the service, Sven came in and took a seat next to Jason. When the time came for visitors to be recognized, Sven nudged him to get up and introduce himself. Jason stalled. He did not care if all the others knew his name, but he hesitated to let Sven hear it. Finally, after Sven jestingly elbowed him two or three more times, he stood and gave his first name only, adding that he was from the United States and was presently unemployed.

Graham led the congregation in six or seven choruses. Then Yoma introduced tonight's teacher as Praba, a preacher-in-training from Delhi, India.

Praba announced his subject: "God's Chain of Authority." For twenty-five minutes he outlined from several passages the authority relationships taught in Scripture. Then he concluded by saying that children were to be totally subject to their parents' authority for as long as their parents lived.

Jason looked over at Yoma, who was sitting quietly. He seemed to know what would come next, and to be willing to let it happen.

And it did.

With obvious respect and love for Praba but disagreeing strongly with his opinions, the Europeans and Americans cited other Scriptures and challenged his views on the extended authority of parents. "That's not Scripture you're teaching, Praba," one of them said, like an older brother. "It's an extension of your Indian culture that you've allowed to color your interpretation of the Bible."

Another Indian, an older man, voiced his agreement with the others and asked Praba if he would rethink his position.

Humbled by the extensive disagreement with his view, Praba said he would take into consideration all their arguments. At his request, the others repeated the references for the Scriptures they had quoted, so he could write them down and study them later.

Finally Yoma spoke up.

"We are learning tonight what we learned last Sunday night. We are learning that the diversity of nationality, the diversity of culture, and the diversity of background in the same church is good. Diversity makes you think. On the other hand, uniformity in a church destroys one's need for thinking. Diversity forces you to ask questions. Uniformity lets you harden in your wrong beliefs."

He rounded out his thoughts with a ten-minute discourse on the astonishing diversity among the twelve apostles, the men God himself personally handpicked to pass on the baton of Christianity to the rest of the world. United on the same team, for example, were Simon the Zealot—an anti-Roman fanatic—and Matthew, a committed collaborator with the Romans. There was the impulsive Peter with his secure belief in himself and his ideas, joined together with the silent, cautious, hesitant Thomas, who easily doubted everything in life. There were the brothers James and John, the boisterous Sons of Thunder so preoccupied with rank and greatness that one wondered how the other ten could possibly endure them—and how those two ever endured each other.

"Did not Jesus know," Yoma asked, "that to put these twelve men together would be an almost unbearable test for everyone involved? Yes—of course he knew," Yoma said excitedly. "And God used those strong individual differences as a tool to sharpen and define each of them into a well-balanced, insightful, effective church-planting missionary. They needed the push and pull of each other's differences. Their differences rubbed them like sandpaper until each of them finally shone like polished steel."

While Yoma spoke, Jason took notes—the first time since his days in seminary that he had written down the thoughts of another man's sermon.

Jason found his mind exploding with questions. He hastily approached the old pastor after the service. "Yoma," he said, consumed with his thoughts, "what about the American churches? They're filled with uniform congregations. They don't experience this diversity you say is so needful. Could it be that they're helpless victims of a single-culture environment, and they're pretty much locked in to an inherently weak system?"

Yoma responded quietly. "The church in America has a great potential for diversity. But Christians there too often run away from it. They start new churches to get away from diversity. Every city maybe has too many churches for the wrong reason. That's where the weakness lies."

"I see what you're saying," Jason responded. "And with so many churches everywhere, a Christian can shop around until he finds one that's totally compatible with his preferences and personality—robbing himself of a diverse environment and all its benefits. After all, as you said, Jesus himself made this diversity a necessary part of following him when he chose his team of disciples—and yet we in America go out of our way to prevent the very thing Jesus made compulsory."

"Ah, Jason learns quickly," Yoma said with a smile.

Jason would have enjoyed talking further, but cut his conversation short since others were again waiting to talk with Yoma. As he thanked Yoma and said goodbye, the old pastor invited him to attend a single-adults get-together the following night. Jason accepted.

On the return bus trip Jason took out a sheet of paper and began a rough draft for his next entry in the Wisdom Book: Diversity vs. Uniformity.

≈   ≈   ≈

HE ARRIVED A HALF-HOUR EARLY to the meeting hall Friday night, hoping to have time for a rich talk with Yoma. In the old Burmese man and his unusual church, he had found a pastor and congregation whose Christian language reached his mind, whose Christian ways reached his heart, and whose Christian presentation—void of heavy manmade baggage—reached his entire being.

But a lingering sadness dogged him as he stepped off the bus and walked toward the meeting hall. For the first time in years he was actually enjoying his Christianity, yet he still needed a friend —a woman—to live it with. And he needed his granddaughter to share it with as a legacy.

Jason entered the unlocked front door and was surprised to see Yoma and a young woman just as they were sitting down in the front row of chairs. Jason thought she must be one of the single adults, and had perhaps come early to talk with the pastor about a personal problem. They turned to see him, and Jason apologized and started to excuse himself.

209

"You are welcome to stay with us," Yoma said to him. He turned to the girl, and added, "It's okay. He is a pastor too. He'll keep in confidence everything we say." The girl nodded her assent.

How does he know I'm a pastor? Jason immediately wondered. *Nobody in Norway knows that.*

Jason joined them and was introduced to the young woman, Carole, a student from England.

Carole began telling Yoma about a variety of personal rejections that were making her life miserable, rejections she attributed to her unattractiveness.

In a world where beauty exists, Jason was thinking, this girl's physical appearance was not competitive even on a minor scale. She was ultra skinny and seemed to have an all-teeth face. In the worldly game of looks, she was definitely a loser.

Yoma, however, seemed to feel her pain. "More people are not beautiful than are beautiful," he told her truthfully. "Maung Maung is one of those not-so-beautiful.

"But we who are not so beautiful have a particular satisfaction that beautiful people never have. We know that those who like and love us do so with a pure motive. Our looks do not decoy them. They are drawn to us, not because of what we look like, not because of the pleasure we give them visually, but because of who we really are, because of the pleasure we give them mentally and emotionally. Their friendship for us is not hollow, is not easily uprooted.

"But Yoma," she said with exasperation, "There's *no one* who likes me or loves me."

"Ah...Carole does have a problem," he rebuked her tenderly. "But her problem is not that she is not beautiful. Her problem is not that she has no friends. Her problem is this: She dislikes herself. She dislikes herself so much that she thinks everybody else dislikes her too."

Carole hung her head. "Maybe there are a few people who would say they're my friends." Then she hastened to add, "But not very many."

Yoma thought for a moment, then asked, "How many people does Carole feel *should* like her?"

"To be honest, Yoma, I guess I'd like the whole world to like me."

"And if the whole world liked Carole," Yoma quietly continued, "would she like herself?"

"I think so. If I knew nobody rejected me—yes, then I would like myself."

Without explanation Yoma abruptly stood to his feet and walked several steps to a large portable chalkboard. With a piece of chalk he drew a large circle.

When Yoma now spoke, Jason thought it was almost with anger; yet the anger seemed directed not at Carole, but at the fact that she was hurting.

"Nobody is accepted by everybody. Nobody, Carole. Not beauty queens. Not American movie stars. Not King Olav. Not even the Lord Jesus.

"On the other hand, nobody is rejected by everybody either. Not the poorest man. Not the ugliest man. Not the meanest man. Not Adolf Hitler. Not even the devil."

With the chalk he scattered several dots around the circumference of the circle, and told her to imagine them representing the billions of people living on earth. "No matter where people stand on life's circle, Carole, it is the same: They have people to the left of them; they have people to the right of them. They have people who find them innocent; they have people who find them guilty. They have people who praise them; they have people who criticize them. They have people who like their flavor; they have people who don't like their flavor. And no matter if a person changes his body shape, changes his attitude, changes his personality, changes his ideology, changes his public status—no matter where he repositions himself on the circle, he will still get it from the left and the right.

"Carole needs to accept where God has put her on the circle. She needs to accept the body God has given her. She needs to accept the many strong points God has blessed her with. She loves children. She is a good speaker. She is a good teacher. She is sensitive to the hurts of other people. She is not lazy. She has good humor. She has the potential to be a good leader.

"If she accepts herself, she will not deny it when other people accept her, when other people say they are her friend. She will believe Maung Maung, for example, when he says that he likes Carole very much, and when he says Carole is a very, very special lady."

Carole had tears in her eyes. Yoma reached out and took her hand, then concluded his exhortation: "However, the most important thing is not whether people accept or reject Carole, not even whether Carole accepts or rejects herself; but whether God, the master and judge of the universe, accepts or rejects her. *And He has accepted her!*

"Carole!" he said, taking her chin and lifting her eyes to meet his. "*He* has accepted you! *He* likes you! *He* loves you!"

As Jason saw Carole break down in tears, he could not help wondering how many hurting people Yoma had helped in his lifetime. He shamefully realized that he himself had never had a heart for the so-called underdog. In a cold manner, without ever trying to feel their pain, he had always told them God did not like losers, and that's all they would ever be if they didn't somehow get their act together.

O God, forgive me! he prayed. *As I grow older, help me be a wise man like Yoma.*

≈ ≈ ≈

THE OLD WOODEN STEPS creaked in the cold late-evening air as Jason and Yoma climbed them. Yoma's apartment was on the second floor of the meeting hall, and was reached by this exposed stairway on the building's backside.

Yoma had invited Jason to join him for tea after tonight's meeting, and Jason readily accepted. They walked into a tiny living room. Through open doors Jason could see a tiny kitchen and a tiny bedroom with a thin mattress stretched across the bare wooden floor. Yoma quietly went into the kitchen, putting a tea kettle on to boil.

In the living room were three chairs positioned around a coffee table. Against one wall was a bookcase stuffed with dozens of record albums, with an inexpensive stereo system sitting on the middle shelf.

Jason seated himself in one of the chairs and watched the old man through the doorway.

"Yoma," Jason asked, "How did you know I was a pastor?"

Yoma brought in two plain white teacups and set them carefully on the coffee table. Then he answered in the way a father would tell a son something that should have been obvious to him: "Jason, Maung Maung has been around for nearly one century. Maung Maung is not blind. Pastor is written all over you. It is also written in many things you say."

He went back into the kitchen, returning soon with hot herbal tea. As he poured it into the cups he asked, "But tell Maung Maung: Why did Jason leave the ministry?"

Jason could not explain it, even to himself—but more and more he felt mysteriously transparent in the old man's presence. Jason found himself believing that Yoma had already discerned his disillusionment and the general reasons for it; only the personal details were yet unknown.

He took a sip of the tea, then said with sadness, "Yoma, have you ever had a family?"

Yoma read through the question at once. His eyes were instantly ignited with empathy. "Maung Maung now understands Jason's pain. If Jason prefers not to talk about it, that will be okay. I know such pain can stretch a man's heart and mind until the man is never the same again."

He spoke slower now, much slower, as his eyes seemed to look beyond Jason to something else. "Thirty-five years ago, Maung Maung lost a wife and son to Japanese war bullets. Still today I miss them. Jason's pain is much fresher. I understand if you wish to keep it inside."

In Yoma's presence, even more than in Corinna's, Jason suddenly wanted more than anything to pour out all the intimate struggles of his heart and soul. And as the night deepened, that is what he did. By the time he finished talking at 2:00 A.M., he had told everything there was to tell. Yoma now knew more about him

—his life, his failures, his feelings, and his longings—than anyone else alive.

Yoma remained silent for several moments. Then, with the sound of somber victory in his voice, he said, "Jason is an unusual student. He does not allow any of his pain to be wasted. He squeezes from it all possible insight and understanding.

"And now he articulates the wisdom of a broken and learned man. God is teaching Jason the language of pain, and Jason is learning well. One day he will become a teacher again, a teacher who will be able to help many hurting people."

Jason knew it was a deeply sincere compliment, and it did more to boost his sense of being than any he'd ever received. He felt as if God himself had anointed his wounded heart with a soothing balm, as if God himself had assured him he would not die to his Christianity after all. His spirit was soaring. Maybe there was hope for him as a Christian.

But would he really ever teach again? Did he really want to?

Yoma asked to pray with him before Jason left, and Jason bowed his head. When Yoma prayed, he prayed to the ears of God, not to the ears of man. Jason almost opened his eyes to see if God had materialized and was standing in the room.

As they stood at the door, Yoma said, "Here is a new entry for Jason's Wisdom Book."

"I'm listening," Jason smiled.

"Life Reviewing versus Life Regretting."

Jason got the message. He mentally filed it away for his book's eighth entry.

≈ ≈ ≈

JASON HAD ON HIS RUNNING CLOTHES by noon the next day, as ready as ever for a run in the bracing winter air. Both frustration and hope were fueling his urge to burn up some energy.

Despite his late hours last night with Yoma, he had been awake by eight o'clock this morning, and quickly continued his phone-calling project. By late in the morning only two numbers on the Karina Nykvist list were not crossed out, and he was mentally casting about for other approaches. If those two numbers didn't lead to her, he would simply have to expand his search. He would ask the central registry for the name of every Nykvist family in Norway. Some of them, somewhere, had to know something about her.

Meanwhile he had decided on an additional tactic: He would find out all the courier companies in Oslo that provided international courier service, then visit their offices and make personal inquiries during the upcoming week.

He stretched his arms and legs for the run, and was just walking out of his hotel room when the telephone rang. He stepped back in to pick it up.

"Hello, Jason. This is Sven."

In his sudden fear Jason said nothing, but Sven quickly filled the silence. "You mentioned the other night that you enjoy jogging. I like it too, and since it's Saturday and I have some free time, I was planning a run through Frogner Park this afternoon. Would you like to join me? I could meet you at the hotel in fifteen minutes."

Jason couldn't think what to answer. The questions rushed and tumbled together in his mind: *Had Sven already found out? Were the police about to arrest him? Was Sven following up a lead, trying quietly to find out more about him?*

Or could the invitation be entirely innocent? Could it be that Sven knew nothing, and wanted only to be a friend?

"Jason, is something wrong?"

Jason remembered his commitment earlier in the week: To stay and face the danger. If the Norwegian police really were after him, it was probably too late to run anyway.

"Pardon me, Sven. My mind was just preoccupied, that's all. Sure, I'll go running with you. I'll be waiting for you in the lobby."

Fifteen minutes later, Jason was relieved to see Sven drive up and get out of his car alone, dressed only in a few layers of sweat clothes. They shook hands. Sven told him it was a ten-minute drive to the park, so they got in the car and drove off.

Knowing Jason's interest in Yoma, Sven steered the conversation in that direction as they drove. Jason learned that the church gave Yoma a salary of three hundred dollars per week, but that he usually gave most of it away. Nobody knew exactly to whom, except that it was normally to strangers in need. They knew with certainty, however, that he had no bank account. He hardly ever spent money on himself, and never on anything he didn't really need.

Yoma was a vegetarian, Sven said, and took only cold showers all year round—"It's better for you," Yoma always tried to tell them.

As for Yoma's teaching, Sven felt that one of the secrets to its power was that Yoma always thought of himself as a student—a man who could learn from anyone and everyone. Because of all that he was learning, his sermons each Sunday tended to be unpredictable. However they were always insightful and biblical; and, as far as Sven knew, Yoma had never given a sermon a title.

Sharing Sven's obvious appreciation of Yoma, Jason found himself liking the police officer. But he still refrained from saying anything about himself or his past.

When they were back at the hotel an hour later, Sven mentioned that he was an avid mountain-climber, and that he would love to have Jason come along with him sometime and teach him the sport. Expressing genuine interest, Jason thanked him for the invitation.

≈ ≈ ≈

SUNDAY WAS DECEMBER FIFTEENTH, Renée's fourth birthday and the fourth anniversary of Hannah's death. In each of the past three years this date had brought a severe emotional downspin for Jason, and this year was no exception. Depression bore down on him, and he felt the strong subjugation of past grief. Carrying the criminal charges that now kept him out of England and away from Renée only made it worse.

At first he decided on Sunday morning to stay in the hotel and not go to church. He felt he did not want to see anybody. But after thirty minutes of wrestling with his emotions, he talked himself into putting forth the effort.

At the church, Yoma had also remembered what day it was, from his talk with Jason the previous Friday night. Standing at the podium for the sermon, he said first, "Today is not an easy day for our new friend Jason. Today, the same as many other days in his past, he is hurting very much because of personal loss. He carries an inner pain in his soul.

"But Jason is a very strong man. He is already learning much from his pain. As a matter of fact, the sermon Maung Maung will give today is a sermon he has learned from Jason. Maung Maung will even give it a title. He will call it, 'Resistance versus Routine.'"

In the next forty minutes Yoma illuminated several psalms whose themes were of strength, suffering, and dependence on God. He closed his sermon by saying, "An easy, routine way of life which many associate with stability and security only gives man stagnation. Entrenched routine only spoils man and makes him simple and weak. On the other hand, progressive resistance in life always has the potential to give man progressive strength, and to make man progressively wiser.

"The truth is this: Most if not all the true wisdom of God, the true insight of God, and the true knowledge of God that a man holds in his heart he has learned from resistance and affliction.

"Resistance makes a man think new thoughts he never considered before. It makes a man ask questions he never asked before. It makes a man seek answers he never sought before. It makes a man beg God for help that he never before realized he needed. These quests, quests of the heart and soul, eventually make a man deeper, wider, taller.

"Therefore man should fear the easy routine way of life that weakens, but he should welcome the resistance-filled life that strengthens and makes wise."

As Jason listened, he wrote. His mind understood the message, and so did his heart. He was probably not yet a true wise man, but one thing was certain: His struggles had definitely expanded his thinking, causing him to fearlessly ask questions and ardently seek answers. He had been taught much, and he prayed now that it was true wisdom he was learning.

He decided his notes from Yoma's sermon and the thoughts it had triggered would become the ninth entry in the Wisdom Book, to be titled "Resistance vs. Routine."

Jason was just writing down a lingering thought on the subject when he heard Yoma announce, "Next Sunday evening, Jason will share with us a truth from the Scriptures that he has learned with God's help."

What? Jason shouted to himself.

After the meeting was dismissed, several people walked up to Jason and told him they would be looking forward to hearing his message. But Jason was speechless, and felt his nerves tie up in knots.

As soon as he could, he worked his way through the crowd to where Yoma was standing. He felt annoyed, and it came through in his voice: "Why didn't you ask me first before you took the liberty to make such an announcement?"

Yoma locked eyes with him, not authoritatively or defensively, but in tenderness. At first he let his eyes alone do the talking. With their depth of human understanding and compassion, they spoke volumes.

Jason succumbed, almost as if he had been hypnotized. He closed his eyes and slowly forced himself to relax. Then he spoke again, the words coming from the ashen side of his heart. "You don't understand, Yoma. I don't want to teach. I'm not ready for that yet."

Yoma broke his silence. "On Friday night when Maung Maung first understood that Jason lost his family, Maung Maung thought maybe Jason was still too sensitive to talk about it. But when Jason demonstrated he could talk about it, and when he explained how much he has learned from it, Maung Maung knew that God was ready for Jason to teach again."

"But, Yoma, I..."

Before Jason could finish, Yoma turned away and left him stuttering under his breath. He could almost see through the back of Yoma's head to the grin of triumph on his face.

Jason turned slowly and left the building, pondering the situation. As he stepped into the parking lot where a few other worshipers were getting in their cars, a new hoard of questions swept over him. *Can I really teach again? How will it feel after so many years? Do I still remember how? Would these people want to listen to me if they really knew me? Has God forgiven me to the point that he will let me teach again? What will I talk about?*

He was lost in his thoughts when he suddenly felt someone take his wrist in his hand, and grip it firmly.

It was Sven, dressed immaculately in his black Norwegian police uniform.

Sven looked at him with cold blue eyes and said, "Is there something you and I need to talk about, Jason Faircloth?"

25

SVEN ESCORTED JASON directly to his car. During the short walk across the parking lot neither man said a word.

Jason began breathing heavily. He could tell by Sven's professional composure that his secret was over. He cursed himself. *I knew I should have left Norway.*

But how did Sven find out, anyway?

Yoma! Of course! Yoma told him!

A bitter resentment moved in and immediately supplanted the love Jason had developed for the old man. *Why? Why in God's name would Yoma betray me? Didn't he believe me when I said I was innocent?*

Sven led him to the car, and they both got in. Sven removed a page of folded newspaper from his shirt pocket, unfolded it, and handed it to Jason. "It tells everything," he said.

There, taking up a full eighth of the page was a black-and-white photograph of Jason. Jason recognized it immediately as a copy of his passport photo. But he couldn't read the accompanying print. It wasn't in English. He wondered if it was Turkish.

Sven spoke up again. "I had a Turkish teacher here in the city translate it for me. It says you were caught smuggling a hundred and eighty grams of cocaine over the border from Nicosia to Lefkosa. Claimed you were innocent, that you had been framed.

But couldn't produce testimonial evidence. Tried in a judicial court, found guilty, sentenced to twelve years. Escaped police custody en route from the courthouse to the jail. Injured a policeman. Stole a motorcycle. Still has not been apprehended."

Jason suddenly felt cold. Sven continued, pointing to the paper.

"You'll notice that someone has taken a red crayon and underlined a couple of the sentences. The underlined sentences are the ones that emphasize your claim of being innocent. Notice also this line extending from those sentences all the way to the margin with an arrow pointing to the other side." Jason turned the page over. "In the same red crayon," Sven said, pointing to some large, handwritten, block-letter words. "It's the name and address of a Nicosia hotel. Under it is the name of a Greek lady."

Jason's mind was having trouble taking all this in. What was this policeman saying?

"Apparently," Sven continued, "there's an underlying message here. Someone is trying either to help prove you're innocent, or to provide some kind of evidence to the contrary. I would like to believe the former." He looked to Jason for a response.

Jason's eyes were glued to the names in red. His mind asked the impossible: Could this somehow be the name of the hotel where he was set up—and the name of the pregnant clerk?

He was almost breathless. "Where did you get this?"

In the second or two before Sven responded, Jason thought of answers: Dimitri, perhaps, or the American embassy in Tel Aviv.

"I found it lying on my desk," Sven answered, "when I stopped by the office yesterday afternoon, right after you and I went running together. It was in a sealed white envelope without any markings—not even a return address. According to the officer there who signed for it, it was delivered in person by an international courier."

"A what? A...*who?*" Jason gasped. No, it was unbelievable—Corinna? "I mean, who was the courier? What was her name? Or was it even a woman? What was the name of the company?"

"Whoa, whoa," Sven said. "Let's take one thing at a time." He reached out and placed his big hand on Jason's shoulder to calm him down. "First of all," he began slowly, "tell me this: Did you knowingly have the cocaine in your possession when you crossed the border?"

"No!"

"You're telling me you're innocent?"

"Yes, Sven, that's what I'm telling you. I was framed! I was set up! I was conned!"

"Okay, okay...I believe you," Sven assured him. He turned and stared out through the windshield, speaking as if he were talking to himself: "So, it may well be that whoever sent this newspaper article, along with the written-in information, is trying to help prove your innocence."

He reached down and cranked the car's ignition. "Okay then. I'll take you to a restaurant and get you something to eat, and you can tell me the whole story, from the beginning."

≈　≈　≈

"HERE'S WHAT I'M GOING TO DO," Sven said, leaning his chair back from the table. For nearly three hours he had listened to all Jason had to say, constantly taking notes when he wasn't interrupting with questions and comments. His interest had deepened as the story unfolded.

"Pending permission from my superiors, of course—but I don't foresee a problem there—I'm going to contact the Greek Cypriot police authorities through Interpol and tell them I've received information from a reputable informant that will possibly disclose a drug-smuggling ring being operated out of this Nicosia hotel. And I'll give them this Greek lady's name, and suggest they check her out as a possible conspirator.

"If they take the information and act on it, and if they're able to find something incriminating in the lady's past and convict her with it, then I'll recommend that they interrogate her about her role in your accused crime. If they can get a confession from her saying she indeed set you up, your name will most likely be cleared.

"But—understand that this is a long shot. There are an awful lot of nonnegotiable variables involved. And if it does work out, it could take months. Just between you and me, though, we can pray and ask God to step in and make it work."

Jason grinned. "Praying about it can't hurt," he agreed. "Thanks, Sven, for wanting to help clear my name."

Then he asked the question that was still holding back his hope. "Well...what now? Do I go with you?"

"What do you mean?" Sven responded.

"I mean, am I under arrest, or what?"

Sven laughed. "Under arrest? You're not wanted here in Norway. I've already checked."

"So...you mean I'm free to go?"

"Free as a sailor."

Jason's relief was indescribable. "Well," he said, letting go a big breath, "now that everything is out in the open and I'm still—at least for the time being—a free man, can I ask you to do me a favor?"

"If it's within my power."

"Can you use your connections to find out if I'm listed as a wanted man in England?"

"It'll require some clever work, so as not to give away the fact that you're residing here, but I think I can probably pull it off."

"And one other thing, if I can be so bold: Can you please find out the name of the courier company and the courier who delivered the newspaper article?"

"Yeah, that won't be a problem. As soon as I take you back to your hotel and get to the office, I'll start working on all of it."

"Thanks again, Sven. Only God knows how much I appreciate all you're doing."

≈ ≈ ≈

IT'S PROBABLY NONSENSE, Jason told himself. It was Thursday afternoon, and he was riding the T-ban back into the central city to his hotel. He had just left the offices of a courier company, the third one in Oslo whose address he had. He'd visited all three this week—and Corinna wasn't employed by any of them. He wondered anew if he was being utterly foolish.

Yet for some reason he couldn't let go of the notion that she was somewhere in Oslo. He was convinced that she was the courier who delivered the newspaper article to Sven's office, though the more realistic part of him asked all the right questions to demolish that possibility.

222

How, for example, would Corinna know he had been set up by the hotel lady in Nicosia? How would she possibly know the name of the hotel, or the hotel lady? How would she know he was now in Oslo? And the most devastating question: If she had somehow managed to miraculously ferret out those facts, and knew he was here in Oslo—why would she remain aloof?

On the other hand, he argued, if the courier who delivered the article was not Corinna, then who in the name of logic could it possibly be?

He had been tempted several times during the week to call and ask Sven if he had been able to acquire the name of the courier. He talked himself out of it each time, not wanting to presume on Sven's graciousness.

Stepping off the T-ban, Jason decided his next plan would be calling every name in the entire Nykvist section of the Oslo telephone directory.

Back in his hotel room, he received another call from Sven. "I don't have time to talk right now," he said in a rush, "but can you meet me fifteen minutes before the church meeting tonight?" He was on duty, he explained, following up a leaked drug-smuggling attempt. He was on his way to a dock-side meeting with a ferry arriving from West Germany.

"Of course," Jason said. "I'll be at the meeting hall at six-forty-five."

After hanging up the phone, he prayed—with genuine sympathy—for the person on the ferry who was about to be caught.

That evening when he arrived at the church, Sven was already there. Jason joined him in his car.

"Good news, Jason," Sven smiled. "I've got the go-ahead to send the information to the authorities in Cyprus. I'll get to work on it first thing tomorrow morning.

"Also—and this news isn't so good—I was able to confirm that you're a wanted man throughout Great Britain."

Jason said nothing, responding only with a bleak expression.

Sven jumped quickly into the silence. "Actually I should say that *for the time being* you are a wanted man in Britain. But don't worry. We're going to do everything within our means to get your name cleared from their files. Hopefully, with God's help, you'll be able to get to England sometime within the next year and find your granddaughter.

"And by the way," he continued, "I tried to track down the name of the courier company and the courier—but it's kind of a funny thing. Nobody in the office can find a copy of the receipt. It's almost as if it disappeared. The officer who signed for the envelope can't recall the name of the company.

"All he remembers is that the courier was, in his words, a stunning Norwegian blonde dressed in pink."

Jason's bearded jaw dropped. And in the church service that followed, his mind could not stop thinking about the description of the courier.

It could not have been anyone else, his inner voice declared. *It had to be Corinna.*

≈ ≈ ≈

THE NEXT DAY he spent three hours at the Norwegian immigration-control office. When he stepped out of the building, he had both a long-term resident's permit and a work permit stamped in his passport.

It was a good feeling to have a more definite status in being here, especially since with each passing day he was feeling more compatible with Norway's climate, culture, and people.

The pleasant feeling was intensified as he walked away from the immigration office downtown and noticed the Christmas decorations being hung. It was only a week until Christmas, but for Norwegians the season was just beginning. He had learned from Sven that Christmas in Norway was a time of relaxation and deep reflection, a time when people wanted simply to enjoy the fun of winter and to contemplate the Christmas Story. The season would last until the middle of January. There would be family get-togethers, church services, candle-lit trees, homemade evergreen wreaths, special breads and cookies, and small, private parties.

In his hotel room that night Jason worked until long past midnight preparing his notes for his Sunday evening sermon. He stopped frequently to pray for God's guidance in this hesitant attempt to re-enter the pulpit. Jason had decided to speak on the subject of "Packaged Christianity."

On Saturday, with the help of some of the hotel staff, Jason scanned the newspapers for advertised apartments and set up interviews with landlords for the coming week. He also spent several hours working his way through the phonebook's list of Nykvists in Oslo. He was thankful most Norwegians could speak English.

≈ ≈ ≈

GRAHAM LED THE CHURCH in all four verses of a peppy song to begin the Sunday night service. Jason noticed, with new respect, how much more confident Graham was in his role.

Yoma walked into the service late, accompanied by a middle-aged American man. Jason had met him only two weeks ago. His name was Rudy, and he was a financial-affairs executive with one of the North Sea oil companies. He and his wife, Joyce, had been attending International Community Church for only a few months.

Yoma and Rudy took seats in the front row. After the singing, Yoma stood at the front, beckoning the American to join him there. "Rudy has something he wants to say," he announced, then sat back down.

Rudy began in a sober tone. "Most of you know me, and you know that Joyce and I have been attending the Sunday services since last fall. I've sat here week after week, and I must confess I've had my heart and mind blown away by the Christianity I've seen.

"Until I started coming here I was never interested in the Christian faith. Back in America most of the people who tried to convert me succeeded only in turning me off that much more. To be honest, I felt they showed little interest in me as a person. They badgered me against my wishes. It was as if they were forcefully trying to convert me for no other reason than to put another notch on their belt.

"But then I came here. I told Joyce—and by the way, there has never been anything wrong with her Christianity; as a matter of fact, her dedicated life has kept me from losing respect for Christianity altogether—I told Joyce last fall I would visit this church with her only once.

"But you people were different," he said, his voice beginning to choke. "You've loved me as a person. I've been in your homes. We've had meals together. You've made me feel accepted. You've even asked my opinion a couple of times about church administrative decisions.

"I've witnessed so many unexplainable things in the lives of the people here. And the more I've been around you, the more I've been provoked to think about God and how I'm accountable to him.

"I realized last night that I could not run from God any longer. So just a few minutes ago, at my request, Yoma prayed with me and I gave my life to Christ." He paused to regain his voice, his eyes shiny with tears.

"I've never felt so clean as I do right now. I've never felt so much at peace. But I realize I'm just what you call a spiritual baby, and I want to grow. So I want to end by saying that I need the help of you people more than ever."

While he took his seat, Yoma stood. He too had tears in his eyes, as did many others in the room. In a fatherly manner he closed his eyes and said simply, "Remember: Jesus compares evangelism with sowing seed, not swinging swords."

Then he prayed. It was the most powerful prayer Jason had ever heard. He felt awed and even somewhat frightened by the presence of God that seemed poised in the room. He wondered now how he could ever have suspected Yoma of betraying his trust and carelessly giving away his secrets to Sven. *Yoma would never do that*, he concluded, *even in the face of a firing squad.*

When the prayer was over, Yoma nodded toward Jason—his only signal that the time had come.

Jason stood. Rudy's words, plus Yoma's prayer and his brief statement before it, had resurrected in Jason's mind his former tactics of avidly beating the Bible over the heads of nonbelievers. He had undoubtedly been among the fiercest of sword swingers. He wondered if he had ever planted any true Christian seeds in anyone's heart in his entire life.

Now, taking his place behind the podium, he felt like a hypocrite. After all, he had never intended to preach again. He had made that vow four years ago. Now he was standing here in violation of those vows, in violation of his intentions.

He looked out around the double circle of chairs. There were more than a hundred people sitting around him, and they came from every corner of the world. The desire to be mature Christians was written all over them. They were ready for him to speak, to feed them.

Someone else should be standing here, he cried from within. *Someone more stable, someone more committed. O God, please help me...*

He inhaled, and exhaled—and began.

"I'm not sure what the situation is in most of the countries represented here tonight," he spoke softly. "But in America, based on my own observation and experience, it's normal for Christians to be given a packaged Christianity. Every aspect is tightly defined and outlined. And there's no admission of the possibility of errors in the way it's all put together. It's practically unforgivable for a thinking Christian to tamper with that packaged shape. Yet it's a form of Christianity shaped mostly by the mere preferences of men.

"And when man, with his peon thinking, packages Christianity to the finest of details, he is bringing Christianity down to a level that robs it of its three most potent elements: the supernatural element, the mystery element, and the faith element..."

For the next twenty minutes, Jason guided the group in exploring Scriptures that richly demonstrated each of those three elements. Then, for an illustration, he told how he almost lost his faith when God did not "perform" in Hannah's situation according to the teaching of his packaged Christianity—a package that said God must always, without exception, respond favorably to the prayer of unwavering faith.

"The Christianity I've experienced here," he concluded, "is a Christianity that sets God free. And you would not believe how refreshing that is for a person who comes out of my type of background. I've been a Christian for over three decades, but like Rudy I can say that what I've seen here blows me away.

"Don't ever take what you have here for granted. Thank God each day for it. And whatever you do, wherever you go, never let anyone persuade you to accept a Christianity that's packaged by man, no matter how attractively it's wrapped."

Jason sat down. He felt a strange fulfillment within. He felt as if he were somehow a spiritual survivor. To be able to stand up and preach again from the heart, after so many years of bitterness, was a step of victory—one that he had not sought.

Yet he was glad this moment was behind him.

After the service Yoma quickly approached him, looked at him with a mentor's eyes, and said with delight, "Yes, there is very much hope for Jason!" Before Jason could thank him, Yoma turned and walked away. Jason wondered why Yoma liked to do that. When he found himself immediately repeating Yoma's last words to himself, he thought, *Perhaps that's Yoma's reason.*

But he would have to think more about Yoma's words later. A dozen or so people were already lined up to express their post-sermon felicitations. The next fifteen-minutes-worth of encouragement and compliments were a thrilling boost for Jason.

The last person in line to greet him was Sven, smiling as widely as ever. He shook Jason's hand, then said quietly, "More good news: The office got word from the Cypriot police authorities about three hours ago. They've agreed to investigate the woman at the hotel."

He slapped Jason's back. "But if you keep teaching like you did tonight, we might never let you out of Oslo—whether your name is cleared or not!"

As Jason lay in bed that night, he felt buoyant, full of life. He even found his mind wandering briefly to an image in the future —a vision of himself holding Renée on his knee, stroking her hair with his grandfather's hand. He wondered: *Is God about to answer my prayer?*

In Jason's frame of heart tonight, he definitely believed so.

26

THE WEEKS ROLLED BY like playful children down a grassy knoll. By late January the Christmas season had become another memory. Jason secured a sixth-floor, one-bedroom furnished apartment near the center of the city, obtained a Norwegian driver's license, and bought a used Volkswagen Passat. With the help of one of the church members, he landed a twenty-hour-a-week job as a financial adviser for a sardine export company, offering ideas to help them increase sales to America. The part-time hours gave him time each day to pursue his other "job": telephoning all the Nykvist families in and around Oslo. He was relentless, refusing to give up his hope of tracking down Corinna.

More and more he fell in love with Norway. There was something endlessly alluring about the land's beauty, which he especially began to appreciate on cross-country skiing trips with Sven. The trips were breathtakingly fun for Jason, though Sven seemed to regard them merely as warmups for the real adventures coming in the summer: climbing Norway's mountains.

In Sven, Jason saw first-hand evidence of the Norwegian tendency to approach life as a modern-day adventure. It seemed to be part of an overall "enjoy life" philosophy—an easy calling for Jason to surrender to.

He found himself being raised to new spiritual heights by his ever-increasing involvement with the International Church. The services were still refreshingly unpredictable. On a Sunday morning in mid-February, for example, the Laotian wife of a British air force officer expressed a prayer request: She was asking God to send a Christian missionary to share the story of Christ with her Buddhist parents whom she had not seen in nine years. The church that night voted immediately to buy her a round-trip ticket to Laos.

As always, the services were filled with substance—the kind of substance that stirs hearts and souls and minds, substance that grabs and won't let go. God was working, visibly changing lives week by week.

The Romanian family was granted political asylum late in March. They enrolled themselves not only in Norwegian language classes, but also in English classes so they could one day take full part in the ministry at the church.

Jason often found himself having tea in Yoma's sparsely furnished living room, talking into the late hours with the old pastor. Under Yoma's wing Jason found himself being spiritually healed, and recovering the noblest of his former passions—to preach God's word and to practice the truth of the Christian message. This time, he knew, his zealous Christianity was different. The old passions had been resurrected in a rebuilt heart. It was a young heart, but a wise, sensitive, and nonjudgmental one. It was a heart that centered its understanding in an objective, Bible-based theology, rather than a subjective man-formed theology. It allowed God the freedom to be only partially understood by mortal minds. Jason was not following a God-in-a-box anymore, but an unfathomable God. Therefore his learning could never be exhausted. The pressure to be a know-it-all was behind him.

The more he grew in his Christianity, the more his thirst for wisdom intensified. By April his Wisdom Book totaled fifteen entries. And more and more he was mindful of trying to apply his accrued wisdom to daily life.

But throughout this momentum of personal spiritual revival, he waited. He waited for the silence of the Cypriot police authorities to come to an end.

Finally, late in April, there came a report that broke the silence. It was a telexed message to Sven's office. Following the case number and the name of the hotel clerk were these words: "No criminal activity uncovered. Investigation ended."

This time Jason did not question God with "why's." But his commitment to exercising faith in a sovereign and mysterious God still did not fully dispel his feeling of being divinely let down.

He realized that in all probability he would never get to see his granddaughter. He tried to come to grips with that fact, but could not. To concede to the permanent sacrifice of his only grandchild on the altar of the unknown was too much against his will and judgment.

For the first night or two after he received the news, even sleep would not come unless he first agreed to pay the ransom of a thousand tears.

Sven redoubled his efforts to give Jason moral support. They made plans for their first mountain-climbing expedition in June. They bought equipment for Jason and discussed everything that could be learned about climbing before the actual experience, especially the dangers. Meanwhile they also gave themselves to sightseeing trips, racquetball, and hours of heart-to-heart talks. Jason found Sven's honest-to-God friendship to be decidedly therapeutic.

And so was the explosion of spring.

With the melting of the snow came the unveiling of the land. By the last week of April all of Oslo was green and budding, and in two more weeks iridescent blooms were everywhere. With the city bathed in flowery fragrances and the warmth of the lengthening days, to feel sad about anything was almost an impossibility.

Jason was smiling again.

In mid-June came his long-awaited first climb up a mountain. Joining Jason and Sven was David Finelli, a 26-year-old New Yorker. He was a teacher and coach at the American junior high school in Oslo, and had recently begun attending the International Church and become a Christian under Yoma's care. The three men had chosen a relatively easy climb on one of the shorter peaks not far from the city. Jason found that Sven's months of exciting hype came far short of describing the actual exhilaration. Jason did well —and was immediately ready for something higher and harder. He was forty-seven, and feeling as strong as ever.

Back in Oslo a week later they joined in preparations for Midsummer's Eve Night on June 22nd. It was the shortest night of the year—in Oslo the darkness would last only two hours—and hundreds of thousands of people all across Scandinavia would be outdoors around bonfires to celebrate.

That afternoon Jason was out on one of Oslo's islands, helping five other men collect firewood for the International Church's bonfire party scheduled there that night. Sven, still on police duty, tracked him down there.

He was flush with excitement. "You're not going to believe this," he told Jason, half-laughing.

Standing with his arms full of dead spruce branches, Jason listened carefully as Sven stumbled through the words in his eagerness to tell what had happened. A week ago, he explained, the Nicosia hotel lady had been arrested for murder. She allegedly killed the man who, it turns out, was the leader of the drug-smuggling ring she had been part of. He was her lover and the father of her child, but apparently had proposed marriage to another woman. Out of jealousy she walked into his home and shot him early in the morning while he was still in bed. She called the police and told them what she had done. They found her sitting in a trance with her feet dangling in the backyard pool.

"She told all about the drug ring after her arrest, and even gave a list of names, from both sides of the border. It led to the biggest drug bust in the history of Cyprus: Nineteen people and four hundred pounds of narcotics.

"All the information was in a telex waiting for me four days ago, when we returned from the climb. I responded right away through Interpol, requesting the Greek police to question the hotel lady about her possible connection with you. They agreed, and I got their follow-up report today at one o'clock.

"Jason, the lady confessed to setting you up, and even identified you for the police from your passport photo that the Greeks had on file. So they brought in the Turkish police to question her, and she told them all about it: the wedding gift idea, the powder envelopes, the illegal visa—everything.

"The Turks," Sven announced with gusto, "have therefore officially removed your name from their police files. And they've already sent word to Greece and Great Britain to do the same."

Sven grabbed Jason's shoulders. "Jason! You're a free man!"

Jason dropped the spruce limbs to the ground and gave the smiling Norwegian the biggest bear hug he'd ever received.

≈   ≈   ≈

WITHIN AN HOUR AND A HALF of hearing Sven's news, Jason had packed two suitcases, notified his boss of his intention to be away for a few days, and begun the four-hour drive south to Göteborg, Sweden. From there he would take the next available ferry direct to Harwich, England. The trip across the North Sea would take approximately sixteen hours, giving Jason time to collect himself and plan his strategy.

He would be in London by tomorrow.

27

JASON DROVE HIS VOLKSWAGEN off the ferry and went through the passport control at Harwich without being detained. That one restriction-free movement caused him to cherish freedom a hundred-fold. He hoped he would never undervalue its greatness.

The ninety-minute drive south to London required extra concentration due to the drive-on-the-left rule. His earlier experience in Cyprus helped; so did the gray weather and unexciting scenery in the countryside, providing few distractions.

But the closer to London he got, the more anxiously he breathed. He was out of the secure surroundings of Oslo, and he felt it. He was alone again in another foreign country. Once more he was a stranger, a nobody. It was just him and his God.

His thoughts were weighted now with the past, and he suddenly felt scared. He tried to prepare himself for the worst. What if Cody and Renée had moved? And what if he could not find them again? Could he emotionally survive another letdown?

The last question scared him most. There was no one around him now to give him support. Why couldn't he just trust God?

His recently revived faith started to vacillate. Past memories raised their ugly heads, and he could not escape their stare—the memories of feeling like dirt in God's sight.

Feeling oppressively warm, even with the car windows open, he wound his way through slow traffic and countless stoplights on the edge of the city. He referred nervously to his map and his memory for directions to the suburb he had visited eight months earlier.

He should have been happy. Instead he felt sifted—sifted of his courage, his purpose, his hope. It didn't make sense.

Suddenly, there was the street.

And then, somehow, he knew Cody and Renée were not there. He could feel it. The neighborhood air was flat with emptiness.

He pulled the car to a stop across the street from the house. He stayed in his car, leaving the engine running, staring at the familiar dwelling.

He almost decided to get out and check, just to make sure. But then he changed his mind. Somehow he knew it would only be futile.

He laid his head on the steering wheel, but he refused to cry again. If Cody and Renée were not there, they were not there. He would promise himself not to think about it anymore. He did not want to pray about it either. He just wanted to leave.

He shifted the car into first gear. Before pulling out into the street, he looked in his rearview mirror to check for traffic. There was no traffic. But what he saw held him momentarily motionless. His eyes were riveted to the image in the mirror of a little girl, a little girl who looked to be four or five. She was skipping down the sidewalk on the opposite side of the street. Her dark, curly hair was bouncing on her shoulders.

Jason reproached himself for even thinking it. But when the little girl turned into the yard of the only London address he knew, he was suddenly overcome.

All of his planned composure was forgotten. He cut the engine and scuttled out of the car as fast as his body would move him.

He shouted the one-word question from the top of his lungs: "RENÉE?"

The little girl, halfway across her yard to the front door, turned in her tracks.

Jason moved away from the car and started across the street. His eyes full of mist, he broke into a half run. "*Renée?*" he tried to call again, but the word came out only in a choking whisper.

The little girl, obviously frightened, hurried up the porch steps and inside the house, leaving the door open behind her.

Jason was left standing at the edge of the yard, his heart pounding in his chest. He paused there for two or three seconds. Then, oblivious to everything but his powerful feelings, he headed for the front door.

As he planted his foot on the first step, a woman appeared suddenly in the doorway. She was wearing a gingham pinafore that looked as if it had been used to wipe up a pound of spilled flour. Holding a wooden rolling pin in her right hand, she looked silently at Jason with the eyes of a mother ready to manhandle anyone posing a threat to her child. Her blistering green eyes dared him to take one more step forward without an explanation.

Jason wiped the moisture from his eyes, and pointed to the little girl hiding behind the woman, holding on to her dress. "Renée Freedman?" he said.

Still tense, the woman spoke nervously, machine-like. "If you're looking for the Freedmans who used to live here, they've moved away."

"Moved away?" Jason asked.

She gave a stiff, affirmative nod, but Jason didn't see it. He placed his hand over his face, trying to sort out his smattered thoughts. "So...Cody Freedman and his daughter don't live here anymore?" He finally managed to force out the words. "Is that what you're saying?"

"Moved somewhere back to the States. In February."

"So, she's not Renée?" he asked, nodding toward the little girl. His mind wanted to deny the mistake it had made.

As the woman slowly moved her head from side to side, Jason turned and headed to his car.

He noticed the name "Murphy" on the gate mailbox.

≈   ≈   ≈

ON THE FERRY late that evening he sat in silence at one of the café tables in the aft of the ship, and did nothing but stare out the window at the churning water. He sat there for hours until his eyes grew heavy with sleep. As he headed for his cabin to go to bed, he concluded that finding his granddaughter was just never meant to be.

But as he lay on the bunk, his subconscious refused to put the matter to rest. In his sleep he was again staring at the blurring water. It was dark and secretive, but for just one moment he saw beneath the waves a little person, her head hanging down. Instantly he knew it was Renée; yes, it had to be. It was a little girl, his granddaughter for whom he had been searching so long.

In the fleeting glimpse — which was all he was allowed — he saw her chained, and alone, and extending her little arms. What was she doing? Why was she there? Was she in trouble? Why was she alone? Why had everyone forsaken her? *My God, I've got to help her!*

He awoke, sitting upright in his bed and shouting: "I'm coming, Renée! I'm coming!"

Sleep did not return to him, but the dream would not go away. What did it mean? Was Renée in trouble? Was someone hurting her?

Or was it nothing? He was so tired. Perhaps he imagined Renée hurting because he had feared it in his heart for four and a half years.

But why wouldn't the fear go away?

Wearily, he wore out all the questions, discovering again that there were no answers.

At about 5:00 A.M. he got out of bed, dressed, and went up on deck. It was time to give the matter to God, once and for all.

In the early morning light he stepped to the railing, and prayed.

"Lord God," he said aloud. "More than anything in all this world I've wanted to find Renée. I've been driven like a possessed man. You know that. For four and a half years I've tried my best to track her down, believing she needs my help. I've begged you.

My God, how I've begged you! I've begged you day and night to help me find her.

"And what have I gotten? Dead ends. Dead ends at every corner. Dead ends that have left me with pain. Dead ends that have just about killed me. And it seems you haven't cared.

"Well, I'm tired. I'm not going to look anymore. I give up!

"There! Is that what you want to hear? Do you want me to shout from a mountaintop, 'You win!'? Is that what you want?"

He bowed his head against the railing, and closed his eyes. His voice began to break with surrender. "I can't beat you, God. I'd be a fool to try.

"So, God, in spite of all my hurt, I'm just going to trust you. Do you hear me? I'm going to trust you. I'm going to trust you with Renée's life. She's yours. Take her. And if I ever find her, and if I'm ever able to help her, it will be only because you have chosen to make it happen. But if I never see her — so be it. I'll accept it as your will."

When he finished praying, he took a last, long look across the sea, then up into the dawn sky. It was silent.

He left the deck, walked down to his cabin, and crawled back into his bunk. He slept all the way to Göteborg.

≈ ≈ ≈

"LET MAUNG MAUNG give Jason a future warning."

Jason nodded his consent, ready for Yoma's boost of wisdom. They were in Yoma's upstairs apartment, drinking a cup of herbal tea following the Thursday night Bible study. After yesterday's disappointment in England, Jason had been eagerly looking forward to refreshment in the presence of this mysteriously wise and selfless old teacher of God. This was their first chance to be alone again.

Yoma, his worn Bible in hand, turned to Psalm 13 and asked Jason to read all six verses in the chapter.

Jason complied. He took the Bible from Yoma and read the psalm slowly and thoughtfully. Then he looked up to await Yoma's instruction.

"The chapter is written by King David. Tell me, Jason. If God truly forgot David, as David says in verse one—then how did

God at the same time truly love David unceasingly, as David says in verse five?"

Before Jason could frame a suitable answer, Yoma fired a second question.

"David also says in verse one that God hid his face from him. At the same time, in verse six, David says God was good to him. How does Jason explain David's contradiction?"

This time Jason made no immediate attempt to answer. He could tell by Yoma's intensity that the pastor was not yet ready to talk about answers.

"In verse two," Yoma continued, "David says he wrestled with many thoughts and had sorrow in his heart every day. But in verse six David says he sang with joy at the same time.

"In verse two David says his enemy was triumphing over him. But in verse five David says God was delivering him from his enemy.

"Does Jason see the discrepancy?"

Jason answered carefully. "Yes, I see what can possibly be viewed as a discrepancy. But I'm sure it appears that way only because I don't understand the psalm."

"Ahh...but Jason does understand the psalm," Yoma corrected him gently. "Yesterday, when Jason discovered that his granddaughter was taken away again, did he feel loved or unloved by God?"

"Not loved," Jason replied truthfully.

"Yes, Jason felt that way. But did Jason believe that way?"

There was silence. Jason thought about the question, then gave a sober answer: "No, I cannot say I believed I was unloved by God. If I really believed God didn't love me, I would have completely given up on him long ago."

"Exactly," Yoma replied. "Jason has felt unloved by God many times, but at the same time Jason has always wanted to believe the opposite. Jason has always wanted to believe God somehow loved him."

The psalm now clicked in Jason's head, and he looked again at the verses. "So, you're saying the apparent discrepancies in the chapter are simply the differences between David's feelings and

David's beliefs? You're saying David *felt* like God had forgotten him, while at the same time he really *believed* God's love for him was unceasing?"

Yoma quietly nodded.

Jason continued with excitement: "David *felt* God had hidden his face from him, but he *believed* God was somehow being good to him behind the scenes. He *felt* the pains of inner sorrow, but he *believed* he had every reason in the world to sing. He *felt* his enemy was defeating him, but he *believed* God's unseen hand would somehow actually deliver him from that enemy." Jason's face shone with discovery.

But Yoma wasn't yet finished with the lesson. "Does Jason also understand," he asked without any letup in intensity, "that King David's strong and certain beliefs about God's love and about God's involvement in his life were the weights that kept him anchored while the powerful negative feelings were trying hard to blow him away?"

Again, Jason thought. "Yeah, I understand. The very fact that David continued in his walk with God means that his beliefs kept him from being beaten by his feelings."

Yoma quickly drove home his last point: "Now—does Jason finally understand why he, Jason Faircloth, has nearly been blown away so many times in the last four and a half years?"

Jason felt as if someone had uncovered him, exposing a nakedness he had for years been trying to hide. He felt the revelation cutting him to the soul. In shame he lowered his head in the presence of the old man of God.

"Yes," he finally said. "I understand now why Jason has nearly been blown away so many times. It's because his feelings have been stronger than his beliefs. His beliefs about God's love and God's mercy and God's providence have been too weak and too uncertain."

Yoma kept silent, letting Jason be pierced by the truth of his own words.

Jason half lifted his head, and spoke again. "Is this the warning you wanted me to hear?"

"Yes," Yoma answered tenderly. "This is Maung Maung's

warning. Jason must once and for all decide what he believes about God's love, decide what he believes about God's mercy, decide what he believes about the misfortunes God allows in his life. Jason must know with certainty what he believes, so that his future will not be destroyed by the many strong winds of negative feelings."

It was true and Jason knew it. His four and a half years of wandering had left him teeter-tottering in his ideas about God's personal love and concern. He had learned many things, but his overall picture of God's love had been left abstract. Only during the last six months here in Norway had his concept of a caring God really grown. And that was due to Yoma and the International Church. They had prevented him from going all the way under. They had been his spiritual lifesaver. They had helped persuade him that God does love, that God does care.

Yes, Yoma was right. He had to settle, once and for all, his beliefs about the loving side of God's character. He already had his directive: to simply believe the person of God as portrayed in the Scriptures, not adding anything to the picture and not taking anything away. Yoma and the church had begun the process; now there was no excuse for allowing it to stall.

"Thank you, Yoma. I'm going to make that decision a priority. And if God lets me live, I promise you that one day soon I'll be strong in my beliefs."

Yoma's face wrinkled with an ancient smile. He placed a hand on Jason's shoulder and said, "Yes, Maung Maung is sure Jason will."

28

"SOMETHING ISN'T RIGHT, Francine," the nurse said, as she entered the central nurses' station on the pediatric floor.

A few feet away Francine looked up from the paperwork on her desk, which was stacked with folders and patient charts.

"She's been lying there six days," the first nurse continued anxiously. "The little girl—Renée—over in twelve. There's been absolutely no sign of her father. Not even a single phone call to ask how she's doing.

"And tonight she's scared. She misses him, and she can't sleep."

Her curiosity sparked, Francine took a folder from near the top of a stack, opened it, and began looking over the information inside. "It doesn't make sense," she said reprovingly. "The man's not even employed, so he should have the time. And he lives close enough. What kind of a father would stay away so long? Especially since the girl is without a mother."

She put away the folder. "What does Dr. Cohen say about her?"

"She'll have her leg in traction quite a while. She'll be here at least four weeks. And after that—well, it was the growth plate of the femur that was broken, right near the hip joint. So the leg will soon be outgrown by the other one. She'll most likely carry a limp the rest of her life." After a pause, the nurse's worried countenance gave way to a slight smile. "And she's such a sweetheart, Francine. You'll find out."

Francine sighed, then stood and abandoned her paperwork. "Well, since this is my first night back from vacation, let me go meet her."

She walked down the hall and into Room 512, where she met the wide, ocean-blue eyes of Renée staring at her.

"Hi, Renée." Francine smiled softly, and moved gently into the room. "I heard you were awake, so I decided to come and meet you. My name is Francine, and I'm going to be here all night long to help take care of you." She started to place her hand on the railing beside the bed, and was surprised when the girl quickly reached out to hold it.

"Where's my daddy?" Renée asked.

"I don't know, sweetheart. But please don't be frightened. If you'll help us, we'll all work together and get you well so you can go home and be with him again. Okay?"

"Okay."

"And do you know how you can help us tonight?" Francine stroked the girl's blonde hair. "By closing those pretty blue eyes and giving them some rest. Can you do that for me?"

Renée gave a quick nod and closed her eyes. Then she popped them open again. "Will you take me home?"

"Well, who knows?" Francine said. "When you're well, maybe your daddy will come and take you home himself. Won't that be nice?"

Renée gripped Francine's hand harder, then said matter-of-factly, "We live in Duffalo."

"Oh, you mean Buffalo," smiled Francine. "Well, guess what? This hospital is in Buffalo too! We're very, very close to your house right this minute. So you rest those eyes; then we can help you get well and get you back to your daddy. Okay?"

Francine expected another nod and at least a long blink from Renée, but the girl's troubled mind had one more question.

"Will Daddy hurt me again?"

≈　≈　≈

ROCK MUSIC WAS BLARING on Cody's car radio as he sat in the driveway of his Buffalo home. He was repeating the battle he'd fought every night this week, in the same place and at the same hour, and with the same result.

His late night hours spent with glasses and bottles and bets and barmaids and streetwalkers were over; now his fatherly duties were striving for what was left of his attention. The battle, however, was hopeless.

In his drunkenness he would think about seeing Renée, and for a brief moment actually plan to see her. Then he would hazily replay in his mind the afternoon—almost a week ago now—when he had last seen her at home.

A small patch of wetness was there on her pants, in between her legs, and he saw it the moment she came through the door. He yelled at her, and made her pull down her pants and panties. Then he shoved her toward the bathroom, hard, twisting her. But her little legs were caught in the clothes and didn't twist when the rest of her did, and something snapped, something broke.

He saw it all again—then immediately wanted only to forget it. He was tired, too tired to go anywhere now but bed. He wanted to forget everything. He wanted to forget life, though he wasn't sure why.

He couldn't even remember why he was here in Buffalo. Was it because he was afraid? He remembered his fear in Cyprus, when the apartment manager told him someone had been there looking for him. In London his neighbor told him the same thing. So he ran away, back to America. Maybe he moved to Buffalo because it was close to another English-speaking country where he could go and hide, in case he ever needed to run again.

29

JASON THREW A FIR CONE in the gushing water and watched the current quickly carry it downstream. It bobbled toward the next curve in the mountain river's path to the sea, and was out of sight in less than half a minute.

At first he hadn't even realized the cone was in his hands. He had been rolling it lightly in his palms while thinking, out here alone, about the decision he was trying to reach.

And now he had reached it: His search for Corinna was over.

Jason had continued to look for her after his London visit, though he vowed not to let it become a consuming priority. He had started accumulating the addresses and telephone numbers of all the Nykvist families in every part of the country. He decided to contact them at his leisure as a kind of long-distance hobby of hope. Now, two years later, he was satisfied he had reached every Nykvist family in Norway either by phone or letter.

Though he would have highly valued seeing Corinna again and having the chance to build an intimate friendship with her, ending the search was no longer as crushing as it once would have been. For some time now both his fantasy and his need for her had been diminishing. He had become so involved in the needs, feelings, struggles, and pains of others that his own interests were no longer preeminent in his life. He was finally learning what it meant to be a servant, what it meant to live for others. With a constant flow of people coming in and out of the International Church, he had no lack of opportunities.

He had also begun preaching two or three times a month in the main services, and was the designated leader of the church's ministry to singles. The singles viewed him as a co-pastor with Yoma, and Jason was constantly in demand to give them his time, conversation, and counsel.

There were also the frequent mountain climbs with Sven and David Finelli in the warmer months, and other sports and activities as well.

His life was filling up.

Being with Corinna, therefore, was no longer a pressing goal. Instead, she was a blissful memory, a memory of an extraordinary woman who had indirectly caused him to come to Norway—where he found Yoma, the church, and his own spiritual renewal. He would never forget her.

He tossed one more fir cone in the mountain stream, then walked back along the short path to the campground where the church was holding its annual week-long summer retreat. He was heading toward the dining hall where everyone was convening to enjoy an evening snack of Norwegian waffles and hot tea.

When he was almost there, he heard his name being called. He turned and saw David running lightly toward him on the path leading from the cabins.

"Jason! A message for you," David said as he approached. "Yoma wants to see you in his cabin when you're finished here."

Jason started to ask for more details, but David shook his head and kept running past him toward the dining hall. "I'm a waffle-maker tonight, and I'm late!" he explained.

Jason thought about following him into the dining hall—he was hungry not so much for the waffles, but for the lively spiritual discussions that occurred around the tables.

A touch of concern for his pastor, however, made him decide to turn immediately down the path toward Yoma's cabin. Yoma had not been part of this afternoon's activities, and Jason wondered why. It was not like him to not be where the people were.

When he approached the cabin—just a square room with a bunk and a table—he noticed that there were no lights coming from the inside. The door was half open. He ascended the three log steps and poked his head inside. In the semi-darkness he started to call Yoma's name when he heard a voice mumbling, "Come in, Jason."

He stepped in, and made out Yoma's outline kneeling on the floor beside the bunk.

"Are you all right, Yoma?"

"Kneel with Maung Maung, Jason," came the solemn reply.

Jason knelt at his side, his mind wondering what was wrong.

Yoma's tone was sober. "Forty-five years ago, Jason, Maung Maung heard the story of Jesus for the first time. It was in the year nineteen thirty-three. A Christian missionary from Britain stopped me on the street one day. He told Maung Maung in Maung Maung's language that Jesus was the same God who created Maung Maung, who loved Maung Maung, who died on the cross for Maung Maung's sin. He said that Jesus was the same God who resurrected from the dead, the same God who ruled the universe. Then he said to Maung Maung that Jesus was the living God who has ears that can hear, eyes that can see, a heart that can love, and hands that can help. He told Maung Maung that Maung

245

Maung's trust in Buddha was futile. He said Buddha was dead, that Buddha was not God. He said Buddha had ears that could not hear, eyes that could not see, hands that could not help, and a heart that could not love. With God shining in the missionary's eyes, he asked Maung Maung why Maung Maung believed so strongly in a helpless little piece of wood.

"Maung Maung never saw the missionary again. But the question the missionary asked...Maung Maung fought with it for many, many weeks. Maung Maung knew in his heart what the missionary said about Buddha was true. Maung Maung knew Buddha was only a piece of wood that had no life, no power. Maung Maung knew that, Jason—because Maung Maung had hoped in Buddha for forty-six long years. Maybe Maung Maung had hoped in Buddha more than most other men. For Maung Maung was the chief of the Buddhist council, the chief Buddhist monk in all Burma."

Until that moment Jason's knowledge of Yoma's past had been shrouded in mystery. There had always been something too sacred about Yoma to try meddling in his background. Out of curiosity Jason had once inquired about it, but Yoma had responded with such a strong and diversionary silence that Jason never felt the freedom to mention it again.

And now, here was a mind-boggling revelation. Jason had no doubt that Yoma was an elite person, but he understood it more than ever now. It was not that Yoma had been the leading Buddhist monk in Burma, whatever power and prestige that might have entailed; rather, it was the fact that Yoma had never exploited that part of his past to gain special recognition. Instead of allowing himself to be promoted as a prized convert to Christianity, Yoma had been simply a servant of all. For Jason, coming from a background where pushing one's superstar status was too often the forgiven norm, this sudden understanding of the depth of Yoma's self-denial made the old man's Christianity that much more stupendous.

Yoma, still in a state of calm earnestness, went on to tell about his Christian conversion five months after his encounter with the missionary. He had secretly obtained a Bible and poured through its pages, discovering for himself the truth of the missionary's words.

"When God showed Maung Maung the truth," he told Jason, "Maung Maung fell down before God with an idolatrous heart and wept. Two days later, when Maung Maung got off his face, he became a new follower of Jesus God."

Yoma described how he publicly denounced Buddha, at the cost of his position and social acceptance and nearly his life. No longer pledged to celibacy, he married. Then came the joyous birth of his son, followed by three years of happiness before the Japanese army invaded and left him childless and a widower.

The next twenty-two years, Yoma said, were a spiritual odyssey that brought him across the eastern hemisphere to Norway. Then came the past fourteen years of ministry at the church in Oslo.

"So you see, Jason, the International Community Church with its many spiritual children is the family God finally gave to Maung Maung. But Maung Maung is now too old to be a teacher anymore." He turned his powerful eyes to Jason. "Now, God wants to give this family to Jason."

Jason only now understood that the sharing of Yoma's life story was part of the old man's final preparations for passing on the mantle of leadership.

"For two and a half years," Yoma told him, "God has prepared Jason to be the leader for this people. God is ready to plant Jason's feet again. He is ready to use Jason's wisdom and Jason's broken spirit to guide this international family. God is now ready for Jason to resume fully his position as a pastor."

Jason was still on his knees and in silence, trying to absorb the full impact of all he was hearing.

"Therefore," Yoma concluded, "Jason must soon ready himself to take the leadership of the church. Maung Maung will talk to the church elders tomorrow morning."

≈ ≈ ≈

TWO DAYS LATER, on a grassy slope behind an eight-hundred-foot hill that shadowed the cabins, Yoma's brown, slender, ninety-one-year-old body was found face down, in a kneeling position. He had been missing from the camp for six hours.

There were no signs of struggle or pain. His death was as mysterious as his life had been. From all appearances, God had simply come and met him during the brightest part of the day, and walked his spirit home.

When he heard the news, Jason thought immediately of Corinna's words: "There are so few good people out there, especially good people who are not naive or self-righteously obnoxious." Yoma was one of those few.

≈ ≈ ≈

WHEN JASON STOOD to give his first sermon as pastor of the International Community Church, he made his message a tribute to Yoma.

"Yoma was a man who understood both people and the Bible," Jason said, "and how to bring the two together. His wisdom was extraordinary. His compassion was limitless. And his selflessness profound.

"Under his pure and powerful ministry, some twenty-four hundred people from more than fifty nations have been a part of this church, and one-third of them converted to Christianity under Yoma's influence. Many came out of Buddhism, Hinduism, and Islam; others out of agnosticism and atheism; and others out of plain passivity.

"For most of the others who were already Christians when they came to this church, being under Yoma's ministry revolutionized their personal walk with God. They will never be the same, and neither will those around them.

"Thirty-four men representing twenty different countries have broken up their careers and gone into various aspects of full-time Christian ministry. Hundreds of others have been changed from mere Christian spectators into Christian activists. They are now scattered all over the world, making an impact for God, and multiplying Yoma's touch.

"This is Yoma's legacy. Yet Yoma chose to die alone, not wanting any fanfare in his death, just as he had not wanted it in his life. I've never known a pastor, or anyone else, who tried harder than Yoma to quell a public build-up of himself.

"In light of his life, I can't help feeling that our twentieth-century churches have failed. At some strategic point they have failed to produce a generation of wise old men like Yoma, godly people who are indisputably wise in their Christianity and who know how to articulate that wisdom, people who selflessly take the younger Christians under their wings and teach them the beauty and power of unadulterated Christianity.

"Yoma's life and leadership should not have been considered so unusual. Rather, it should have been considered normal. For all of us who knew him, we can say that we have had the privilege of seeing what Christianity should be."

Jason lifted open the front cover of his Bible. The inside cover was filled with handwriting.

"I would like to read some of the statements I've heard Yoma make," he said. "Many of you heard him repeat these words many times, and they characterized his pastoring:

> *Evangelism should have as many different approaches as there are people.*
>
> *Christian growth is the lifetime process of personally discovering what is inherently valuable, and what is not.*
>
> *The local church should be more than just a preaching station where people come and sit front-to-back as spectators, and listen to a one-hour lecture before returning home. It should be a spiritual support group where Christians get into one another's lives.*
>
> *The essence of the Christian walk is to live contrary to human nature.*

"And finally, this one:

> *An easy, routine way of life which many associate with stability and security only gives man stagnation. Entrenched routine only spoils man and makes him simple and weak.*
> *On the other hand, progressive resistance in life always has the potential to give man progressive strength, and to make man progressively wiser....*
> *Resistance makes a man think new thoughts he never thought before. It makes a man ask questions he never asked before. It makes a man seek answers he never sought before.*

It makes a man beg God for help that he never before realized he needed. These quests, quests of the heart and soul, eventually make a man deeper, wider, taller.

"Of all the people I've ever known, Yoma was a man deeper, wider, and taller.

"When I arrived in Norway two and a half years ago and started attending the church regularly, I once asked Yoma why the church didn't take some of its money and have this old building renovated. Yoma looked at me with his teacher's eyes and said, 'Jason, the building is not important; the people are important.' For the next thirty months I saw him put that belief into practice.

"Yoma honestly lived for God by living for others. I know. I was one of those 'others.' My standing here today as your pastor is a direct tribute to Yoma's selflessness. He reached out to me when no one else even knew I was hurting. God used him to salvage my life.

"As your new pastor, I want to follow Yoma's example. I want to give my life away to people, and I want to stay in a constant state of learning. Therefore, as I teach you, I want you to help teach me. I need you to correct me, to question me, to challenge me, and even to disagree with me. I need you to keep me in check so we can all grow together."

≈ ≈ ≈

JASON HAD LEARNED the biblical concept of "teaching men to teach others" from Yoma, and in the next decade he put it into continual practice at the International Church. He became a master, like his mentor, at mobilizing men and women and helping nurture their spiritual gifts to fruition.

During that decade, fourteen of those people, representing eight different nations, became full-time pastors and missionaries to join the other International Church "graduates" scattered around the world. David Finelli was one of them, and after eight summers of climbing mountains together with Sven and Jason he returned to the U.S. to plant an international church in the heart of New York City, with full financial support from the Oslo church. The attempt succeeded beyond anyone's imagining. After two years Liberty International City Church had grown from five people—the number in David's family—to more than five hundred. The Oslo church was mushrooming as well. Even before David left it had more than doubled in size and was approaching four hundred people. The growth was welcome, but Jason saw that on such an expanded scale, not everyone could have enough opportunities for the active participation needed to discover and develop each person's spiritual gifts. The solution, Jason decided, was to divide the congregation into groups of about one hundred. Each group would be a self-governing, self-supporting sister church to the others. And each would be co-pastored by two men of different nationalities.

The plan worked beautifully. It provided smaller groups for more personal relationships, while at the same time mobilizing more people into active ministry roles. The division also developed a surprising camaraderie between the sister churches. They were still one big special family, and each of the four groups bore the same name—the International Community Church of Oslo.

In New York, David regularly corresponded with Jason and followed with keen interest the inception and implementation of the sister-church program. As his church in New York quickly increased in size, he and its leaders decided the Oslo model would be right for New York as well. But he knew it would take at least a year of hard work to get it going, and orchestrating the monumental set-up required more leadership than he could provide. He needed help.

Two and a half years after leaving Norway, David returned to meet with Jason and the Oslo congregation. He had a plan.

On a gray and damp October day, Jason went to the Oslo airport and met David on his arrival from New York. Traveling with him was Art Weizman, a Jewish Christian and one of David's first contacts. Art impressed Jason as a stable and thoughtful person, someone whose feathers never got ruffled. Yet behind his easygoing manner there was an obvious fire for God and for serving God's people. Jason's impression confirmed the positive reports about this new young potential leader he had been reading about in letters from David.

On the following day, Jason and hundreds of people from all the sister churches met together to listen to David's proposal, which he had already outlined privately for Jason. With a photographic slide presentation showing many of the people and places involved, David explained his vision for establishing as soon as possible a network of at least six sister churches located throughout the New York metropolitan area.

"As you in Oslo can appreciate, it's a complex undertaking," he said. "For example, it could take three or four months just to complete the logistical task of locating and securing the rental facilities that meet all our criteria, such as being strategically separated from one another, and being close to a subway station or bus stop."

The biggest task, David emphasized, would be selecting and training the twelve to sixteen men required for the co-pastor spots in the sister churches.

David ended his presentation with these words: "Your example here in Oslo is a unique and extremely valuable new ministry approach. And when it's carefully adapted to our conditions in New York, I believe it will be the answer to the overgrowth problem at Liberty International City Church.

"But, my brothers and sisters, the church has already outgrown my leadership capabilities, and I alone cannot implement such a huge effort. I need help.

"I need the help of your senior pastor—Jason Faircloth."

David's desire, he continued, was to have Jason come for one to two years and guide the New York church through this sweeping transition, just as he had done in Oslo.

The people then prayed together, discussed the matter, and quickly voted their heartfelt decision: By the end of December, they would give Jason up with full pay for as much as two years to help David achieve his objective.

A much wiser man now at age fifty-eight—and looking it, with his beard and hair that were mostly white—Jason was returning to America after a dozen years away.

He was going to New York.

PART THREE

1987-1989

30

"WHERE TO?" asked the fat driver of the taxicab.

"Three-sixty-eight Lakeview Drive," Renée told him, slurring the words.

It was two o'clock in the morning on December 16th. She had enough alcohol in her blood to make her legally drunk, but not enough to ruin her party spirit. Before attempting to crawl into the back seat of the cab, she put her bag of birthday gifts down on the snowy curb and gave her girlfriend one last thank-you hug.

"It was a great party, Cindy. Couldn't have been better."

"I guess I did go all out," laughed Cindy. "But you're worth it, girl. All sixteen years of you!"

"Oh, Cindy—" Renée said, starting to bite her lip. "I'll never have a friend like you. I wish you weren't moving. California might as well be China."

The driver tapped his horn.

"Well, I still have another week in Buffalo," said Cindy, as Renée turned with irritation to get in the cab. "We'll spend it together, I promise. Good night, Renée. I'd better get back and see if there's anyone else who isn't too smashed to go home. Oh, it's going to be hell cleaning up before Mom and Dad get back tomorrow!"

Renée laughed and stumbled into the taxi, waving goodbye.

On her way home she rested her head against the cab's back door, her mind replaying the evening's most memorable moments of dancing, laughing, petting.

Then she thought of home. She wondered if her dad would be waiting up to beat her again. She had grown to hate him. For as long as she could remember he had treated her like an animal.

She wanted him to die. That's how much she detested him. Three weeks ago she was utterly disappointed when the doctor released him from the hospital and said he would survive the close bout with death brought on by his bad liver. *If he doesn't die,* she thought, *then I will. And why not?*

She suddenly caught the driver staring at her in his mirror.

"Do you mind if I give you a compliment?" he asked nervously when he saw her look up.

She knew it would be nothing more than a pass. She wasn't naive. She knew how guys thought. She had given up her virginity when she was fourteen, and since then had had sex with four different guys. Men were all the same: They just wanted to have a good time with what a girl had. But for the moment, in her bitter contemplations, she felt she could use a positive comment, even if it did come from a bald, triple-chinned cab driver.

"Yeah, lay one on me, big boy."

Before he responded, the cabby first pulled the car into a small grocery store parking lot and stopped. He turned on the interior light. Leaving the car engine idling, he turned in his seat, as much as his extra poundage would allow. He looked at her, his face wiggling with nervousness.

Renée slowly slid her hand to the door handle.

"I noticed you when you walked out to the cab," he told her slowly.

"Yeah?" Renée responded coolly. "So?"

"I couldn't help but catch your limp."

"What about it?" she asked, her anger rising.

He grinned. "It turns me on," he said, emboldened by his own momentum. "How about it? I've never made it with a girl who has a limp."

She automatically lifted her arm. With her open palm, she wanted to slap him. "You pervert," she snapped, her voice suddenly filled with hate.

The cabby just sat there, frozen in awkwardness. His big face was an easy target.

Poised over her head, Renée's hand vibrated in its cocked position. But she never used it. Instead, she spat on the back seat of his car, opened the back door, and jumped out, slamming the door behind here.

≈≈≈

IT WAS 3:15 A.M. when she finally slid the key into the keyhole at home. Still tense from her experience with the cabby, she was no longer thinking about her dad as she stepped into the darkness of the front room.

When Cody suddenly grabbed her by the arm, she almost fainted.

"Do you know what time it is?" he growled.

She tensed, bending her shoulders. Out of habit, she readied herself for the expected blows. But they did not come.

Instead she found herself being pushed backward. Unable to oppose Cody's strength and his flabby 285 pounds, she was quickly pinned by her shoulders to the living room wall.

She could smell whiskey on his breath.

Only once before had she tried to fight him. The effort had only energized him into giving twice the abuse he ever had before. He had so bloodied and bruised her face that she stayed out of school nearly three weeks. She had never fought back since.

"Where's Vanessa?" she stammered, hoping to distract him with mention of his latest live-in mistress.

He ignored her question. He just stood there, keeping the pressure on her shoulders, staring at her through the darkness. Their heavy breathing was the only sound piercing the silence.

When Cody finally spoke, his words were strangely quiet. "Even in the dark, you're beautiful." He moved his right hand from her shoulder to her face-length blonde hair, and started running his fingers through it.

Renée automatically jerked. When she did, he returned his hand to her shoulder and slammed her to the wall again.

"What's wrong?" he continued. "Don't any of the guys ever tell you you've got a nice body? Don't they ever tell you how much you turn them on?"

This is absurd, she thought. She tried squirming loose again.

Cody held her tight, then stepped in closer and pressed his full body against her.

"Get off me!" she shouted.

Cody had his lips to her forehead. "You're not still a virgin are you?" he said sarcastically. "At sixteen? Do you need your daddy to show you about the birdies and the bees?"

"Stop it!" she screamed in hysteria. "Get off me!"

Before she could react further, she felt his lips press against hers. She suddenly felt sick. In a desperate bid to free herself, she tried to lift her right knee to his groin.

Suddenly she was being thrown through the darkness. She crashed over the coffee table and landed painfully on her back between the table and the couch.

Before she could recover, she saw Cody standing over her. Even in the darkness she could see what was written in his eyes.

She watched him unbuckling his pants.

Already realizing in sickening anguish that her words would do no good, she begged him:

"No, Daddy. Don't. *Please don't!*"

31

JUST OUTSIDE THE CUSTOMS AREA at New York's JFK Airport on the last day of December, Jason was greeted by a group of sixty excited people holding a banner that read "Welcome to N.Y., Jason!"

Their cheers and applause were triggered as David stepped out from the crowd to embrace him. Standing with David was Art Weizman.

Within a few hours, Jason, David, Art, and other leaders from the church had already begun a four-day council session. When the four days were over, their strategy for implementing the Oslo model had been decided:

In the early spring they would break off a group of eighty people from the central congregation to form the first sister church. Two months later they would break off another eighty people, then another eighty in two more months, and so on. The mother church, as long as it contained the bulk of the people, would continue acting as a support group to help each new church stand on its own.

Within each sister church, smaller cell groups of twenty or fewer people would meet together weekly for Bible study and prayer. This would provide an even more intimate spiritual support group for everyone, providing ample and needed interaction. It would also allow those with the gift of teaching to bring that gift to the surface in the small-group context. These people could then be groomed and trained to fill the ever-expanding list of leadership positions.

Jason would spend his time directly with each set of co-pastors, working with them night and day for eight weeks until the next sister group was broken away. David, meanwhile, would oversee the committees and make sure everything was running on schedule.

Hopefully, by the summer of the following year, the present congregation of 580 would be transformed into eight self-supporting and growing congregations, each with two leaders who were trained to mobilize others.

The plan was shared with the full congregation the following Sunday. A vote was taken, and the plan was approved enthusiastically. A facilities committee of twelve men and four women was formed to begin searching immediately for the right building for the first sister church.

Jason, for now, would concentrate on the task of training the co-pastors—of whom Art was the first chosen. Jason immersed himself in his new calling, particularly thankful that he had something to distract him from his difficulty in getting readjusted to America. David had warned him to expect a period of reverse culture shock, but Jason was surprised it was so intense and came so quickly. It almost threw his optimism off balance. After his long absence, America's peculiarities now seemed more pronounced and almost exaggerated. Americans seemed over-fat and over-loud, their cars too big, and their roads too wide. The women wore too much makeup, and the newspapers focused too much on crime and scandals. Americans seemed to shop mostly at gigantic stores with a ridiculously unlimited variety of junk, and to eat mostly at fast-food restaurants where the joy of dining was a joke. Most senseless of all was the incredibly fast pace of living that robbed everybody of everything but their unwanted fatigue. It all seemed so...so excessive.

He was already looking forward to his return to Norway.

≈≈≈

WITHIN TWO YEARS AFTER JASON ARRIVED, the people of Liberty International City Church witnessed a phenomenon they could only accredit to God. Their adventure and the fruit it bore was incomparable to anything the people had ever experienced.

Not only had all eight sister congregations been established on schedule—but each one had already far outgrown its original eight-people core.

When the first sister church to be broken away grew quickly to nearly one hundred and fifty people, Jason and David recognized the potential of keeping the multiplication momentum going. They immediately laid plans for that group to divide again, with one of the two co-pastors joining with each of the halves, and other co-pastors selected to assist them. Soon the pattern was adopted for other groups as well, and by the fall of the second year, five of the original breakaway groups had been divided again.

Now there were thirteen self-supporting congregations, ranging from seventy to about a hundred and twenty people each, and scattered strategically throughout the boroughs of New York. Following the example of the Oslo church, they collectively kept the same name—Liberty International City Church—and together elected David as their senior pastor. In a system of accountability, David and Jason met together with the co-pastors once every three weeks to report on progress, assess needs, and make decisions.

Once every six weeks all the congregations met together under one roof, usually in a rented basketball gym, to nourish their spirit of purpose. This group now numbered about thirteen hundred people from more than two dozen nationalities—an awesome reminder of God's power. At least half the people were recent converts, having been won to Christ by the other half. Doctors had come to Christ. Drug addicts had come to Christ. Entrepreneurs and street people had come to Christ. Even a professional ballerina had come to Christ.

With God's help the people had broken through barriers of race and class and religious backgrounds. They now stood together, united as Bible believers, learning from one another and having their hearts and minds stretched by the experience.

The church did not have a television or radio outreach, a Christian school, or an advertising campaign. But it did have people—people whose eyes had been turned upward, whose hearts had been conquered by the purpose of God, and who had worked hand-in-hand with God to bring about what had happened. In less than two years they had seen more evidence of a personal and life-changing God than most people see in a lifetime. And their motivation and mindset was not recognition or dynasties or fame, but simply *people*.

In the center, spearheading it all, was Jason. The church had been ripe for expansion before he came, but God had used Jason to give a fruitful direction to the church's energy.

At his insistence, the people acknowledged that Jason was just a servant and not someone to be put on a pedestal. Nevertheless they fell in love with him. They saw him as a mysteriously selfless and wise sixty-year-old man who symbolized the essence of Christianity.

They were saddened to realize his two-year visit was quickly drawing to a close. It was not that they feared his departure would leave their ministry void of direction or momentum; they had already learned too much from him for that. But he had worked his way into the permanent places of their hearts, into the kind of relationship for which goodbyes are never easy.

The person who was saddest was David. There were no mountains nearby to climb, and little time to climb them anyway, but he and Jason were together nonetheless, scaling other heights. Never before had David experienced a relationship with a man on the level he had come to know with Jason. Besides working with David, Jason was also living in an extra bedroom in the home of David and his wife Patricia and their three children. The two men had enjoyed a continual exchange of bold new ideas, serious reflections, confidential thoughts and feelings, tears, and even unrestrained laughter.

Jason was having to face his own sadness about the departure as well. David, more than twenty years younger, was like a son to him. So many others had also become like family to him. They had even helped him readjust to the wild American culture.

Yet his longings for Norway were also growing stronger. His beloved Norway, it seemed, was the land where he belonged. He was anxious to return to the people there and share in detail the marvels he had seen and learned. He was already savoring the quiet fireside conversations, the cozy teas, the walks in the snowy evergreens, and the grand vistas from the conquered mountaintops.

On the last day of November he booked his return flight for December 14th—just two weeks away. He wanted to be in Norway in time for Christmas.

≈ ≈ ≈

HE WAS DRIVING UP David's driveway, having just returned from picking up his ticket at the travel agency, when he saw Patricia come running toward him in an obvious state of panic. He immediately knew there was a serious emergency of some kind. He started to jump out to meet her, but saw her frantically waving for him to stay in the car.

She slung the door open on the passenger side and jumped in. She was colorless. "It's Art and Ginny—they've been in an accident," she blurted out. "Queens Hospital. Hurry!"

Jason had the car backed out of the driveway before Patricia could get her seatbelt on.

Art Weizman and his wife, Ginny, had become David and Patricia's closest New York friends in the months when the Liberty Church was first beginning, and the friendship had only deepened over the years. Ginny, with her vibrant and outgoing temperament, was the perfect mate for Art to help round out his ministry. Eight months pregnant with their first child, she was the happiest mother-to-be anyone could remember knowing. She was an encouragement to everyone who met her, and the church adored her.

As Jason raced the car through the city blocks as fast as he dared, Patricia told him through her tears that Art and Ginny's car had been hit by a truck. She did not know the details; David had called only five minutes before Jason had pulled up, and said only that it was bad. He had asked her to meet him at the hospital as soon as she could.

At the hospital they rushed into the emergency ward and found David sitting on the edge of one of the waiting room couches. He had his head in his hands, crying, and did not hear Jason and Patricia when they entered.

"David?" Patricia asked, her tone echoing her worst fears.

David looked up, his eyes bloodshot.

"*David?*" she asked again, her voice trembling. David looked at her, his beaten expression answering her question.

Art and Ginny were dead.

Patricia threw herself into David's embrace. Holding her in his arms, David looked over her shoulder in a broken, lost voice. "Why, Jason? Why did God let them be killed?"

Jason made no attempt to give an answer. He simply stepped in and wrapped his arms around both of them. He was smitten with grief, as well, and wanted to convey to them that he, too, was sharing in their agony.

After a few minutes of standing there, trying to absorb the shock, David began telling what he knew of the details.

Art and Ginny apparently had been on their way home from one of Ginny's pregnancy checkups. They were stopped at a traffic light at the end of a highway exit ramp. A flatbed eighteen-wheeler, loaded with several tons of lumber, had come down the ramp behind them, and the truck's brakes must have failed. Art and Ginny's car was crushed from behind, bulldozed across the street, and slammed head-on into a metal utility pole. Between the truck and the pole, the car was crumpled into a pile of twisted metal and shattered glass. Art and Ginny were trapped in the car for nearly an hour before firemen cut them free. Art was already dead. Ginny, with a faint pulse, was rushed here to the hospital, but died in the emergency room. The eight-month-old fetus died with her.

David first heard of the accident through a phone call from Frank, Art's brother. Frank had been contacted by police, and made it to the accident scene before the bodies were taken from the wreckage. It was there that he had pieced together the details.

Patricia's tears were streaming, and David was again embracing her. He was staring at Jason, his face an expression of a thousand questions and a thousand pains.

Jason knew they were undergoing a faith-shaking loss. From his own past, he knew that their lives in the next few weeks would be in emotional and mental upheaval, and perhaps spiritual upheaval as well. He prayed silently that their Christianity— far deeper and more solid than his was when he lost Lorene and Hannah—would stand up under all the negative questions and feelings.

"It's okay to grieve," he told them in a heavy-hearted but emphatic voice. "God doesn't expect you to detach yourself from your feelings. As a matter of fact, one of the best things you can do right now is to run to God and tell him exactly what you're feeling, even if the feelings are negative, and about him.

"Listen to me!" he said strongly, to get their undivided attention. "You have the right to share your wrong feelings with God, as long as your attitude is a help-me attitude and not a rebellious attitude. God encourages it. The Bible is filled with examples. Moses did it. Asaph did it. David did it. Others did it too. God put them there to show us that it's okay. He knows we need that type of emotional outlet. Do you hear me?"

With a new burst of tears, David nodded an affirmation. Patricia, however, acknowledged nothing. She looked as if she wanted to scream.

"It's okay for a Christian to hurt, Patricia." Jason spoke with quiet intensity, as if he were a father speaking to his confused daughter. He stepped closer to her and pulled her head to his chest, gently patting the side of her head. "It's okay," he said again.

Patricia broke into a muted scream of agony, and Jason held her while she wept.

Then he asked David, "Where's Frank?"

David told him Frank had walked over to the hospital's administrative wing to try to sort out insurance and other matters. David and Patricia agreed to go on out to the car to wait for Jason, while he looked for Frank.

Jason found him just concluding a conversation with a hospital official. Frank looked up when he saw Jason coming, and greeted him with a teary squint and a tight handshake.

Because of Art's influence, Frank had become a Christian three years earlier. At age twenty-six and single, he had become a rising young leader in Art's congregation. Jason knew him to have many of Art's strengths: stability, thoughtfulness, and compassion.

Jason spoke first. "You're going to make it, Frank."

Frank took a deep breath. "My gosh, it hurts, though."

"I know, Frank. I know it hurts."

"God understands too, doesn't he?" Frank's question was a request for reassurance.

"Yes, Frank. God understands. I know that, too."

"Then...do you think that, since you and God both understand—" Tears appeared in his eyes. "Do you think you might pray for me, and ask God to help keep me strong? I think I really need that, Jason."

Jason reached out and took both of Frank's hands, squeezing them tightly in his own while he prayed. He was still clasping them when he closed out his prayer.

He looked at Frank. "Is there anything I can do to help you here?"

"Nothing could help me more than what you just did."

"Can I help you by just staying with you and being company?"

"No, that's okay. I'll be all right." Frank's voice was like that of a hurt child, but one who was exceptionally brave.

Sensing that Frank wanted to be alone for a while, Jason promised to pray for him, then stepped away.

As he turned and walked along the shiny hallway floors leading toward the front lobby, he whispered another short prayer for Frank, then began praying for himself as well. He begged God to use him as a pillar of strength and consolation to those hurt most by Art and Ginny's death.

Still praying, he approached two large glass doors and failed to notice a young woman dressed in a white hospital gown and robe who was approaching the doors from the other side. He opened one door and almost pushed it into her, then caught himself. He stepped back, pulled the door toward him, and let her pass through first.

"Please forgive me," he quickly apologized, "for being so careless."

The woman shuffled slowly through the doorway without a response, without even making eye contact.

Jason looked back at her. She was young, perhaps in her early twenties. She had a detached expression about her, a look of emptiness. Her hair, reddish-black and unkempt, fell around a pale and overly thin face. Her eyes looked as if she had long ago given up on life.

Jason could not help but hurt for her. With all the other heavy weights now burdening his mind, he found himself feeling angry at the intrusions of pain that so mercilessly and randomly beat the life out of people.

He was suddenly wanting deeply to reach out and help the girl in some way. But he was only one person, limited and finite. And he was needed by other people, like David and Patricia, who were waiting for him now.

So he only stood and watched her passively, with an aching heart.

The young woman quickened her pace, and rambled away with a limp.

32

JASON CANCELED his scheduled appointments and spent the rest of the evening with David and Patricia. Frank, too, showed up at the house. Jason rustled them up a supper of soup and a salad.

They spent the evening making and answering phone calls, discussing the details for Art and Ginny's funeral, and praying together for Art and Ginny's surviving family, and for their congregation. They also made plans for the following day: David and Patricia would finalize the funeral plans, and Frank would make trips to the airport to pick up his parents and two other brothers, who would all be flying in from Toledo and Denver. Frank said he also had some insurance papers to drop off at the hospital, but Jason volunteered to take them by for him the next morning.

Jason's plans for his final two weeks in New York were simply to help out in the present circumstances as much as he could. "Dear Lord," he prayed, as he drove the next morning to the hospital, "use me as an effective servant. Use this tragedy somehow to make us all aware of how fleeting life is, so we'll give our priority to doing the things that count."

At the hospital he quickly took the insurance documents to the proper office on the administrative wing, then headed back toward the car.

Passing a waiting room on his way out, he happened to turn his head and glance through the room's open door. His feet carried him three more steps, then he stopped in mid-stride.

He walked slowly back to the door, and looked in again. There, sitting alone, was the hopeless-looking young woman he had almost knocked down with the door yesterday. She was facing a television mounted on the wall, but seemed oblivious to the cartoons that were showing.

He stepped into the room, but she did not look up at him.

His heart was captured again by the girl's look of detachment and aloneness. To him, the girl looked as if she were a sad and abandoned human island without a sole connection to the rest of humanity. He felt compassionate. And he found himself overpoweringly moved to say something to her.

He walked closer, and stood in front of her.

For the first time, the girl's eyes met his.

"I was just passing by," Jason said softly, "and I couldn't help but notice that you looked awfully lonely. I was just wondering if you might need someone to talk with."

"What do you want to talk about?" she responded distantly.

Jason's immediate impulse was to say, "Anything you want." But that sounded too vague. "Let's talk about loneliness," he answered.

"What do you know about loneliness?" she shot back cynically.

The distant look was gone from her eyes. *At least she's now here in the room with me*, Jason thought. He tried to sound gentle and defenseless: "I have been its victim a few times. And I know from experience that it can sometimes make you want to give up on life."

For a split-second the girl's eyes had a faint gleam, as if she thought she had found someone who might understand. Then they went defensive again, as if she were trying to hold in check a premature conclusion.

"You're a doctor, and you know that from experience?" she blurted out. "Yeah! From talking to your patients, maybe. But not from experience."

"I'm sorry," he smiled, "I guess I should have introduced myself first. My name is Jason Faircloth. I'm not a doctor. I'm just temporarily working here in New—"

"You're not a doctor?" she said roughly, cutting him short. "I thought..." Her face conveyed angry discomfort. She stood, and walked toward the door.

Jason responded, "But if you'll just give me a chance to—"

She was already out the door. Apparently she had no intention of talking to a strange man.

Walking to the door, Jason looked down the hall and saw her

limping around a corner into another hallway. He wanted to follow her, but didn't want to make a scene.

He let her go.

≈≈≈

TWO DAYS LATER Jason was sitting with hundreds of other mourners in the gymnasium where Art and Ginny's funeral was held. It brought to mind vivid memories of Lorene and Hannah's funerals, the only others he had witnessed that equaled this one in size.

As the service proceeded he was still reliving those memories when a young woman from Art's church began singing a solo. Jason knew the young singer—her name was Marlene, and Art and Ginny had visited her at random in her apartment sixteen months earlier. At the time, she was an active groupie of heavy metal bands. Pregnant with who-knows-whose baby, she had been only two days away from a planned abortion when Art and Ginny shared with her the claims of Christ. As a result of that visit and many others, and the subsequent discoveries that took place in her heart, Marlene kept the baby, eventually became a Christian, and let God turn her life around.

Her song, one she had written herself in memory of Art and Ginny, was about the life-saving and life-changing impact a dedicated and loving person of God can have on other people.

As Jason listened to the lyrics, touched by their significance, he wondered again about the lonely young woman he had seen in the hospital. Should he try to talk with her again? Would his persistence make a difference in her life, as Art and Ginny's persistence had made in Marlene's? Maybe he should not give up on her so quickly. To know that he could possibly make a difference, and yet not put forth the effort to find out, simply hurt too much.

As Marlene finished her song and David made his way to the microphone to speak the eulogy, Jason quickly promised himself he would try one more time. He would go back to the hospital tomorrow.

≈≈≈

THE NEXT MORNING Jason was one huge, sympathetic heart yearning to help someone.

After asking for the young woman by description, Jason was

given her room number. He found her there, sitting asleep in a chair. He head was leaning sideways, resting against a corner wall. Her arms were crossed and her legs were tucked under her, as if she were either cold or frightened.

Jason stared at her for a few moments. He noticed her face had a worn and beaten look about it, as if it had been made to look old before its time. As he stared more intently, he noticed that hidden beneath those telltale signs of excessive experience and heartache there seemed to be a latent youthfulness and a potential beauty. It led Jason to change his mind about the girl's age. He guessed that instead of being in her twenties, she was probably still a teenager, maybe eighteen or nineteen. And it now appeared obvious that the reddish-black color of her hair had come out of a bottle.

His eyes then were drawn to one of her crossed arms that was exposed below the elbow-length sleeve of her gown. It was massively scarred with needle marks. He wondered if the heroin use had been the cause of her problems, or only a symptom.

He prayed, asking God to help him show her the way of hope.

He started to sit on the edge of her bed and wait. Then he decided it would be less awkward for her to be awakened by his nudge than to wake up on her own and find him just sitting there. He decided to wake her.

Before he did, he disappeared from the room for a few minutes and came back with a cup of coffee, reasoning that it would make him look less threatening.

He then squatted at her side, another nonaggressive gesture, and reached out and silently shook her arm.

"Wake up," he said tenderly. "I've got something for you."

When she opened her eyes, when flinched strongly, as if she thought someone was going to strike her. The movement caught Jason by surprise.

"I'm sorry," he apologized quickly but softly, "I didn't mean to scare you."

"What?" she demanded as her eyes tried to focus on him. "Who are you? What do you want?" she asked, with a mixture of confusion and fear. She was curled up in the chair frightened.

Jason instinctively started to reach out and touch her arm again, but in light of her apparent fear he let his hand rest on the chair arm instead. "I'm a pastor," he said calmly. "I met you in the TV room about three days ago. Remember? I just came by to try to talk to you again. I want to be your friend."

The girl just gazed at him, apparently recognizing his face, but still leery.

"It's a cold day outside," he spoke again, interrupting her stare of confusion and suspicion. "I thought maybe you would like a cup of hot coffee." He held out the still-steaming drink so she could take it.

She looked unsure of what to do, as if no one had ever politely served her anything before. Finally she reached out nervously and took the cup. "I don't understand," she half-muttered. "What is it you want from me?"

"I just want you to let me be your friend, that's all," he said warmly.

"I still don't understand. I don't even know you." Tears appeared in the corners of her eyes. "Why do you want to be my friend?" Her voice was trembling.

"Do you have any friends?" Jason responded. He guessed the truth before she answered.

"Yes, I..." She paused, and her shoulders sagged. "No, I haven't got any friends."

"Then that's why I want to be your friend."

She took a sip of coffee, still looking as if she wondered what he really wanted.

"The doctors—they told you about me, didn't they? They sent you in to talk to me."

"No, I'm not connected to the hospital," he said persuasively. "My name is Jason."

His voice still gentle and warm, he went on to patiently tell her more about himself, his reason for being in New York, and his reasons for recently coming here to the hospital.

She listened, hearing every word.

"And no," he said in a level voice, "nobody has told me anything about you. The only thing I know about you is what I've seen written in your eyes and in your face."

"And what's that?" she replied defensively, suddenly sounding more like a teenager.

Jason answered softly, sympathetically. "Loneliness. Hopelessness. Misery. Depression."

"And so you've come to tell me about God, or preach to me, or what?" Her tears had vanished. She appeared on the verge of getting upset.

Jason so greatly wanted a chance to get into her life somehow. He could feel the reflection of her fear and her emptiness. He knew what the girl needed. She needed hope. She needed God.

God help me, Jason prayed, and he almost started to cry.

"Yes," he conceded, "I want to tell you about God."

"Well, don't bother," she snapped. "I've never seen any evidence of him. I don't believe in him."

Eighteen years earlier, Jason most likely would have reacted to such a response by thinking, *Go to hell, then,* and walking out. But in those years he had learned what it was like to be alone, cynical, and without hope.

He had already decided to be persistent in his effort to reach this girl for Christ. But he knew he had less than two weeks left in New York. In the meantime he wanted to introduce her to a lot of potential friends—people from the church, people who would gladly befriend and help her.

"Well, even if you don't believe in God," he said, without losing any of his positiveness, "and even if you refuse to let me tell you why I do, I would still like to be your friend."

He saw the tension slowly leave her. She sat speechless, searching for what to say.

"You really mean that, don't you?" she finally asked, with confusion in her voice.

"Listen," Jason said with a smile of relief. "People can't live without hope. We both know that. Now, I've only got a week and a half before I fly back to Norway, and I know that's not a lot of time. But I can't think of anything that would make me happier than to be able to visit you every day during that time, and just be a supportive friend. And I'd like to introduce you to some other guys and girls living here in New York who can open up their lives to you as well."

The confusion was gone from her face. Instead she now looked as if she simply didn't care.

"Look," she said, "I'm not just a lonely girl who doesn't have any friends. I'm a hooker, a drug addict, and an alcoholic. Life doesn't hold anything for me anymore. Do you understand? I really don't want to make any friends. I just want to die."

The truth didn't scare him away. Jason reached out and placed his old hand on her young shoulder. With a spirit of purpose, he dared to ignore her statement of self-rejection. "How much longer are you going to be here," he asked.

"About two weeks," she said, looking confused again.

"Okay, then," Jason said. He smiled, and gave a squeeze to her shoulder. "I'll be here every morning at nine o'clock."

She was speechless again.

"By the way," Jason asked as he stood to leave. "What's your name?"

She paused as if wondering again if this man was for real. "You must be crazy," she said, a crooked smile breaking out on her face. "But if you really want to know, my name is Daytona. Daytona Richards."

33

WHEN DAYTONA SAW the flowers in his hand the next morning—a half-dozen long-stemmed red roses—she did not know quite how to respond. Jason's way of relating was totally foreign to her. This was the first time in her life a man had given her flowers. Her suspicion still fought to convince her that his kindness was for an ulterior motive. Nevertheless, she appreciated the new attention.

"They're pretty. Thank you."

"Any lady stuck in a hospital deserves some flowers," Jason replied.

After a moment Daytona said slowly, "I told you yesterday I'm nothing but a cheap hooker. So why are you trying to treat me like a lady?"

As before, Jason could almost hear the self-hate in her voice. "If God is willing," he said, "to forgive people and forget their past, then I would be a real hypocrite not to do the same—especially since I'm one of those whom he's forgiven."

"What have you done that was so wrong?" she asked.

Jason closed his eyes. "I'm a murderer," he said. "I took the lives of two human beings: my wife, and my teenage daughter."

Daytona looked at him skeptically. It was not that she put it beyond anyone to commit such a hideous crime; her life had already revealed to her the evil a man can do. But Jason, in her opinion, appeared far too sensitive and considerate.

Jason saw her disbelief. "It was eighteen years ago," he told her. "I didn't kill them premeditatively, with a physical weapon. But I drove them to their deaths just the same—through emotional abuse."

"What did you do?" Daytona asked, her voice low-keyed.

To answer her question, Jason decided to go ahead and tell her his life story, praying as he did that it might establish a common bond with her.

He told her first about his family, then his early years in the ministry. He told her about his destructive attitude, and how, step by step, it had worn down Lorene and Hannah to levels of intolerance. He told how Hannah ran away and was missing for eighteen months. He told about Hannah's marriage, her child, and her death. He told about Lorene's death, and his own subsequent disillusionment, his leaving the church, and his suicide attempt. He told about his search for Hannah's baby, his granddaughter, whom he had never found.

Daytona was listening, almost spellbound.

"At one point," Jason told her, "I traced her to London, only to find that her dad had taken her for a long stay in the Mediterranean."

At those words, Daytona quickly shifted her eyes to the window, and stared through the glass with consternation. A London row-house had flashed in her mind. So had the Sphinx. But she did not know why. She did not even know what the Sphinx was. Why had such a strange sight suddenly come into her mind? And the house—it was like no other architecture she was familiar with.

The thoughts were awkward, mysterious.

Jason stopped in the middle of his next sentence, and asked, "Are you okay?"

Daytona snapped out of her puzzlement. "Oh...yeah, sure. I'm fine. I just got lost in some crazy thoughts, that's all."

Jason paused, wanting to be sensitive. "Anything you feel a need to talk about?" he asked. "I don't have to finish my story. I guess it was maybe starting to get too long, anyway."

"No, no," Daytona said assuredly, slightly shaking her head. "It's really nothing worth talking about. Besides, I want you to finish your story."

The common denominators of pain, loneliness, hopelessness, and confusion were already drawing her to Jason. The law of So-I'm-not-alone—you've-been-there-too was in effect. "I want to know what happened," she said.

What was exceptionally interesting to her was that Jason, who according to his own words had once almost given up on life, now appeared to be so normal, so stable. He could talk about his past so openly. He had learned so much from his struggles, it seemed. He had won. He was a conqueror, a survivor. He had beaten the odds.

She continued listening as Jason told about his drug escapade, his flight to Norway, and the healing and restoration he found there.

"God, how I envy you," she finally told him. "After all you've been through, you seem so happy now."

Jason's response was simple and straightforward. "Just as there was hope for me, there's hope for you too, Daytona. You don't have to lie down and let life beat you."

The words, spoken with such certainty, sparked a flicker of hope in Daytona's heart. But it died out almost as quickly as it had come to life. She wanted so much to believe there was hope, but it seemed like a ghostly tease. To grasp for it seemed both futile and punitive.

"I only wish!" she said, resigned to her emotional wasteland. "But it'll never happen. Not for me. It's already too late."

Jason probed cautiously. "Can you talk about it?"

Daytona wanted to open up. Sitting before her was a caring individual, the first person who had ever wanted to share and understand her pains. But to tell him about all those pains was to relive them one by one, and she so desperately wanted to forget them. They were her enemies.

Already she started to quiver, as if she suddenly was chilled. She buried her face in her hands, and began sobbing.

Slowly Jason placed a hand on her shoulder, refusing to say anything.

A minute later, Daytona lifted her head. "All right," she said in a downbeat tone. She was wiping away some tears from her face, and trying to hold back another flow. "I'll talk about it."

She swallowed, paused...then began.

"My father raped me on my sixteenth birthday," she said, forcing herself to be brave. "It was almost exactly two years ago. That was the beginning of the end."

All of Jason's sympathies were immediately engaged. He realized at once that he would need to handpick the person from the church to work with Daytona and be her friend after he left. The person, preferably a woman, would need to know Daytona's language of pain.

"I hated my father anyway," she continued, "because he always hated me. But after that I literally couldn't stomach the sight of him anymore.

"Instead of killing him, like I wanted to, I left home. It was in the middle of the night, about an hour after he…did what he did." That was in Buffalo, she explained, where she had spent most of her life. That night she caught a bus to New York City, taking about a hundred dollars and a single suitcase filled with clothes. She got a job cleaning floors, tables, and restrooms in a fast-food restaurant. For the first ten nights she slept wherever she could—the bus station, a subway stairwell, a hospital waiting room. When she got her first paycheck she moved into a run-down, one-room apartment.

One night she saw some streetwalkers. They were wearing ultra-tight pants to advertise their bodily goods, and waist-length minks for warmth. She stood and watched. In thirty minutes, all the girls had been picked up by men cruising by.

Her mind started whirling. Could she do it? She knew her body was attractive. But was it attractive enough? She wondered how good the money was.

A few nights later she drummed up enough courage to approach one of the streetwalkers. The lady said her name was Melissa. Daytona asked her about getting into the work, and found that in one hour she could earn ten times her hourly wage at her cleaning job.

The money was right. A few days later she linked up with Melissa and Melissa's pimp. They told her in detail what to do.

The first night she raked in more than two hundred dollars. She was hooked.

The money hooked her, and so did her new friends—especially her pimp. Knowing she smoked marijuana, he got her to try hard drugs, and she enjoyed the escape. Then came harder drugs. By the end of her first year working the street she was addicted to heroin. She was taking in as much as five thousand dollars a month, but most of it went for her habit.

From her heavy drug use, she started feeling and looking bad. Not as many men would pay to be with her. Her income started to slide. She could no longer afford the daily fix she needed. She started stealing. Her pimp demanded that she generate more revenue, and threatened her. She took to getting drunk. Finally her pimp beat and raped her, and kicked her off his turf.

A few weeks later her landlord locked her out of her apartment for being three months behind in rent. In desperation she decided—for the first time since running from home—to call her dad in Buffalo. With all the new horrors in her life, and after a year and a half away, she momentarily managed to suppress her hateful feelings toward him.

The only answer on the other end of the line was, "Daytona who?" It had been the ultimate rejection—to be purposely cut off by her own father when she was lying at the bottom of life.

She was now almost eighteen. She had no family, no friends, no money, no place to live, no education, no job.

Then she discovered she was pregnant.

She didn't know who the father was, but the child was a little life growing inside her. Somehow it became her last hope. The baby—this innocent baby—was someone she could love, and someone who would love her in return.

She was going to raise him in the right way, and help him learn all the right things in life. She would teach him to be proud. And she would always stand by him, always. When he stood strong and tall, she would be the proudest mother alive. Her own mother had abandoned her when she was a baby; but *this* baby—and this baby's life—would be different.

She had a lot to decide, and she thought about it all the time: What would she name the baby? Where would she choose to raise him? What school would she send him to?

That bundle of life inside her gave her wings, wings to fly above everything else in life. For the sake of the baby—and with no money for her habit anyway—she went through the nightmare of withdrawal from the drugs. For the sake of the baby she stopped drinking.

Then one morning, Halloween morning, she was down by the harbor. She was going to wash her face in the water. The sun was rising, and she was feeling good. She was wearing a coat she'd found in a dumpster a few days earlier—a man's coat, several sizes too big, but it was warm. She was telling her baby in her womb good morning.

As she walked across a parking lot she saw three boys behind an old wharf building, on a concrete overhang that reached out over the water. They were near the edge of it. The oldest one looked about sixteen or seventeen, and the other two a lot younger. It looked like they were doing a drug deal. They saw her, but she guessed they could tell she was just a street-dweller, because they didn't seem to mind. The two smaller boys looked awfully young, she thought. But she'd heard that a new drug, crack, was around, and was being pushed on preteens. Poor kids, she thought.

She turned away from them and started down a concrete stairway leading to the water. She took three or four steps down. Then she heard tires squealing, and the roar of a car engine. She stopped and looked back. A black sports car was screaming across the parking lot, with smoke coming from its back tires. It was heading toward the boys.

They started running, but one of the younger boys was knocked off balance. He fell from the concrete overhang into the water. The other two kept running and disappeared behind the other side of the building. The car braked and nearly slammed into the wall.

Daytona thought it must be undercover police, but two young guys jumped out. One of them had a pistol. They went to the edge of the overhang and shouted something to the boy in the water. The one with the gun aimed it, and fired three shots.

Daytona put her hand over her mouth to keep from screaming, and ducked down next to the steps to keep from being seen. She decided to stay there until the car drove away. Three or four minutes passed and she heard nothing more. What was wrong? Why weren't they leaving? Had they seen her? Were they sneaking up on her?

She panicked. She stood and peeked up over the top step. The two guys from the car were still on the overhang, looking down into the water.

She looked the other direction. On the other side of the parking lot was a junkyard piled with wrecked cars. Between it and the parking lot was a three-foot drop-off and a wire-link fence. She thought she could make it over the fence and hide behind the junked cars.

She ran for it. After she started running, she found that the heavy coat was slowing her down. She was still fifty or sixty feet from the fence when she heard the car doors slam and the engine start.

She knew she had to get out of the coat. She started peeling it off as she ran, and finally got out of it. She got to the fence and climbed up. She heard the car racing closer.

From the top of the fence, there was at least an eight-foot jump to the dead grass on the other side. She hesitated only a second, and then jumped.

But her shoe, or her shoestring, or something got snagged in the fence. It caught there as she careened off balance. Only when her body weight was below the top of the fence did her shoe rip loose. But it was too late. Completely disoriented, she fell to the ground, landing on her back. She told herself to get up and run, but her body wouldn't respond. She felt numb all over.

Just before she blacked out, she saw the two guys on the other side of the fence, staring at her. The one with the gun was pointing it at her.

When she came to, she was shivering. She looked up at the fence, and saw no one. She was alone.

She slowly started to sit up, and knew she was hurt. She felt something wet between her legs. She looked down and saw the blood. Her pants were soaked. At first she thought she'd been shot. Then she thought she'd been raped.

But the sudden pain she felt in her abdomen told her differently. She was miscarrying. It must have been the fall.

She backed up against the parking lot wall. The pains got stronger. She got ready, and squatted.

She spoke to her dying baby. "I tried...I tried to be a good mother. I'm sorry. Please, please don't hate me."

In half an hour the miscarriage was over. She got up and

walked several blocks, and at the first busy street she threw herself in front of an oncoming taxi.

"And to show you what a failure I am," Daytona told Jason, bringing her story to an end, "I couldn't even kill myself. All I got was some broken ribs, a punctured lung, and a brain concussion."

Jason's attention and emotions had been fixated by her account. Never had his heart gone out to anyone in such a consuming way. Everything in him yearned to love the broken life sitting before him—to love her with God's redeeming and life-changing love. He silently pleaded for God to come to her rescue.

Jason reached out and took her hands. "Daytona?" he said emotionally, but without flinching. "Do you think you could accept the friendship-love of an old man?"

She stared back, with tired, thirsty eyes. She was sure she had already felt that love. She felt herself drawn to him, with a bond deeper than she had ever known.

"Listen," he told her. "I just had an idea. Some of my colleagues may not understand it, but I'm going to carry it out anyway. And I'm going to do it for nobody else but you: I'm going to delay my return to Norway. I really don't have to be back until the twenty-ninth anyway. Going back on the fourteenth was just for personal reasons. It's not something I can't change for a friend. That way I'll have an extra two weeks with you."

Daytona knew he really meant what he was saying, though for the life of her she still could not understand why a professional and a stranger like Jason would reach out to love a nobody like herself for no apparent reason.

Jason waited for her response

Finally she spoke. "What makes you so...so *different?*" she asked tenderly.

Jason smiled. "God," he said.

34

THE NEXT MORNING at nine Daytona was opening a gift-wrapped box tied with a bright red ribbon. As Jason watched her take off the wrapping, he was silently, fervently praying that God would let him be a life-changing influence in her life.

She pulled the gift out of the box. It was a compact, leather-bound Bible. Jason had even had her name printed in gold letters on the outside cover.

She turned it over in her hands, feeling with her fingers the gilt-edged pages. "A Bible?" she asked.

"You can read it at your leisure," he said. "God will tell you in his own words how he changes a person's life, and how he makes them...different."

She looked bewildered, and wasn't even opening the cover to look inside.

"You've never read the Bible, have you, Daytona?"

"No," she answered softly. "But...even if I wanted to...I couldn't."

"Why is that?"

She decided not to try hiding the truth. "I can't read," she replied. "It's my own fault, though. I never took school seriously, that's all."

He tried not to look surprised. "Well," he said, "in that case, maybe I can read it for you sometime—if and whenever you'd like to hear what's in it."

She looked down, and for the first time opened the cover. "What about now?" she said, as she flipped a few pages.

He could tell she was serious. "Sure," he said, caught somewhat off guard.

She handed the Bible to him, and when they were both comfortably seated, he turned to Isaiah 53. "I'm not sure what you know about the death of Christ," he said with the voice of a sensitive teacher. "But that's what this chapter talks about. I'll read it through slowly, then we'll talk about what it means."

The thirty minutes that followed brought questions to Daytona's mind that had never occurred to her before. She had heard of Jesus' crucifixion. But did it really happen? How did he "die for our sins," as Jason put it? What did that mean for her right now? Jason said Jesus willingly died because of his personal love for everyone—"and for you, Daytona," he had said. She was overcome by the thought that it could be so personal. It was all so new.

When it was time for Jason to leave, she told him she wouldn't mind hearing more the next day.

≈ ≈ ≈

JASON MET THAT AFTERNOON with Marlene, the young woman who had sung at Art and Ginny's funeral. He had been thinking more and more that Marlene would be one of the best candidates for befriending Daytona.

As he told Marlene the full story, he could tell she was deeply moved, and that she had an immediate desire to reach out to Daytona. So when he asked her to do just that, she gladly agreed. She was leaving the next day for a holiday trip to a friend's home in Virginia, but would be back a few days after Christmas. Jason could introduce her to Daytona after her return. In the meantime, she promised to pray every day for her.

Jason also talked in the afternoon with David and Patricia, and together they made plans for Liberty International City Church to "adopt" Daytona after her release from the hospital. For as long as she would allow them, the church would provide her with food, lodging, work, friendship, encouragement, and direction. Temporary lodging would be in an apartment house only five blocks from David and Patricia's, where two of the single girls in the church had an extra bed.

With the door wide open now for a long-term ministry to Daytona, Jason felt tremendous relief. Sleep came easily to him that night.

In Queens Hospital, however, Daytona was restless. She was helplessly burdened with a multitude of strange new thoughts— of Jason, of Jesus, of her own life and future. She was tempted to somehow hope again, but she could not see her way clearly through all the bold, unfamiliar questions.

When she finally drifted off, it was due only to sheer mental fatigue.

One of the night-shift nurses found her asleep at two-thirty in the morning. The closed Bible was in one of her hands, resting over her heart.

≈ ≈ ≈

DAYTONA FIXED HER HAIR the next morning for the first time since being admitted into the hospital.

Jason immediately thought she looked prettier when he entered her room. She seemed to be radiating a slight bit of energy—a new energy, a promising energy. *Her beauty is emerging,* he thought, surprised to see such a change in such a short time. He saw it in the hairstyle, the genuine smile, the air of new life.

Jason told her first about Marlene. She gave his news only a neutral response.

"What will you read about today?" she asked, changing the subject with a smile.

"More about God and his love," he said. "This time from the gospel of John." He started with the first verse in the book and read all the way through the fifth chapter, offering very few words of explanation this time. He simply read the words, slowly and clearly.

As he read, Daytona was struck by the atmosphere of intense tranquility that seemed to settle over the room. She did not know why it was there, or what to call it. All she knew was that the calming, beautiful words of the Bible as Jason spoke them had somehow gently pushed her into the realization that there was a God. Suddenly she knew she believed, believed in both God and his Word. It was a majestic belief, a want-to belief.

When Jason finished reading, Daytona asked, "Do you really believe God can make me different?"

His answer was a quick and unequivocal "Yes."

"And do you really believe God loves me?" She asked it slowly. Her overwhelming desire for the answer to be positive made her fearful that it wouldn't be.

Jason went back to John 3:16 and read it to her again. "I not only *believe* God loves you, Daytona, I *know* it."

"But if he knows all that I've done, like you said before—how could he possibly ever love me?"

She held her breath while he thought about his answer.

"Daytona, I can't tell you how or why he loves you, or why he loves me, or anybody else. But he does love you. And that is an irrefutable fact.

"To begin with, he chose—out of a heart of love—to take your place on the cross, at the punishing-end of God's justice. He was punished for your sins.

"And secondly, as the all-powerful Savior who conquered death and rose from his own grave, he wants you to be reconciled to him. He wants to take away the distance between you and him; he wants to bring you close, right into his arms. He freely offers that reconciliation to you. You can receive it, just as you are.

"Daytona, for God to do all that—it had to be love."

She sat silently for a few seconds before pouring out her words from a yearning soul. "Then if he died for me, and wants to save me—that's what I want him to do. I want him to forgive me. I want him to make me a Christian."

The unexpected words sent a flood of joy sweeping over Jason, striking him momentarily speechless.

"Jason, I know I told you last week I didn't believe in God. The reason I told you that is because I'd never seen him. Well, now I do believe in him, because for the first time in my life I've seen him. I've seen him...in you."

That morning, Daytona gave her heart to Christ. She was born again.

35

JASON'S DAILY VISITS grew longer and longer. Daytona, in her new relationship with God, found herself hungering for every morsel of spiritual truth Jason could feed her. The newly discovered words of God were like a promising rainbow to her, and she could never get enough. She had so many questions, questions sparked by their daily Bible readings, that Jason found himself not only her friend but her personal Bible teacher as well. And teaching, he knew, took time.

He gave the extra time gladly, however. He never grew tired of watching God take broken, confused people and miraculously stamp his divine reflection on them bit by bit. It was particularly satisfying for him in Daytona's case, considering the depths of her misery. Besides, she had already captured a big piece of his heart. In a fatherly sort of way he had already grown to love her.

He had failed to foresee, however, that during their daily heart-to-heart exchanges, Daytona would grow increasingly dependent on him—and in a crazy teenage way, even fall romantically in love.

To Daytona's credit, the romantic feelings for him were totally unplanned. It was just that she had never been treated so well by a man before. Not a single man had ever valued her, respected her, showed a real interest in her feelings, or related to her with tenderness and sensitivity. Now she was receiving all of that from a confident, intelligent, and gentle sixty-year-old man who was clean and attractive, and who in some ways looked more like an energetic forty-nine-year-old.

It took only a week and a half of being on the receiving end of that treatment before the woman in her started automatically to respond.

Her feelings were first brought to Jason's attention three days before the hospital dismissed her. Knowing Daytona would soon be out in the real world again—and no longer wearing hospital gowns—he had gotten Patricia's help in picking out a new outfit for her. It was a lavender dress in a fashionable button-up-the-front design. She tried it on for him, and it was a perfect fit. When she saw herself in the mirror, she gave Jason a big hug.

The question that followed, and the way it was asked, tuned Jason in to her emerging feelings.

"So, you really don't have a girlfriend?" Her eyes shyly reflected her suggestiveness.

Realizing that time, if given a chance, would only complicate the situation, Jason chose to deal with the matter then and there.

He was certainly not a stuffy old man. Had he given himself permission, he could have easily yielded to being more than just a friend to her. But he was wise enough in his older years to understand that feelings alone were too shortsighted to serve as a guide for life-important decisions.

"I think you and I need to sit down and talk," he told her. With all the sensitivity he possessed, he explained to her the impossibilities of a romantic relationship between them.

"I know," Daytona finally told him, haltingly, after hearing his sensible reasons. "I couldn't help dreaming, though." Realizing her dream would never be anything more, she tearfully threw herself into Jason's arms, a frightened young girl finding refuge in the only person in the world who really cared about her.

"Promise me," she begged, "that you'll never stop being my friend. Please!"

"I'll never, never, for any reason stop being your friend, Daytona," he reassured her. "And I never want you to stop being mine either."

"Never!" Daytona said emphatically through her tears. *Never.*

≈ ≈ ≈

ON FRIDAY AFTERNOON, when Daytona checked out of the hospital, she discovered at the hospital cashier's desk that her hospital account had been balanced to zero. "A Mr. Faircloth just paid both the hospital and doctor's bills in full," the cashier told her, holding the check in her hand, and reading the amount: "Eleven-thousand three-hundred and seventy-eight dollars and eleven cents."

Jason at that moment was bringing his car around from the

hospital parking lot. As he pulled up at the main entrance to pick her up, Daytona was standing in her new dress at the front doors, crying.

Jason parked the car with its emergency lights flashing, and got out.

"What's wrong?"

"How am I ever going to repay you?" she asked.

"Repay me for what?"

"For eleven thousand and whatever dollars, that's what."

"Just forget it ever happened. Now then, let's get you to your new home."

"Forget it ever happened?" she protested.

"Listen, Daytona," he told her. "It was a gift. You don't repay gifts. So forget it. Consider it a closed issue."

"But—"

"But nothing," he interrupted, extending his hand to help her into the car. "Where's your coat?"

She knew he was trying to change the subject, and refused to follow the lead. "I don't have a coat. I lost it on the day I lost my baby," she said bluntly. "And now, to get back to what we were talking about, I just can't forget a gift of eleven thousand dollars."

"All right," Jason conceded. "There is one thing you can do for me as a means of repayment." Both his countenance and his tone of voice became sober. "Never lose your heart for God. Whatever happens in your future, whether good or bad, never lose your heart for God."

Daytona heard the words. She knew they were not a demand, but a plea. She had already learned from him that God was the consummation of all wisdom, all truth, all power, all love, all life itself. She understood, in theory at least, that once a person came to God it was then ultimate futility to walk away from Him. Where would one go if he walked away from the first, final, and only source of everything that was good and right?

Daytona, even in the newness of her walk with God, already understood Jason's plea.

"All right," she said, just as soberly. "It's a deal."

They both climbed into the car, and Jason pulled out into traffic.

Daytona started crying again.

"I'm listening," he tenderly coaxed her. "Talk to me."

She kept on crying, staring out the side window.

Jason waited.

Fifteen seconds later, when she felt she could no longer hold it inside, she blurted out her fear. "I don't want you to go back to Norway," she sobbed. "How am I ever going to make it without you?"

Hearing of her burden and feeling some of its weight, Jason wanted to stop the car at once and give Daytona his full attention, but there was simply no place right then to pull over. To compensate, he reached out and took her hand. He squeezed it, and sighed.

"You're going to make it," he told her with confidence. "You'll be in the hands of some of the most loving people in New York. And they're going to be much more to you than I could ever be." He reviewed for her again the arrangements that had been provided for her, and promised her she would like her new friends.

"I just can't believe these people will completely accept me, knowing my past and all." Her fears were obvious.

"Oh yes they will," Jason smiled.

Minutes later, Jason at her side, she stepped into the apartment she would be sharing. Waiting eagerly inside for her were a dozen people—all young single adults, she would soon learn, who were part of Liberty International City Church.

Framed by balloons, a big sign in red letters on the living room wall said, "Welcome, Daytona!"

≈   ≈   ≈

"ARE YOU SETTLING in okay at Tanya and Stephanie's?" asked Jason with a smile, as he and Daytona sat down together at David's church on Sunday.

"It seems to be going okay," she answered. In the last day and a half she had found to her unfolding surprise and slight confusion that Tanya and Stephanie treated her not only as an equal, but almost as a celebrity.

She liked Tanya and Stephanie—but it was obvious to her that they were both naive about the dark side of life. Consequently, though they treated her far beyond her expectations, they still couldn't relate to her with the wisdom, understanding, sympathy, and insight that Jason could.

How will I ever make it without him? she painfully asked herself again.

Right now, in church, it was only the presence of Jason at her side that made her feel safe. This was the first time she had ever attended a worship service of any kind, and her emotions were a little shuffled.

Once she got into it, however, she was more comfortable. She realized that instead of just two people worshiping God and studying his word together, as she and Jason had been doing in the hospital every morning, there were about a hundred and fifty sharing the same experience. It was fascinating to realize that probably every person in the auditorium had a personal relationship with God the Creator, just as she did. It made her more in awe of the greatness of God's love.

David's precise and vivid Bible lesson added to the thrill. He talked about the thoroughness and exactness of God's forgiveness. It was a message that touched the heart-chords of her new Christianity, helping her realize more fully the truth of her clean standing with God.

After church that afternoon she lay down at the apartment and tried to sleep, under doctor's orders. But sleep wouldn't come. There were too many new and breathtaking thoughts floating around in her head. A week earlier Jason had read to her from the Bible that she had passed from death into life through her conversion to Christ. She was not sure how, but the introduction to a church family with so many brothers and sisters in Christ, all of whom seemed to genuinely care for her, seemed somehow to be proof that she was alive in a way she had never known before.

At four o'clock she got up to begin getting ready for a dinner engagement at five. Jason was going to take her, Stephanie, and Tanya out to a Chinese restaurant before the six-thirty evening service.

Stephanie and Tanya were already dressed and ready, so she

had the bathroom to herself. A hot shower! A comfortable apartment! New friends! A new life! Love! Hope! Goodness! Could it really be happening? Standing in the spray of the steamy hot water, she leaned against the pink shower wall and cried tears of thanksgiving.

When Jason arrived, it had been snowing heavily outside for the last hour, the first snowfall of the season. Jason got hit with three snowballs as they went out to the car—but only because he threw first.

In the car, when the laughter subsided and the mood became more serious, Daytona began asking a few questions about the morning sermon. Forgiveness was still an astounding subject to her. At Jason's encouragement, the other girls shared in the answer-giving.

At the restaurant Daytona, seemingly unable to keep quiet, continued to dominate the conversation with her questions and the heartfelt sharing of her afternoon thoughts and feelings. But Jason, Stephanie and Tanya loved it.

Oh, thought Jason, *the unjaded beauty of Christianity in its romance stage!*

≈ ≈ ≈

"PEOPLE FORGIVING PEOPLE" was the title David gave to his sermon that evening. It was, he said, a natural follow-up to his morning sermon on how God forgives people.

The message was a piercing one for Daytona. To follow the pattern of Christ, David said, we must forgive all who have offended us. The words would not stop echoing in her head. Was it really God's will for her to forgive her pimp, and the hoodlums who caused her to lose her baby? Most of all, was it God's will for her to forgive her dad? Could God, in all fairness, really expect her to do that?

She struggled with the thought all the following week—all through the snowy mornings while cheerfully tagging along with Jason on his last few errands of business, all through the afternoons when she tried to rest, and all through the evenings filled with dinners, Christmas parties, church meetings, and a shopping trip with Jason. He had given her six hundred dollars to buy needed new clothes.

It was a perfect week in so many respects, a week of developing friendships and of just being close to Jason. But the thought of forgiving her enemies, especially her dad, hung persistently in her head and refused to release its grip. That, along with trying to prepare herself to say goodbye to Jason, was the only distraction to the week's delight.

By Thursday, Christmas Eve, she had decided she would not have any real peace of mind until her questions about the "forgiveness" thing were brought to the surface and answered. And if they were going to be talked about, she wanted to talk about them with Jason, in person, before he left for Norway. She valued his wisdom more than anyone else's.

That evening she was with him at a special get-together for four or five families at David and Patricia's house. But with all the spontaneous conversations going on, it was almost impossible to catch Jason when he had a free moment. She made a bid when she saw him break loose from a group discussion and head for the snack table.

"I've got to talk with you," she blurted out, as Jason stacked a few quarter-sized tuna salad sandwiches on his plate.

Jason could tell that whatever was on her heart was something serious. "Sure," he said. He gestured toward a couch near the Christmas tree.

When they were seated, she told him, "It's about the sermon David gave last week, the one about Christians forgiving their enemies. Ever since hearing it, I've been troubled by something I need to know. Is it really necessary to God that I forgive my father for doing what he did?" She asked the eye-to-eye question in a two-ton whisper.

Jason knew the principle of forgiveness in God's word, and he knew David had treated it fairly in his sermon. He told Daytona so. Nevertheless, in this case he did not want to give Daytona a simple yes or no answer. He wanted her to come to the right decision on her own.

He told her that God could be trusted, and had to be trusted, to honor those who honor his word. He quoted 1 Samuel 2:30—"Those who honor me I will honor." Because he wanted Daytona to know that God wasn't unfair, he emphasized that God sometimes performed miracles to honor in a significant way those who purposefully obeyed his word against their own interests and reasoning.

He decided to say no more. It was obvious to him that God was already working in Daytona's heart over the matter. So he felt the most prudent thing to do was to let Daytona wrestle alone with God until she came to her own conclusion.

At that point he excused himself, and got up and left her. He had to force himself to do it. He had grown to love her deeply, and even felt responsible for her. He truly believed he could feel her present pain.

As he turned and rejoined the mingling crowd, he prayed ardently for God to settle her heart and give her the courage to do what needed to be done.

When Jason walked away, Daytona was left staring uncertainly around the room, her eyes glimpsing the red and green calico wreaths, the white scented candles, the fresh greenery, the array of Christmas cards around the door frames, the festive Christmas tree at her side, laden with its hand-painted wooden ornaments. Her searching stare lasted perhaps forty-five seconds. Then she broke into tears. How could she ever forgive a man who had raped her, especially when that man was her father?

That night she lay in her bed, wide-eyed. Her soul churned, it seemed, for hours. She forced herself to relive the rape and the mass destruction it had caused. Without self-resistance, she once again relived her original explosion of hatred after the rape, an explosion so big she still felt its shockwaves two years later.

And yet, the only thing she kept hearing from God was, "If you forgive men when they sin against you, your heavenly Father will also forgive you. But if you do not forgive men their sins, your heavenly Father will not forgive your sins." It was the verse David had used in his sermon. Her own personal sense of justice continued to oppose those words. After all, if anybody on earth deserved no mercy, it was her dad; she was profoundly sure of that.

But no matter how much her spirit protested, grappled, and

fought, God seemed to stubbornly yet gently transcend all her opposition with his message of unconditional love.

At one point, when she momentarily dozed from exhaustion, she had a dream. She saw Christ hanging on the cross, and she and her dad were standing alone only a few feet away. They were each holding a hammer and spikes in their hands. Together they had nailed Christ to the tree. A voice from the cross was praying, "Father, forgive them both; neither of them knows what they do."

When she snapped out of the dream, she knew immediately that the battle had to end. It was obvious what God wanted.

≈ ≈ ≈

AN HOUR EARLIER than she was expected that morning, Daytona was knocking on David and Patricia's front door. It was seven o'clock, Christmas Day.

"I apologize for coming over so early," she said when Patricia opened the door, "but I need to talk to Jason. It's important."

She was ushered into the den, and sat down on the couch beside the Christmas tree while Patricia went to tell Jason she was there.

The moment he walked into the room Daytona was on her feet and almost in his face. "Can you go to Buffalo with me to see my dad?" she asked, with fiery determination cresting in her eyes. "As hard as it's going to be, I've decided I want to tell him about my conversion—about Christ. And I want to tell him I forgive him. I want to tell him..." She paused, and finished slowly: "...that I love him."

The first thing Jason felt was humbled. He knew he could not begin to imagine the psychological barriers Daytona had to work her way through in order to make that decision. One of Yoma's sayings came to his memory: "The essence of the Christian life is to behave contrary to human nature." He knew that what he was seeing in Daytona was that kind of Christianity. He was proud of her.

"Of course I'll go," he said. They could go the next day, Saturday. The trip by car would take about eight hours each direction, so they agreed to leave at four in the morning.

36

ON THE RIDE TO BUFFALO, Daytona sat in the passenger seat cuddling a big pillow. When she wasn't talking nervously she was staring out the car window with an expression of deep thought.

After one period of quietness, Jason said, "You know, Daytona, I'm proud of you. What God has done in your life in the last few weeks is a powerful tribute to the beauty of his love. And I'm equally excited about the marvelous things he's going to do for you in the future."

Daytona didn't underestimate what God had already accomplished for her—in fact, she was still overwhelmed by it all. But her optimism about her future didn't match Jason's.

"If you were going to stay here," she told him, "I think maybe I could make it. Without you, I'm not sure."

"You're going to make it, Daytona," Jason said, trying to bolster her. "David, Patricia, Stephanie, Tanya, Marlene, the church; they're all going to stand beside you.

"Besides," he added, "the fact that I'm leaving doesn't mean I won't be a part of your life anymore. I will."

Daytona looked at him with a strong expression of doubt, as if asking just how he planned to manage that.

He read the question in her eyes. "I'll buy a portable tape recorder," he continued. "We can correspond by tape." He had already realized that written correspondence would prove too difficult for her, because of her reading handicap. "And in the beginning," he said, "maybe I can even call you by phone a couple of times every month. We'll stay in contact. I promise you that."

"It won't be the same," she told him.

She was right, Jason knew. It wouldn't be the same.

"Well," he said. He knew he was going out on a limb, but he said it anyway: "Who knows? Maybe it will work out for you to come and visit me sometime."

"In Norway?" she asked, taken by surprise. Her face lit up with a hopeful smile.

"Yeah. In Norway."

She stayed in a good mood the rest of the way to Buffalo.

≈ ≈ ≈

CONFRONTING THE PLACE AGAIN with all its stinging memories, Daytona had to fight to keep from reverting to her old hatred and fear. Looking at the house from the car, she prayed quickly and fervently that God would help her overcome the negative pull.

Jason took her hand and joined her in prayer, saying the words out loud.

They got out of the car and moved across the snow toward the house. It was run down, much more than Daytona had remembered. The screen on the front door was partially ripped from its frame, and was dangling stiffly. The window shutters, once a deep gray, were faded to a white-ash color. The peeling white paint on the front-porch awning looked even worse.

At the foot of the porch steps, she turned to Jason. "Don't be surprised at what we find or how we're treated. Be prepared for literally anything."

Jason nodded his understanding, then asked, "What's his name?"

"Huh?" she asked, missing the meaning of the question.

"You've never told me your dad's name. What is it?"

Daytona realized it was true. In all the pained conversation with Jason about her father, she had never referred to him by name. It really didn't surprise her, though. Her hatred for him had made her despise his name, even to the point of refusing to speak it. Until now.

"Coe," she finally spoke from her silence, finding it awkward to repeat after so many years. "His name is Coe."

Daytona led them up the steps to the front door.

After a moment of hesitation, she reached out and pushed the button. Underneath was the name "Freedman," written years earlier with a felt-tip pen. It was in its little metal frame, covered with a piece of hard clear plastic that had grown dingy with time. Jason saw it, but didn't look at it closely enough or long enough to decipher it.

They stood and waited.

Daytona rang a second time, then a third.

Still no one answered.

Then she tried the door. It was unlocked. She opened it and stepped inside. She looked, but did not see anyone. But she did see the couch and the coffee table—the rape site of two years before. Her stomach knotted up. Suddenly she felt that she was being raped all over again, just by the vivid memories. She heard herself groan. Feeling as if she were going to lose it, she turned and threw herself into Jason's arms. She had to stay there for a few moments until she could catch her breath.

Jason held her tightly. When he was convinced she was going to be okay, he pointed down the hallway and said, "Listen."

There were television sounds coming from one of the back bedrooms.

"Daddy?" Daytona called, hoping to quickly get her mission over with.

No one answered.

With Jason behind her, she slowly started to walk the length of the hallway. Images of the past demanded her attention as she scanned the familiar settings. She fought to suppress the flashbacks.

"Daddy?" she called again. *O God, help me,* she prayed.

She paused at the doorway to her old bedroom and looked inside. The room was untouched. Nothing had been moved or cleaned; it was exactly as she had left it two years earlier.

It was bizarre, almost spooky. Her mind reeled. For a moment she felt dizzy. Reminding herself of her purpose, she shook off the daze, then headed for her dad's bedroom at the end of the hallway, the room where the television sounds were coming from.

When she reached the door, she paused. Before she looked inside, she took a deep breath. Then, under the momentum of it all, she stepped slowly into the room.

What she saw was a pair of legs extending from a deep lounge chair. From her point of view, facing the back of the chair at an angle, the legs were the only sign of life she could see.

"Daddy?" she questioned.

Whoever was in the chair neither responded nor moved.

Daytona walked slowly to the front of the chair, knocking over a bottle she hadn't noticed in the dim light.

Jason saw Daytona suddenly lose herself in a hard-breathing, emotion-rending stare.

"Daddy?" Daytona finally said again, her voice almost a whisper.

The man, slumped over in the chair, slowly rolled his head to a straight-up position, and with effort, opened his eyes. He looked as if he had not moved from the chair in days. There was stubble on his face. His eyes were red and heavy-looking. The hair on one side of his head was matted down flat. On the other side it was wild and tangled, sticking out in all directions. His skin was yellowed, and his body appeared somewhat bloated. He smelled of urine.

Daytona was afraid to touch him. She stood there, looking.

The man locked in on her stare. His eyes looked deep and distant. He continued for about fifteen seconds to probe her with his penetrating stare, as if he were trying to remember who she was. Then he spoke, his voice nothing more than a strained whisper. "What brings you back?" There was no distinguishable emotion behind his words.

In that instant, Daytona saw her father as she had never seen him before. Instead of being full of hate, she found that her heart was filled with a strange sense of pity. Instead of seeing a man who had abused and raped her, she saw a destitute human being who needed help.

"I've come home to tell you that I love you, Daddy, and that it doesn't matter anymore what you did. I forgive you. And I want you to forgive me for hating you, and for running out on you."

The man continued to look at her with an unbroken stare. His mouth hung open like a stroke victim's.

Daytona knew he needed medical attention, but she was more concerned at that moment that her dad understand her message than anything else in the world. Possessed by her purpose, she knelt down in front of him. Ignoring the stench that assaulted her senses, she reached out and took his hands. "Do you understand, Daddy? What happened in the past isn't important anymore. I want us to start over again."

The man blinked at her, as if trying to comprehend.

"I found God, Daddy," Daytona continued. "He's changed my life. He's—"

"You got religion?" he interrupted, his muffled words more a statement than a question.

"Yeah, Dad. I got religion."

"Who's that with you?" the man asked, abruptly changing the subject, his attention span appearing to totter.

"He's a friend." Daytona motioned for Jason to come closer. "His name is Pastor Jason Faircloth. He's the man who helped me find God."

"Hello, Coe." Jason spoke for the first time since entering the room. He did not extend his hand; already it had registered with him that the man was showing no signs of responsive physical movement, not even toward Daytona, except for the slight roll of his head. Coming closer and viewing the man head-on, he was even more aware that something was wrong.

"Pastor Jason Faircloth," the man suddenly said, as if he were speaking to the air. He rolled his eyes toward Jason, then almost immediately rolled them back to Daytona.

"I was in the hospital in New Yor—"

"Paradoxical," Coe interrupted with a whisper, as if he did not hear Daytona speaking. Then he started mumbling something that was unintelligible.

Daytona turned and looked to Jason.

"He's sick, Daytona. We need to get him to a hospital."

While Daytona continued her effort to talk sense with Coe, Jason found a telephone on the nightstand by the man's bed, and called for an ambulance.

≈ ≈ ≈

"HIS PROBLEM, as you probably know, is alcohol related," the doctor said to Daytona. She and Jason had been in the hospital waiting lounge for nearly an hour now, waiting for his report.

"His liver is cirrhotic," he continued, "and only barely functioning. His body is literally saturated with toxic poisons that have backed up into his system due to the liver failure. What we're going to do is administer some drugs to try to help eliminate some of those poisons. And we'll give him some medication to reduce the water retention. But I'm not going to offer you any false hopes. He's in a critical state. I've seen some people in his situation die within the day, and I've seen others pull through and live for two or three months."

Daytona was neither surprised nor shocked. Instead she felt angry—not at God and not at her father, but at the circumstances. She kept the anger inside, but she had come so far and hoped so strongly that things would work out between her and her dad. Had she waited too long? What if her dad did not regain coherency? Would he die without knowing that Christ loved him and wanted to give him new life? Would she never get to reconcile herself to her dad and have a peaceful relationship with him? Was it all too late?

When the doctor had left them, Jason turned to Daytona and said, "It looks like we need to sit down and talk."

Daytona's secret anger was turning into fear. Her desired plans for the next three days were being reshuffled beyond her control. She knew what she and Jason had to talk about: the likelihood of her staying in Buffalo. It was a decision that would mean saying goodbye to Jason here and now, instead of next Tuesday as she had planned.

Over soft drinks in the downstairs cafeteria they talked about it. The dying rays of a winter day's sun were coming through the windows next to their table.

After an hour of discussion, when the sunlight had disappeared, Daytona finally decided that the right thing to do was to stay.

She grew misty-eyed and started to choke up.

In their minutes left together, Jason tried as much as possible to help reestablish her emotionally, mentally, and spiritually in her new and unexpected circumstances. He told her that until she moved back to New York City—or until she decided she should not move back—he was sure he could arrange for the church to send someone to visit her on weekends, so she wouldn't lose her support group entirely. He would also ask them to help her find a church family in Buffalo that could be a support for her here. And he himself would call her from Norway once every week or so to encourage her and see how she and her dad were doing.

It was time for Jason to leave. But he, too, was feeling the pain of having to say goodbye. She meant too much for him to just walk away and make a clean break.

Daytona tried to be brave. "You know," she told him with a tight lump in her throat, "I've been through a lot of different kinds of pain in my life, but I've never had to go through the pain of having to say goodbye to someone I loved so much." Before breaking into a freshet of new tears, she was barely able to finish her words: "And I think it's going to be the worst pain of all."

Jason held her tightly. He had not foreseen that he would be the cause of so much pain. Feeling desperate, he almost decided then and there to invite her to move to Norway with him. He had definitely thought about it several times in the last week or so. But he had already concluded that the complications of such a move were far too great.

Besides, he reminded himself, that possibility had now been forced completely out of the picture anyway. Daytona's dad needed her now.

While Jason was still convincing himself that the wisest decision had been made, Daytona looked up and momentarily stopped crying. "I owe you everything," she said. "You're the best friend I've ever had. And you always will be, even if I never get to see you again." Her voice broke as she sobbed, "I'll never stop thinking about you."

Jason sighed heavily. His heart was breaking. But before he could respond with words of his own, Daytona continued.

"I suppose if you were still the holier-than-thou person you used to be, we never would have met. You would have passed me by like everybody else. But God has turned you into a one-in-a-million person, Jason Faircloth. You're the most tender human being I've ever known. Whatever you do...don't ever change."

Jason squeezed her firmly. He was a sixty-year-old human being who had been broken long ago. And he knew Daytona was right. If he was still the same man as in his Atlanta days, he would never have given the time of day to anyone like her.

"Daytona," he finally managed to say, "People who have been —not just hurt, but actually broken by their afflictions, will always tend to be more sensitive to the hurts of others. That's why, if you never lose your heart for God, you're going to be one of those rare and sensitive people too. You'll be far more effective at loving people than I've ever been."

To draw some of their attention away from their heartache, Jason interrupted their lingering, and suggested they get permission to try talking to Coe once more before he had to leave.

"Yes," the nurse told them when they found her. "If he's awake. But if he's still asleep, you need to let him continue resting without any disturbances."

They peeked in his room. But it was quiet. He was still sleeping.

They stepped back out into the hallway. Jason tried to prepare himself to say his final farewell. But it suddenly dawned on him in the middle of his thoughts that he was about to leave Daytona in Buffalo without any means of transportation.

"Do you have a driver's license?" he asked her.

She looked at him strangely. "Yeah. Why?"

"There was a car in your father's driveway when we were there this morning. Is it Coe's?"

Daytona nodded that it was.

"Well, it just occurred to me that it would be a real inconvenience for you if you had to stay here without a car. On my way out of town, why don't I take you by the house again, and if you can find the keys, you can drive the car back to the hospital."

Daytona was grateful that he had thought of it.

The ride back to the house gave them extra time together, but the additional minutes seemed to be a mockery. Daytona was quickly being buried in an avalanche of silent depression.

Jason tried to solace her with more words of hope and encouragement, but it was useless. Her heart was already hurting too much.

Under the porch light at the house, she fumbled with the key, trying to fit it in the front-door keyhole. Beside her, Jason's eyes fell tiredly and unintentionally on the name under the doorbell button again. The thought struck him that the name he was looking at was not "Richards." He almost started to give the matter his attention when Daytona suddenly dropped the key to the porch floor.

He reached down and got it for her, then unlocked the door.

It took them fifteen minutes to find the car keys. Then they were outside again.

On the front porch, Jason prayed with Daytona one last time, thanking God for her friendship.

At her request, he wrote down his Tuesday flight number and departure time. He also wrote down David and Patricia's phone number, and Stephanie and Tanya's as well. He told her he would ask Stephanie and Tanya to pack up her clothes and other necessities and mail them to her. And he promised he would explain to Marlene what had happened, and ask her to be one of the visitors from the church who would drive up to visit Daytona.

Arm in arm, they slowly walked down the porch steps and across the snow-covered yard to the street, where his car was parked and waiting.

"I'll call you Tuesday morning," Jason promised, surprised that it was such a struggle to get the words out, "before I leave for the airport."

Only when he had said farewell to Lorene and Hannah at their grave site eighteen years ago had Jason ever been part of such a heart-wrenching goodbye. It was not that Daytona was pleading with him to stay, or begging him to take her along. She had obviously accepted the impossibility of both actions. It was the untold agony she was feeling that was making it so hard for him.

Together beside his car, Daytona embraced him tightly and sobbed on his chest. They stood there for several long minutes.

Then Jason got in the car.

He rolled down the window, and cranked the engine.

"I love you, Jason Faircloth," Daytona told him, holding his hand through the open window.

"I love you too, Daytona."

As he put the car in gear and started rolling forward, Daytona held tightly to his hand and started walking alongside the car.

Jason looked her in the eyes one final time. He could not deny how much he had become attached to her. In reality, she had become the closest female friend he ever had.

As he accelerated and broke the hand-hold, he fought to not look back. But the effort was useless. Staring helplessly into the rearview mirror above him, he saw Daytona falling to her knees on the streetside.

With his heart in his throat, he cried out to God to take care of her.

37

JASON'S MIND KEPT being collared by thoughts of Daytona all during Sunday and Monday. Several times he started to go to a phone and call her. But he resisted the temptation each time. He felt it would only be turning the screw tighter, multiplying her anguish. He would wait and call her as planned on Tuesday.

On Monday evening, his last night in New York, all thirteen congregations of the Liberty International City Church met in a gymnasium for a farewell fellowship for Jason. There was food, music, testimonies, and a closing prayer from David. He asked God to honor Jason "in a very unique and significant way" for his willingness to leave Norway to come and help them.

≈   ≈   ≈

SHE HAD BEEN RIGHT. The pain of losing one's best friend was the worst pain of all.

Daytona had spent three uncomfortable nights in a waiting room at the hospital. Losing Jason had driven her to self-pity, pulverized her hopes, and robbed her of her appetite. She felt like a giant teardrop whose destiny was never-ending sorrow.

No consolation came until she went in to see her dad early on Tuesday morning. Coe was awake and somewhat alert for the first time since being admitted to the hospital.

"I'm glad you came back," he told her. His tired eyes and slow movements made him appear slightly drugged.

She had never dreamed of hearing those words from him. She reached out and took his hand.

"I'm a lonely man," he said fearfully. "I need you."

Daytona knew his period of coherency might not last long. Having his listening ear, she once again conveyed to him her message of forgiveness. She spoke with a tired but determined heart. "I want you to find God too, Daddy." To the best of her ability she told him how to do that, drawing on all she could remember from the Bible study sessions with Jason.

Coe appeared moved, but not quite understanding. "I'm glad you found God," he finally told her, squeezing his hand.

Daytona was overcome. She started crying quietly as she stared down at his tired face. She wondered why a moment like this with her dad had to be so long in coming.

In the next hour and a half Coe passed in and out of sleep. Daytona stayed at his side, holding his hand. She prayed that God would somehow help him come to an understanding of the truth.

At nine o'clock a nurse stepped in and asked if she were Daytona Richards. "A Mr. Jason Faircloth is calling long distance for you from New York City." The call was being transferred to a phone in the waiting room.

Daytona quickly stood up from Coe's bedside to move toward the hallway.

He gripped her hand tightly, refusing to let go, and she turned back to him. His eyes suddenly were wide open, reflecting what she interpreted as fear that she might be leaving him.

"It's okay," she quickly reassured him. "I'm just going to the phone. Jason's calling long distance and waiting to talk to me. I'll be back in a minute."

Coe still held her, his eyes suddenly appearing to go out of focus. He said in a slow, stop-and-go manner, "I'm glad...you...found your grand...father...too." Slowly he let go of her hand. He was drooling.

She was momentarily disturbed by the nonsense he was talking, but too anxious to get to the phone to dwell on it.

"I'll be right back," she told him again. She nearly ran down the hall to the phone.

Jason greeted her warmly and told her he was just leaving the house. David and Patricia were taking him out for a leisurely brunch, and afterward they would head for the airport in plenty of time to check his baggage for the five o'clock flight.

The lump returned to Daytona's throat. It felt like a colossal stone threatening to take away her breath.

Jason asked about her dad, about her, and about her last couple of days. She answered with a forced composure, but the moment of reality was too much for her. Soon she could not even talk clearly.

Jason tried to soothe her as best he could. He told her he had met with Marlene, who was planning a trip to Buffalo to see her in only a week. Then he reminded her again of his promise to call from Norway.

For Daytona, it was an almost unbearable farewell all over again. When she hung up the receiver after the last goodbye, she was shaking and gasping for breath.

Instead of returning immediately to Coe's room, she ran to the nearest restroom, hid in one of the toilet compartments, and cried.

She emerged from the restroom twenty minutes later, and walked to Coe's room out of sheer resolution. All the happiness she had felt earlier with her dad was now gone. She did not want it to be that way, but it was.

When she was with him once more, Coe started mumbling again, his eyes half-closed.

"Is your...grandfather living in...New York...now?"

306

"I'm sorry, I don't understand, Daddy." Daytona sounded almost agitated. Mentally she was only half there.

A few seconds later he repeated the question.

"I'm sorry, Daddy, but I still don't understand."

"Your granddad...Jason...Faircloth. Your mother's father. I asked...if...he's living in New...York now." He was looking up at the ceiling.

"Jason Faircloth? My mother's father? What do you mean?"

Appearing as if he were straining or even insane, Coe continued. "Your mother...your mother...was Hannah Faircloth, daughter...of...Pastor Jason...Faircloth of Atlanta. She was the...most beautiful girl...I...ever laid eyes...on."

Tears started slowly to seep from Coe's now swollen eyes. Daytona labored in her mind, trying to understand why he would talk like this.

"She...died...after giving birth...to...you. In Miami. I...died with her...Daytona."

"Died?" Daytona subconsciously raised her voice, trying to force Coe to remember the truth. "My mother left you. Remember? She walked out on us. Abandoned us." But even before she had finished speaking, her mind started spinning. How did her father know Jason had been a pastor in Atlanta? How did he know Jason's daughter lived in Miami? How did he know she died after giving birth to a baby girl? *It's impossible*, she told herself. *He never even met Jason before Saturday. He couldn't possibly know those things. He couldn't...*

"I killed her," Coe suddenly spoke up again. "I...let her die. My...fault. Never...never...forgave...myself. Never forgave. Never told...you...or...anybody."

Stunned by what she was hearing, Daytona's heart started to pound so hard she felt paralyzed by the sound of it. In chaotic silence she stood and stared at her father.

Until that moment, Coe had kept his eyes focused on the ceiling. When he finally turned his head and looked at her, he appeared to be seeing a thousand miles beyond her. "I didn't mean...to let her die. I...really didn't. I couldn't...couldn't...help it. I...couldn't..."

He seemed to be losing himself inside his memories, his voice diminishing into mumbles.

Daytona was trying to regain her composure, her thoughts racing a million miles an hour.

"Daddy, I need to ask you a couple of questions," she told him, almost forcefully.

She waited for him to stop his muttering, then asked nervously, "When I was a little girl, did we ever live in London and go on vacation in the Mediterranean?"

"Cyprus," he said, the word just a whisper. "Hannah would...have loved it."

For Daytona, the truth was coming like a tornado.

"Daddy," she said, carefully articulating every word in her next question. "Was Hannah Faircloth, my mother and your wife, a runaway?"

She waited for what seemed an eternity before he responded.

"She was sixteen...when she ran. But she..." Coe broke into tears.

The whole picture was coming abruptly together. Daytona was left standing in shock from the mental overload.

When she was finally able to vocalize her thoughts, she asked one more question. Her voice now was an eerie monotone, almost as if she had put her detonated emotions into a deep freeze. "Do you know why my mother ran away?" she asked.

Coe, lying on his back and looking again at the ceiling, started to shake. Anger appeared in his eyes, and when he spoke it was in his voice. "Because...Faircloth was...a religious fanatic...who treated her...treated her like...a piece of trash."

To Daytona it was as if she were hearing an exact replay of Jason's stories. She suddenly understood, as impossible as it sounded, that the man who had reached out to her when she was utterly forsaken, the man who had helped her find a new life in God, the man who had become her best friend in all the world, was her own flesh-and-blood grandfather.

She stood there in silence, letting it all penetrate her mind.

Suddenly she blurted out wildly, "He's leaving! I've got to get to him!"

Leaving Coe in a state of uncertainty about what was happening, she jerked up her purse and darted out of the room with lightning speed.

Running down the hallway, she slid around one of the corners and fell down on the freshly mopped floor. Her mind, in a state of frenzy, did not allow for the registration of either pain or embarrassment. She just sprang to her feet and kept moving.

When she reached the pay telephone near the waiting area, she frantically tore through the contents of her purse to find her list of phone numbers. She almost started crying before she found it. Finally, with David and Patricia's number in hand, she force-fed some coins into the phone and quickly punched out the numbers.

What am I going to say to Jason, she nervously wondered as she waited through the first three rings. *How can I get him to believe me, to believe I'm really telling the truth?*

But the chance never came. No one was at home.

Daytona quickly tried to collect herself and to think rationally. How could she get the message to him before he got on his plane? Who else could she call? Of course—Stephanie and Tanya. She tried their number. But before she finishing striking all the buttons, she remembered that they had both gone to visit Tanya's parents in Rhode Island until after New Year's. Nevertheless, she rang through to their apartment anyway. She just hoped against hope that for some reason one of them might be at home. But they were not.

"Darn it!" she shouted after the sixth ring.

What was she going to do now? She did not have the number to David's church, or to any of the congregations. She remembered a lot of first names of the church people but no last names, so she couldn't call Information for their numbers.

She quickly looked at the clock on the waiting room wall. It was 9:35. Jason's plane was scheduled to leave at five.

In another split-second decision, she was off and running back to Coe's room.

She went immediately to his side. She grasped his hand in hers and then gave him her message. "I'm going to New York City, Daddy." She let go of his hand and grabbed her coat lying over the back of a chair. "I'll try to be back sometime tomorrow. I promise."

Coe said nothing. A look of fear flickered in his eyes as he saw her put her arms into the coat sleeves.

Daytona did not know whether to feel sorry for her dad, or to feel cold and calloused toward him for lying to her these last eighteen years. As she stared down at him, with her emotions in a vicious spin, she understood for the first time that her father was a hurt man who had been running and hiding all his life—a man hopelessly trying to escape guilt and reality.

That emerging insight—painting a new and clear picture in her mind—suddenly brought sympathy into her heart. She knew it was not in her anymore to be cold or calloused toward him.

She walked closer, leaned over, and gently planted a kiss on his brow, something she could not recall having ever done before.

She decided to take time for at least a brief explanation. "Until about fifteen minutes ago, Daddy, I didn't know Pastor Jason Faircloth was my grandfather. But now I've got to get to him in New York. I can't let him leave without letting him know he's finally found his long-lost granddaughter." Those last words brought fresh tears to her eyes.

She thought at that moment of her mother, Hannah Faircloth, Jason's daughter, who had loved this man whom she herself had hated.

Then she remembered. "Daddy—that picture. Of my mother. Do you still carry it in your billfold?" He had once told her that he never allowed it out of his possession. It was a photograph of Hannah standing in front of a silhouette dog sign in Miami. It was the only picture of her mother she had ever seen.

Coe didn't respond. With his eyes closed, he appeared once again to be lost somewhere in the darkness of his mind.

Daytona searched the room until she found his billfold in a drawer in a stand by the bed. She opened it and quickly went through it. When she found the picture, she felt a rush of elation. She took it out of its plastic sleeve and held it tightly in her hand.

Before she left the room, she went to her father's side once more, promising him again that she would be back as soon as possible. When she squeezed his hand, he opened his listless eyes and gave her a languorous stare. She kissed him once more on the forehead, and left.

As she rushed out of the hospital and into the car, she started praying as never before, pleading with God like a desperate child. *Please let me reach Jason before he leaves.*

Sitting wildly alert behind the wheel, she raced the car nearly to its limit. She ignored the speedometer, refusing to even look at it. She raced. She had to make it. She just had to.

One hour passed, and another. It started to snow.

After three and a half hours, the snow was still falling. It was beginning to slow her down. Her optimism turned to pessimism. She began to worry. Her legs started cramping. *O God,* she prayed, *let me make it!*

After four hours her back was hurting, but she continued to race the car through the blowing snow, at high speed and high risk. She kept pushing herself, though she now feared more than ever that she wouldn't make it.

Just after four o'clock, when she neared the airport, she pulled out of her purse the flight information Jason had scribbled down for her and quickly memorized it.

≈ ≈ ≈

JASON HAD JUST SAID his final farewells to David and Patricia before moving through the passport checkpoint and into the international flight zone at the SAS terminal. He was now trying to focus on what lay ahead instead of what was past.

He stopped at one of the international newsstands and bought a Norwegian magazine. The prospect of being in Oslo within the next ten or so hours was already stirring deep longings within him. In New York, it was true, he had felt a strong kinship with the ministry and with the people. But in Norway he had always felt additional kinships with the land, the sea, the culture—everything that made Norway Norway.

As he made his way through the throngs of moving people and walked toward his plane's departure gate, he thanked God in his heart for his life-changing years in Norway, and for letting him have a ministry in a land he loved so much.

He was eager to return. Two years away was long enough.

≈ ≈ ≈

DAYTONA WAS FOUR MILES from the airport when she heard the time announcement on her car radio: 4:30. She was fighting heavy rush hour traffic. She was too close now to give up. She had to keep pushing.

A new flush of adrenaline shot through her body.

She started cutting from lane to lane, moving into every available empty pocket in the traffic, trying to outwit the countdown of fate.

Just when she thought she could make it, the traffic stopped. All she could see ahead, under the low-hanging, gloomy clouds, was an endless line of tail-lights.

≈ ≈ ≈

IT WAS 4:40 when Jason and the people at his flight-gate area were given their boarding signal. Jason was one of the first to go through the boarding-pass checkpoint near the entrance to the plane. His excitement was building.

As he stepped on board he greeted the Norwegian stewardess who was welcoming passengers, then proceeded to his designated seat midway down the length of the fuselage. It was just behind the wing. It was a window seat, his favorite. He put his coat in the storage compartment overhead. Then he sat down and placed his briefcase beneath the seat in front of him.

He adjusted himself in his seat until he was comfortable. Then, relaxed and high-spirited, he opened his Norwegian magazine to settle in for some light reading.

≈ ≈ ≈

WHEN THE TRAFFIC FINALLY started unclogging, it was 4:46. A few minutes later Daytona entered the SAS terminal parking area, bringing the car to a screeching halt, half on the street and half on the sidewalk, at the terminal's front entrance.

Leaving the car illegally parked, she jumped out and raced through the building's electronically activated glass doors.

When she entered the building, her eyes, like high-tech movie cameras, started zooming in to the overhead information boards that displayed the departing flights and their gate numbers. She immediately scanned for the flight number she had memorized, and found it. The gate number was thirty-six. The boarding light beside the gate number was already flashing.

She looked at the board clock. It was 4:52.

She ran through the terminal's hallways like a madman, following the signs to Gate 36. As she ran up escalators and pushed herself through a maze of corridors, she glanced at every clock she passed: 4:54...4:56...4:59...

She reached the passport checkpoint that led into the international flight hall. In desperation she shot past the security guards before she could be stopped.

With the shouting guards immediately on her heels, she kept surging ahead.

≈ ≈ ≈

INSIDE THE PLANE, Jason buckled his seat belt in response to the flashing seatbelt signal. He looked at his wristwatch. It was 5:02.

From his seat he could see a flight attendant closing the plane's entry door. The plane's engines were already running. They would soon be taking off, his favorite part of air travel.

≈ ≈ ≈

THE TWO GUARDS caught Daytona just as she entered the Gate 36 waiting area. As she fought to free herself from them, she broke into tears and screamed, "Don't let that plane leave!"

Her arms were outstretched toward the plane, as if she thought she could hold it back with her own strength if she were only allowed to.

The guards were unnerved by her hysteria. At first they simply tried to ignore the seventy-decibel message she was trying to deliver. It was all they could do just to hold her on the spot. But as she kept screaming, "Don't let that plane leave!" with increasing intensity, the guards suddenly grew fearful. They signaled for the gate manager to have the flight stalled until they could calm the girl down and get more information out of her.

Only then did Daytona start to cool down. When the guards started to escort her to another area of the terminal for questioning, she begged them with tears to hear her out there on the spot.

For the next twenty minutes they listened until they finally understood and believed her story.

≈ ≈ ≈

JASON LOOKED AT HIS WATCH for the fourth time since the captain of the plane announced the delay over the intercom. They were already a half-hour late.

The delay, the captain had said, was due to security reasons.

Out the window he could see snow blowing across the airplane wing. Then he turned his eyes to the front of the plane, and saw a flight attendant talking to a man in uniform who apparently had just boarded the plane through the reopened door. Jason noticed them engaged in a serious-looking conversation for perhaps a minute. Then the attendant disappeared in the direction of the cockpit.

In a minute or so the captain's voice came over the loudspeaker again. "This is Captain Olsen speaking. If there is a passenger on board by the name of Jason Faircloth, can he please report to the exit door at the front of the aircraft. I repeat: If there is a passenger on board by the name of Jason Faircloth, could he please report to the exit at the front of the aircraft."

Jason's head suddenly felt heavy. *Who's been hurt?* he immediately wondered. *Is it David? Patricia?*

For the next few seconds, as he approached the flight attendant at the front door, he was burdened with an attempt to prepare himself mentally for the tragic news. *Help me, God,* he prayed almost fearfully.

The flight attendant waved him on through the narrow passageway.

Where the corridor joined the waiting area, his eyes automatically focused on a small group of people about fifty feet away. There were officials in uniforms and suits. And there was—*Daytona?* Jason had to do a double-take. Yes—she was there in the middle of the group. But how could it be?

As he walked slowly nearer, with everyone standing in silence, he was captured by Daytona's haggard, rumpled appearance. She looked almost sick. It was obvious she had been crying.

His first thought was that Coe had died. But then Daytona's cold stare burst into a giant, effervescent smile, a victorious smile, as if she had just conquered the world.

He was stumped. Had Daytona gone mad? Had she come all the way to New York City and gotten him off the plane just to see him one more time, to try to pressure him not to leave? He didn't know whether to be miffed or to try to be controlled and understanding.

He started to ask what was going on when she burst out of the group and threw herself into his arms full force. She started crying so hard she couldn't talk. She squeezed his neck so tight he thought he was going to choke.

"What are you doing, Daytona?" He finally managed to squeak out his question.

Daytona let go of his neck, hurriedly reached into her purse strapped to her shoulder, and pulled out the photograph of Hannah. She handed it to him, her hand shaking with nervous excitement.

Jason took the picture and looked at it. It was so worn with use —so smudged, bent, and frayed—that the image of the girl in the picture was almost beyond recognition. Suddenly, to his total surprise, Jason realized he was looking at a picture of Hannah. His mind sparked. He remembered the dog-shaped sign he had seen in Cody's back yard in Miami. The picture had to be at least nineteen years old.

But where did Daytona get it? Did she get him off the plane just to give him this picture?

"It's an old picture of my daughter," Jason told Daytona. His statement sounded more like a question.

Daytona was already digging through her purse again. Quickly she pulled out her driver's license. In a slow, stuttering, nervous whisper, she asked him, "Does the name on this license mean anything to you?"

Jason already knew Daytona's name. He gave her another stare of confusion, but then, at her prompting, held the license up close and slowly read the name to himself: Daytona Renée Freedman. He lowered the license and looked again into Daytona's eyes. His mind raced, then did a retake. He read the name again. Daytona—Renée—Freedman. *Daytona—Renée—Freedman.*

The name exploded in his head. *But—it doesn't make any sense. It isn't possible that—*

"The lady in that picture is my mother," Daytona told him. Her voice reverberated with the tension of her suppressed emotions.

Jason bombed her with a stare. Was he hearing what he thought he was hearing? His mind instantly and automatically tried to refuse it. "That's not possible," he tried to tell her. "You're... you're Daytona *Richards*." He looked at the license again.

"Only because I was married to a pimp for seven weeks," she quickly said in clarification.

"But...but your father. His name is Co—"

Then it struck him like a blitzkrieg. With lungs nearly bursting from a giant inhalation, he looked Daytona deeply in the eyes.

"Renée? Renée Freedman?" he asked. "Daughter of Cody Freedman of Miami and Hannah Faircloth of Atlanta, Georgia?"

"Yes!" Daytona smiled. "Yes! Yes!" Then she cut loose a "*YES!*" so loud it echoed throughout the terminal.

In a moment of indescribable elation, Jason and Daytona threw themselves into each other's arms. As he whirled her around and around, lost in their shouts of unimaginable joy, there was no one else in the whole world who existed at that moment—just him and her.

The outlying group of onlookers, having been kept at a distance by the officials, did not understand every detail of what was happening, but they saw enough to be touched. They too were smiling, laughing, and crying—even clapping. It was the timeless spirit of human beings reacting to the contagious emotions of others. And what they saw that day left a lasting impression they would never forget.

Neither would anyone else who heard the story of Jason and Daytona.

Cody, however, would never hear. He died that evening, alone.

When Jason finally put Daytona down, they stood for perhaps four seconds, silently looking into each other's shining face.

And then the laughing, dancing, shouting, and crying erupted all over again.

And again.

And again.

And again.

EPILOGUE

TWO SUMMERS LATER, during a visit with Jason to Norway, Daytona stood at Yoma's grave site and spoke a debt of thanks that had persistently resided in her heart: "I never got to meet you, but I've heard so much about you. Thanks for what you did for my grandfather. Thanks for making a difference. Thanks for caring."

With those words barely off her lips, she realized from all that had happened that a sacred baton of unadulterated Christianity had been passed down to her, not to be dropped, but kept alive. Jason's often repeated words rang in her mind: "Let God have your life, let wisdom guide your life, and let people be your life."

≈ ≈ ≈

"I read about 250 books each year, and this new novel from Questar is the best I've read in ages. Not only does it tell a gripping story I could hardly put down, but along the way it blows the doors off 'packaged' Christianity. As the amazing adventure unfolds, valuable insights come forth that make it a must read for every Christian in America. In fact, if you read only two books this year, make one the Bible—and the other **Wisdom Hunter**."

Paul Griffin, Senior Vice President, Multnomah School of the Bible

"This book is insightful and fun to read. It's Christian fiction with a punch and with a message."

Tony Compolo, Eastern College

"**Wisdom Hunter** is a novel that readers will likely not be neutral on: they will either agree or disagree, and strongly at that."

Jeff Whitfield, *Henry Herald*; Atlanta, GA

"As one who has never cared much for so-called inspirational reading, I found this book refreshingly different. It was not written in a preachy style. It did not seek to force principles down the throat of the reader. Arthur's writing gives the reader credit for having common sense."

The Valdosta Daily Times, May 13, 1992, Valdosta, GA

"**Wisdom Hunter** is mesmerizing—in part because of its intriguing plot, in part because of its insights into human nature, but mostly because of its emphasis on the search for and practical application of wisdom as we deal with the unanswered questions in our own lives."

Tim Philibosian, *The Rivendell Report*, April 1992, Aurora, CO

"I'm always reading three or four books at once and it takes a while to finish any of them. I never read just one at a time...until I began **Wisdom Hunter**. I read it in two days! A record time for me. I couldn't put it down...If you cry out for the freedom and mercy of a soft heart toward those that you despise; if you have lost your joy in a Christianity that is all work with no kindness or compassion—**Wisdom Hunter** is especially for you."

Ron Lindeboom, *The Christian Chronicle*, Oklahoma City, OK

"The depth of feeling shown and the theme of seeking a deeper spiritual walk are definitely strengths in this book... The story line and ideas presented are of high moral caliber and merit a reading by any fan of Christian fiction."

Richard Nilsen, *Bookstore Journal*, Colorado Springs, CO

"Everyone on our staff has read it and feels this will be the big book of the year. What Peretti's books did for spiritual warfare, **Wisdom Hunter** does for the issue of legalism in the church."

Dave McShea, Fresno Bible House, Fresno, CA

"The best novel since Peretti! I haven't read a quality book like this in a long time."

Joanna Hicks, Sign of the Fish, Raleigh, NC

"This is a gripping, real-life drama, challenging the depth of your commitment to Christ. The powerful ending will grab your heart and invigorate your faith in the sovereignty of God."

KenMcEachern & Kathy Herman, Better Books Christian Center, Tyler, TX

"It's rare to find a novel dealing with human spirituality and faith that holds you right on the edge from cover to cover as this book does. **Wisdom Hunter** affirms that after the Cross still comes the Resurrection."

Lee Ellis, Catholic Book & Gift Shop, Tulsa, OK

"Once we started reading we could not put it down. It's entertaining, inspirational, and thought-provoking—it blows away the chaff from real Christianity."

Ann Wolf & Jackie Johnson, Sonshine House, Newark, DE

"This author knows how to write! What a pleasure it is to read something so well-conceived."

Mary Risely, Christian Herald Family Bookshelf, Chappaqua, NY